elvispresley®

elvispresley

The Man. The Life. The Legend.

Pamela Clarke Keogh

SIMON &
SCHUSTER

London · New York · Sydney · Toronto · Dublin

A VIACOM COMPANY

Also by Pamela Clarke Keogh

Audrey Style

Jackie Style

First published in Great Britain by Simon & Schuster UK Ltd, 2004
A Viacom Company

1 3 5 7 9 10 8 6 4 2

Simon & Schuster UK Ltd
Africa House
64–78 Kingsway
London WC2B 6AH

www.simonsays.co.uk

Simon & Schuster Australia
Sydney

A CIP catalogue record for this book
is available from the British Library

ISBN 0-7432-6332-4

Printed and bound in the United States of America

For my brother, Peter C. Keogh,
with love and gratitude;

Bernadette Castro,
who sang for Berry Gordy;

and Fitzwilliam Michael James Anderson,
who is definitely TCB.

contents

Before Elvis, there was nothing.

—JOHN LENNON

prelude

ELVIS PRESLEY WAS ON *The Ed Sullivan Show,* and the kids did not understand what the fuss was about. If they had even heard of Elvis ("Elvis *Pretzel* singing 'Heartburn Hotel,'" some of them thought the deejay said on their little plastic radios), they knew he was a singer whose voice attracted them. They had never heard anything like it. Now, seeing him for the first time playfully blub blub blubbing his way through "Don't Be Cruel," they saw he was grown-up, sort of, but a kid like them, too. They could tell by the way he looked at them—he knew them, knew what they were thinking. Elvis . . . *Elvis.* They said his name and felt the first stirrings of love. He knew what was in their hearts and spoke directly to them.

The adults saw Presley and thought, *What the hell was that?* If they were particularly threatened, they might shoo the kids away from the television set, as if he were contagious and could somehow teach them about sex through the fuzzy black-and-white image. But since this was 1956, Dad probably just cleared his throat and left the room shaking his head, *These crazy kids . . .*

Elvis was the first. Before the Beatles, before the Rolling Stones, before U2, before Sean Combs, there was Elvis. The original Slim Shady, he was black and white, rhythm and country, hot and cool. His appearance on *Ed Sullivan* ripped the 1950s in half, and America was never the same. He could not have seen what was coming—the Colonel, who wanted to make him into sort of a hip Perry Como (if such a thing can be imagined) certainly did not. And for himself, his wildest dream, the one beyond imagining, was to be in the movies like Tony Curtis. But whatever happened, he was game.

In the beginning, Elvis did not understand the audience's ferocious response to him. But he quickly learned to harness it, toying with his screaming fans like a lover. Onstage, something came over him. He was a different person—freer, able to express himself, musically articulate as he never was in conversation. People loved him and he gave their love back to them in kind.

Did the kids even know why they liked Presley? They knew their parents hated him, which was a start. His concerts were an almost Dionysian release. After the placid tones of Frank Sinatra and Tommy Dorsey, rock and roll was a safe place for American teens to go berserk. The great seducer, Elvis left them spent, stunned. They had never seen anything like him: He was so totally *different*, that's for sure. This beautiful man who loved his mama, wore mascara, and sang like an angel.

The first superstar, Elvis was almost pure style. Tolstoy believed that one critical way to judge art was if it got a response—either good or bad. *Everything* about Elvis was provocative. His clothes, his hair, the way he sang, the way he moved on stage, his half-kidding sneer. Adults, church leaders, the great dull morass that makes up acceptable society considered Elvis a joke, but Leonard Bernstein recognized his impact. Talking to Richard Clurman, an editor at *Time* magazine, he proclaimed, "Elvis Presley is the greatest cultural force in the twentieth century." What about Picasso? Clurman wondered. This kind of parrying was common at the Time-Life Building. "No," Bernstein insisted. "It's Elvis. He introduced the beat to everything and he changed everything—music, language, clothes. It's a whole new social revolution—the sixties came from it."

In terms of style, there were three distinct Elvises. The 1950s' Hillbilly Cat beloved by fans is considered the purest Elvis. In his slouchy Lansky jacket Presley played country rube to New York City television audiences. The 1960s' Hollywood Elvis—onscreen, he plays racecar drivers! Roustabouts! Twins!—presented a more clean cut (some would say neutered) Elvis acceptable to middle America. And finally, there was the 1970s' Vegas Elvis—the glitz, the glamour, the behind-the-scenes shenanigans. Elvis is no longer the wide-eyed country boy happy to be here. Spend enough time in Oz and you just know there is some heavy stuff going down. In Bill Belew's hand-studded jumpsuits, Elvis is no longer a singer, but the greatest entertainer in the world. He is quite simply, the King of Rock and Roll.

ELVIS BLEW INTO the complacent center of the 1950s and tore them apart. Like Audrey Hepburn, Grace Kelly, and Jacqueline Kennedy Onassis, three other style icons of the twentieth century, he came along at precisely the right time.

Television, then in its infancy, and the first teenagers with spending money and a world view apart from their parents joined forces to make Elvis a star. Asked why he became the phenomenon he did, Elvis said humbly, "The people were looking for something different and I came along just in time. I was lucky."

Elvis' style worked because it came from his life. Presley (possibly the most distinctive looking, and sounding, man in the entire world) was no publicist's creation. Instead, he lifted his style—which was, essentially, himself—from Beale Street, church, the army, Hollywood, and finally, Las Vegas and the road.

No one looked like Elvis before he came on the scene. He was a stunning original—a shambling Memphis Beau Brummel, the bad boy (albeit with very good manners, because his mother would have killed him if she thought he was getting a big head), a Southern James Dean who reached audiences through his music.

Elvis had a keen visual sense not only in how he presented himself onstage, but in his homes, the cars he drove, the women he dated, even the guys who surrounded him. His pure, idiosyncratic style was all the more remarkable because he was completely untutored. Elvis instinctively recognized the transformative power of clothing—and, indeed, his very life—to simultaneously draw attention to himself and set himself apart from others. Dean Martin, the level-headed, golf-addicted, Rat Pack crooner Elvis idolized, also recognized this. "In a tuxedo, I'm a star," he said. "In regular clothes, I'm nobody."

By high school, Elvis was using his wardrobe as an extension of his personality. A shy, dreamy boy with few friends and no discernible talent or ambition, he wore lace shirts when other boys his age wore khakis and madras shirts, refusing to cut his hair to play on the football team.

Presley came to think of himself as a "freak," set apart by the superstardom of his life and all it demanded of him. His talent was so extraordinary, his rise to fame so absolute, that nothing in his past, or his family's past, prepared him for it. But then again, what could possibly prepare *anyone* for that almost crippling kind of attention?

Unlike some celebrities who hide from the public's attention, Elvis believed he owed everything to his fans. During the 1950s, whenever a teenager was reported missing, the local Memphis police checked the front gates of Graceland, in case she had run away. Elvis always stopped to sign autographs and pose for pictures, no matter how tired or busy he was, reasoning, after all, that they made it all possible.

Elvis had an almost mystical relationship with his fans that continues to this day. By the end of his life, his connection with his audience was so absolute that there was no downtime for him. In the 1970s, he had his costume designer, Bill Belew, designing his offstage wardrobe as well. Unlike other public figures who made very clear delineations between their public and private lives, by then there was no separation between Presley's professional and personal life: He *was* Elvis.

ELVIS AFFECTED HISTORY and, in turn, became history in a way that we, who recognize his influence—in fashion, in music, in cultural expectations— do not. Today, he is so linked with a singular moment in time that he is also a stylistic adjective used to describe a manner of dressing, living, and even behaving.

But while icons like Audrey Hepburn and Jacqueline Onassis, for example, are aspirationally associated with European couture filtered through classic East Coast style, for a time Elvis became the punch line of late-night jokes and cheesy impersonators, raucous living, and zero impulse control. Except onstage or in the recording studio (to him, the only places it mattered), Elvis did not have the personal discipline of Audrey or Jackie.

But at the beginning of the twenty-first century, now that we are able to take a more studied view of Presley's extraordinary talent (which, at the end of the day, is what counts, really), this initial, hasty opinion is finally being recast.

The first thing that Elvis represents, perhaps his most compelling contribution, even today—is freedom. Total, absolute, and utter freedom. Freedom from parents, crummy jobs, school, people who don't understand you. Elvis was not part of the Establishment, and never wanted to be. Instead, he created his own world.

A man with the childlike personal conviction to do exactly as he pleased and the money and creative imagination to back it up, Elvis lived a life millions of people fantasize about. To do what you want, be who you want, drive, escape, *live* the way you want. Elvis' voice—so intimate, so pure, awakened something in those who heard it and gave them the freedom to be themselves, too. Bruce Springsteen felt it. "It was like he came along and whispered some dream in everybody's ear, and somehow we all dreamed it."

There is also Elvis' dark side, as necessary to his style as his voice or his Cadillacs, for his darkness offsets his vast charisma. In the phrasing of his words we hear longing, regret—for things he can no longer have: his twin brother, his mother, the perfect dream of home, lost innocence. How simple his desire must have seemed when he stepped off that truck and walked into Sun Studio, smiling shyly to the woman behind the desk.

In Elvis, we hear the longing of America. Those lonely whistle stops. A dog barking on a country road. A man who got onstage and sang to twenty thousand, who hated sleeping alone. This longing, this loss—both his and ours—and the endless search to fill it, built this country.

Finally we see that Elvis is America, like rock and roll or blue jeans. For better or worse he inhabits our energy, optimism, and goodwilled rambunctiousness, as well as our short-tempered, childish, and occasionally violent side, and reflects it back to us as clearly as any mirror. As Jimmy Carter said, "Elvis Presley was a symbol of the country's vitality, rebelliousness and good humor."

Elvis does not possess the disciplined, flawless French style of Audrey and Jackie, nor Cary Grant's cool Savile Row tailoring. How dull that perfection can be at times, after all. He was not a tiresome intellectual—but out on the road, searching, pushing forward, *reaching* the people. Elvis is not the voice of the city; we leave that to Frank Sinatra and Cole Porter. In Elvis, we hear the South, the West, churchgoing folk, truck drivers with one more haul to go before daybreak. Even today, Elvis speaks for them.

Like the true America, Elvis is not properly schooled, but has unerring instincts; how to move an audience, but mostly, how to sing. Jerry Leiber, who cowrote "Hound Dog," "Loving You," and other hits, says, "He had an incredible, attractive instrument that worked in many registers. He could falsetto like Little Richard. He could sing. The equipment was outstanding. His ear was uncanny. His sense of timing was second to none." Elvis singing to us: how intimate like love, how trusting, that voice in your ear leading you through the dark. Our modern prayer. Through his songs and through his life, he conveys the inchoate desire of this gorgeous heartbreaking country of ours.

Dead at forty-two, worn out finally and alone, Elvis tested the Zen koan as few are given the opportunity: What would you do if your life were pure possibility? If you could have, or do, anything you wanted? In the end, Elvis faltered. Paradoxically, the man who had all the freedom in the world closed up upon himself, retreating to Graceland.

Yet for all his perceived faults (and who is anyone to judge another's life?), Elvis did not fail to live in the time he was given. Like few men, he chased love—

both giving and receiving; believing in its power like he believed in God. With his genius, he recognized that love and its transformative possibility of redemption, perhaps even more than his talent, could save him.

He may have made a few bad judgment calls—some fans and cultural critics judge him as harshly as any ex-wife, but his lowest moments were higher than most men's highs.

Finally, we see that Elvis had all the dreams of man: youth, talent, physical perfection, artistic exuberance. Once possessed, they can never be taken from him. But none of it was enough to save him. Is this our American story? In the end, like all great loves—like the world itself—he will break our hearts. His voice and some small measure of innocence are the only things that will outlive him.

And us.

> If Elvis had worn a white button-down oxford
> cloth shirt, he would still be driving a truck.
>
> —HAL LANSKY

memphis **days**

IT IS THURSDAY, JULY 8, 1954, the close of another hot summer day in Memphis. The sun is just setting as Elvis comes roaring in, almost slamming the door off its hinges. "What's wrong?" His mama jumps at the racket, always fearing the worst. "Nothing," he says, setting his radio on the kitchen table, turning the dial to one station, and telling her not to touch it no matter what. "Make sure you and Daddy listen to Dewey Phillips tonight, and don't tell nobody. I'll be back." "What's going on?" she wants to know. Oh Lord, this boy has her so worried. He can't—he can't sit still, he is too skittish, amazed. "See you later, Mama." With that he heads outside, the street and the soft night the only thing to contain his energy.

He ends up at the Suzore number two movie theater over on North Main, where he worked as an usher before he got the job driving a truck for Crown Electric. He walks in right in the middle of a double feature, barely registering the images on the screen. Roy Rogers and Trigger. Good. He slouches low, legs sprawled over the seat in front of him totally against the rules of the theater, chewing bunches of red licorice. His feet crossed at the ankles beat an edgy staccato.

Outside, there is music in the air in Memphis: gospel, rhythm and blues, jazz. There are piano chords, the foot-stomping faith of a church choir, the hard bass of the sharecropper. Music in his head, in his walk, in the tap-tap-tapping of nervous fingers measuring a bravado beat only he can hear. This music is realer than anything he has ever known. He is poor, he is hungry. Beneath his extraordinary politeness—he has the docility of a house servant—wells the rage of an outsider with nothing to lose and nowhere to go but up. He wants to get the hell out. He comes from nowhere, has nothing. He is anxious for knowledge, for worlds he cannot imagine. These words, this song, this chorus inside his head. Everything, he will say and prove later with his success, is for his mama. Yes, music in the air in Memphis.

OUTSIDE, HIS DREAMS TOOK SHAPE ON BEALE, blessed Beale, the soul of Memphis. In the end for good Southern boys, all dreams begin on Beale Street.

Sam Phillips, founder of Sun Records and the man who discovered Elvis, first visited Memphis with five boys from his church and the only thing they wanted to see was Beale. He'd heard so much about it. He knew that W. C. Handy was from Florence, Alabama, his hometown. He knew Handy had come to Memphis and wrote the blues on Beale Street. And there was nothing, *nothing* Sam wanted to see more than that. It was pouring down rain the morning they arrived, five boys in a '37 Dodge convertible. They drove up and down Beale at four in the morning—and it was everything he had heard. There were folks dressed fit to kill, winos, clean drunks, people from the farm just looking, looking to make sure they didn't miss anything. Beale was the center of the black universe. "They had been saving for years, some of 'em, to come to Beale Street and spend the weekend," Phillips observed.

For Sam and his friends, Memphis was *it.* "At that time," recalled Phillips, "Memphis, Tennessee's main street was the prettiest, widest thoroughfare—you would have thought I was in Germany on the autobahn."

On Beale, as in life, the sacred and the profane bumped right next to each other. You saw things you would never see back home. There were grocery stores, nightclubs, pawnshops by the handful, bars, honky-tonks, liquor stores, restaurants—the Old King Palace, which, in its heyday, sold more beer than any place in the country; Pee Wee's Saloon; and the Culpepper. Johnny Mills had the best barbeque in town—Frank Sinatra always went there when he played the Peabody Hotel. One of the clubs, The Monarch, was so disreputable that the wives called it "the castle of missing men." On Thursday night, the Palace Theater had the "Midnight Rambler," and white folks would come in and go to the movies from 11:45 until one or two in the morning. There were loose women, blues men who never saw the light of day, rooming houses with just one bathroom, and one numberthree washtub for fourteen people. You had to get up pretty damn early in the morning for that bathtub.

Mrs. Jackson had one of the finest rooming houses in the city of Memphis. Count Basie, all the big bands used to stay with her. She had the best fried chicken you would ever want to eat. Tony's Fruit Stand was on the corner of Beale and Main, run by an Eye-talian—he did nothing but print money. The old One Minute Restaurant had a ten-cent hot dog that was unreal. It was owned by a Greek fellow who knew how to make hamburgers and hot dogs. You couldn't get into the place it was so good. During the Depression, farmers came by horse and wagon to trade butter and eggs. The Handy Theater was over on Park Street. Leonard Bernstein went down there after he had a concert at the auditorium. He stayed up all night playing piano with the guys. Unreal.

There was a little club at the corner of Beale and Second, behind the liquor store. Bernard Lansky, who runs Lansky Brothers' clothing store, recalls seeing a man walk out the front door in broad daylight, his throat slashed from ear to ear with a carpet knife. He dropped down dead and no one blinked an eye. "Nobody pushed or nothing like that, they just step aside and walk down the street," he recalled.

ELVIS AARON PRESLEY was a kid who was different and needless to say, he loved Beale. He lived with his mama and daddy, Gladys and Vernon, in the Lauderdale Courts, public housing really, but a step up for them. A step they were most grateful to take. He went to high school at Humes, where the white kids went, and majored in nothing, really. There was never any talk of college. Any money he earned from his after-school jobs was handed over to his daddy on Friday afternoon to help the family. Years later he would say about college, "I'd like to have gone, but I never thought about it. We just didn't have the money."

In his uncertainty, in his anonymity, Elvis was like millions of other American kids. Going to the movies, listening to his radio, scrapping a quarter to buy a burger and a shake—he loved french fries but wouldn't touch the ketchup. Wondering what might happen next.

"I was a nobody, a small town kid in the big city, without a dime in my pocket, not too good in class, kinda shy . . . and the other guys wore GI haircuts," he said later. "I wanted to look older, be different. I guess mostly I wanted to be noticed. My hair, the black shirt and pants I wore did it. But don't think I didn't take a lot of kidding from my friends. Still, I stuck with it. I guess I always knew if you want to stand out in a crowd you gotta be different."

Like most boys his age—he was eighteen—Elvis loved girls, cars, and music. And was wildly particular about his looks, how he *presented* himself to the world. He was terrible about his hair, taking hours—it seemed—to comb it, using three different kinds of grease to get it to stand the way he liked. Elvis wanted to look like the hard men you saw in redneck bars. His chief style influence was from the truckers who roared down Highway 78 on their way to New Orleans. "They were wild looking guys, they had scars," he recalled. "I used to lay on the side of the road and watch them drive their big diesel trucks." His daddy, too, drove a truck—although it was, admittedly, for just a few months: "My dad was a truck driver and I admired him and other truck drivers I knew. Most wore sideburns and mustaches. So when I was sixteen, I grew sideburns to look as much like them as possible."

At Humes, his favorite colors were pink and black, a wild statement when most boys his age wore khakis and madras shirts with loafers. Elvis didn't care. Well, he *did* care, he wanted to be part of the gang. But he wanted to stand out, too. "It was just something I wanted to do," he said. "I wasn't trying to be better than anybody else."

And he was shy beyond belief, that was the other thing. He looked as if he would just about fall over if you said boo to him. But then he wore those crazy clothes, just looking for attention, itching for a fight, almost. To an outsider it didn't make any sense.

Elvis barely had two nickels to rub together but he knew one thing—you want smooth threads, you got but one place to go: Lansky on famous Beale Street. And when you get there, ask for Bernard.

Bernard Lansky was raised in south Memphis. Growing up, his daddy had a dry goods and grocery store with one gas pump. He went to Riverside grammar school and then South Side High School. Asked his favorite subject, he laughs— "Makin' money." After that it was the college of hard knocks; in other words, the army. "Uncle Sam took care of me then."

Like pretty much everybody else during Korea, Bernard was in the army for three and a half years. He started out in Fort Bragg, North Carolina, and from there headed up to Fort Knox, Kentucky.

When he got out, it was back home to Memphis. By then, his dad had bought a second store, this one on Beale Street, because Bernard's brother, Guy, had just gotten out of the army and had nothing to do. Mr. Lansky Senior still had the grocery store and dry goods store on Kansas Street, so the boys got into the surplus business.

Nothing was planned. It was just that after the war, styles were loosening up and people started buying fatigues. Folks wanted the stuff because it was cheap—you could get a cap or a shirt for fifty cents, or fatigue pants for $1.95. Then surplus started thinning out and they had to start thinking of some other kind of line, so they went into the menswear business.

As Bernard recalls, "People thought we were crazy down on Beale Street, going into high fashion merchandise." It was a good move. Other shops on Beale sold simple clothes for farmers—four-button overall pants, cotton dresses for the ladies. When Lansky Brothers started, they were the only store in all of Memphis carrying this kind of merchandise. "We had all the kids, people in high school—had the blacks, and the whites used to come in and shop with us because we had fashion. We had something that nobody else had.

"You want to look clean as Ajax? Lansky's is your place!" says Bernard Lansky with no small understatement. Because there are two things Bernard Lansky knows—clothes and people. He could always talk to anybody. Not immodestly, he says, "I was number one because I knew how to put the language with the people. I knew how to *communicate*. You know, a lot of people go to college and learn all that English and stuff, I knew what was happening, I was down here with the people."

You go to Lansky's and Bernard—who is there, even today, every morning at 6:00 A.M.—or one of the boys will take care of you. Bernard describes his style philosophy. "A man walks in and I see he's got the wrong tie on. You got to know what will look good on 'em. You don't put no rock-and-roll clothes on a man goin' be working in a bank or something.

"You know, different people buy different things. But you can tell. When you go into one of our stores you better know what to put on the customer. Know what kind of business—first thing you do, 'Hey, how you doin', what's your name, sir? By the way, what do you do?' Right away, you know what you're going to put on that customer. I've been here a long time, I know what's happening."

The whole thing started, like so many things, with the black entertainers. Rufus Thomas, the number-one man in Memphis who had recorded "Bear Cat" with Sun Records, bought some wild stuff from Lansky. He'd visit the shop, open his coat, and say, "Ain't I clean? Lansky—that's where I buy my clothes!" The blues guys who played Beale needed some sharp threads so they would stand out. I mean, you can't be dressing like a damn farmer when you're onstage. "A lot of these entertainers used to come in here—black and white. In fact, it was all black at first and then the whites started seeing what they were wearing, they liked what they were wearing. So they used to come in here and buy the same thing."

By the mid-1950s, *everybody* knew about Lansky's. All the musicians shopped there—B. B. King, just off a tractor with $2.50 and a guitar, and the gospel groups, James Blackwood, who favored Swedish knits. The gospels were great for business because they used to come in and buy 'em as a group of four or five guys, gamblers from California and Vegas who dropped some big green. They got a lot of people from Nashville, or Arkansas, down in Mississippi. Kids in from the country who could barely afford to look.

After starting out with a small shop that sold surplus goods, Bernard and Guy added some jewelry and a small pawn shop; expanding, they bought the stores on either side, the upstairs, which had been a rooming house, and eventually, the entire building and the lot next door for $90,000. In 1955, Lansky sold everything a man could want—they had two, three thousand suits in the place. There was no end to Bernard's inventiveness. They had the finest piece goods—silk, wool, and mohair. They had their own in-house tailor shop. If they didn't have what you wanted, they would show you some material and make it for you, whatever you had in mind. "I guarantee you, on Friday and Saturday you couldn't find a parking place around here with all the people picking up their clothes," recalls Bernard. They had shirts, ties, a shoe salon, hats, even luggage.

The place was so jumping, there were ten salesmen on the floor. Ten besides Bernard; his wife, Joyce; Guy; and their sons. They had a tailor shop with six men working full time. Wherever they saw a need, they filled it. Bernard was every-where. He was the Donald Trump of Beale Street without the ego and the dubious comb-over. On Sunday, he dressed the windows himself. "I knew what to put in those windows, I wouldn't let anybody do it but me 'cause I knew what was happen-ing. People looked at our window—it was just like looking at a morning paper, 'cause he's going to see something different."

The consummate salesman, Lansky knew that his windows, his shop, hell, the guys working in the back wrapping packages, had to be giving 110 percent be-cause they were all representing Lansky's. If Lansky was taking care of you, you were taken care of. "You had to look sharp—when you get out on the street you were my advertising, you were my billboard. People knew what was happening, they'd say, 'Hey man, this guy has been to Lansky, I got to go shopping there.'"

Elvis knew about Lansky's, of course he did. Right around the corner from the Loews, he walked by it all the time, studying Bernard's display like it was the label of a 45.

Bernard saw him looking in the windows—a tall skinny kid with crazy hair and eyes that made you look twice. He had no money, Bernard knew, but that never stopped anyone from becoming a customer, from forming a *relationship* with Lansky. Once you knew Bernard, you were a friend for life.

In his white shirtsleeves, Bernard walked out onto the sidewalk to talk to the boy. It was a slow afternoon. "Hey," he said, friendly, "why don't you come on in?"

The boy looked shocked. "Ah, no, I—" he stuttered.

"Come on, come on in. . . ." Bernard was welcoming, he had all the time in the world, holding the door open. He knew this boy, had seen his ways in the farm families, shy seeming and not good enough, almost as if he didn't deserve to be there.

Bernard took him in and showed him around. "Everything he saw, he was like a kid in a candy store," he recalled. Elvis was entranced. He picked up and ran his hand along it all—the patterned jackets with velvet collars, the tuxedos, the black pegged no-back-pocket pants (a Lansky original), $65 alligator shoes.

"But Mr. Lansky, I don't have any money."

Bernard waved the thought away. There was something about the kid he liked. He was so personable, you could tell he *wanted* people to like him.

"But I tell you what—when I get rich I'll buy you out!"

"Hey, do me a favor," Bernard said and smiled, with a fast comeback, "just buy from me—I don't want you buying me out!"

They laughed, getting along fine. This boy—what was his name, Elvis?—was a kidder just like him.

That Friday Elvis came back and put a shirt on layaway; cost about $3.95, that was a lot of bread at the time. "Look at that—you're starting your wardrobe!" Bernard said, like he's talking to a Rockefeller. Elvis smiled. He was on his way.

SAM PHILLIPS WAS COCKY. Damn straight Sam Phillips was cocky. He had The Dream and saw it as few others did. "I will say unhesitatingly that if God gave me anything at all, he gave me the intuitive powers, not to read minds but to feel souls." Like Lansky, and Elvis, too, school was not a big draw for Sam. "I don't think I truly learned too much from books," he said. "Certainly I learned how to read and how to write, a few simple math formulas." But *curiosity* is what Phillips had. Curiosity and an almost manic amount of energy. At the end of the day, experience was what Sam was after, and you'd never find that sitting in a schoolroom. "God knows I learned from people, I learned from animals," he reflected.

Phillips was in radio. He came to Memphis at the age of twenty-two with four years of broadcast experience already under his belt. He started out at Muscle Shoals' WLAY, then moved on to Decatur, Alabama, Nashville's WLAC, and finally arrived at Memphis' WREC in the summer of 1945 with his wife and infant son. Short of singing on the air, he did pretty much everything that needed to be done at WREC— announcer, producer, maintenance man, and broadcast engineer, overseeing the big band broadcasts that were presented every night high atop the Hotel Peabody Skyway.

At the basement offices of WREC, Sam met Marion Keisker, a divorcée who had even more radio experience than he did. A native Memphian, she had made her radio debut at the age of twelve on the weekly children's show *Wynken, Blynken, and Nod* and was a familiar voice to anyone who had listened to local radio over the past twenty-five years. A 1938 graduate of Memphis' Southwestern College, where she had majored in English, she had been the host of the very popular *Meet Miss Kitty*, where she interviewed visiting celebrities five nights a week, as well as the nightly broadcasts of *Treasury Bandstand* from the Peabody Skyway.

Bored with the autopilot performances of the big bands he produced, Phillips was on the lookout for something alive, something *authentic*. A restless man with a rogue ear and a prowling sensibility, he was drawn to Beale Street, to the sounds of the rough country blues players. Forget "In the Mood"; he decided that these were the people he wanted to record.

Unfortunately, no one at WREC (with the possible exception of Marion Keisker who had, in the interim, fallen hopelessly in love with him) shared his vision.

Sam knew without any doubt that artistically, he was able to discern what was different. The music he was after was not the safe sound coming out of Nashville and the Grand Ole Opry, or worse, the Establishment up in New York City, the Dorseys and the Frank Sinatras, smooth boys who were on the inside and working the rail.

No—Sam heard the rhythms of this country, sharecroppers picking cotton on someone else's land, those who were always just a little behind. In their music he heard "the elements of the soil, the sky, the water, even the wind, quiet nights, people living on plantations, never out of debt, hoping to eat, lights up the river, that's where they used to call Memphis."

That was The Dream. Would he ever find that voice?

For Sam Phillips believed in greatness. That was both his blessing and his curse. He believed he could sense it as clearly as he felt the wildness of the Mississippi River. He believed, too, that he was the one who could pull it out of the humble people who walked into the studio.

Born in 1923 on a farm in Florence, Alabama, Phillips had a love for this country, a love of music and the people who worked the land. "I heard the innate rhythms of people that had absolutely no formal training in music. Didn't know one note from another, starting in childhood, and when I got to Beale Street where there was a big black population. To see that and to see the black people especially, that came to Memphis . . . that struck a certain chord in me, and it resonated."

But how to get there? Phillips was already working eighteen-hour days—putting in a full day at the station, going to his makeshift studio late in the afternoon, returning to the Peabody in the evening for the Skyway broadcasts until midnight, then back to the studio to oversee the recording of a cotton patch farmer singing blues on a bare-bones guitar.

Sam was working himself to death, that much was clear. He had already had one nervous breakdown in the forties, from stress and overwork, and was hospitalized twice at Gartley-Ramsay Hospital, where he had received electroshock treatment. It was, he said, the only time in his entire life he was scared: twenty-eight years old with a wife and two little boys, Knox and Jerry, as well as his mother and a deaf aunt depending on him. How could he make it work? For once, his belief in himself faltered. He quit the radio station in a moment, though, when his boss, Hoyt Wooten, made a sarcastic comment about why he had been away.

"Mr. Wooten, you are a cruel man," he said, and left WREC forever.

There was one thing to do. Sam Phillips decided he had to open his own little studio. "I don't have any money, but I can build it with my own hands," he decided. He and Marion found a place on Union Avenue and The Dream took shape.

Fifty years before anybody was into yoga, meditation, Buddhism, or reading Pema Chödrön, Sam Phillips was down in Memphis, an authentic Zen warrior. He recognized that the road he was on was beyond difficult. And he had no way of knowing, in the end, how it would turn out. Still, he pressed forward. "I wouldn't spare myself these hardships," he decided. "I couldn't spare myself these hardships, except one way—not do it. Not *attempt* to do it. That wasn't satisfactory with me. I had to do it. If I did it, and it failed, I was still a hell of a winner. If I didn't, against all odds, then I would have been a failure. Period. Maybe nobody would have known that, but I would have."

In January 1950, with Marion's help, he opened Sun Records, and the Memphis Recording Service, a two-person operation—consisting of, well, Sam and Marion. As she recalls, "With many difficulties we got the place and we raised the money, and between us we did everything—we laid all the tile, we painted the acoustic boards, I put in the bathroom, Sam put in the control room—what little equipment he had always had to be the best.

"I knew nothing about the music, and I didn't care one bit," she continues. "My association, my contribution, my participation was based totally on my personal association with Sam in a way that is totally unbelievable to me now. All I wanted to do was to make it possible for him to fulfill his vision. All I wanted to do was to do what would make him happy."

Phillips' business card read: "We record anything—anytime—anywhere. A complete service to fill every recording need," and they meant it. He recorded funerals, weddings, the conventions that came through the Peabody Hotel. If someone was breathing and came in with $3.98, hell, Sam would record that, too. He didn't even begin to think of having his own record label, but he started recording some of the blues singers. B. B. King for RPM Modern Records on the West Coast. Then Leonard Chess (he and his brother Phil ran Chess Records out of Chicago) came through town and Sam played "Rocket 88" by Jackie Brenston and Ike Turner (considered to be the first rock-and-roll record) and it blew him away. It was the biggest record Phillips had ever had. "If you got fifty thousand sales on a record, that was a big sale. We got this and sold five hundred thousand, that's the equivalent today of probably ten million damn records."

There was a money dispute with the Chess brothers, so Sam, who never liked having partners anyway ("When you cheat me out of one damn dollar, you got a problem"), decided to record his own music. And where did the name "Sun" come from? "I don't know," he says now. "I guess I'm just a country boy. And I know what happened when the sun came up on the farm. It's a happy type of thing, it's three letters that would look good on a 45." For all his messianic idealism, though, Sam was still a realist: "At the same time, I didn't think that the label made much difference anyway—it was going to be what we could create."

So Sam had his own fiefdom, Sun Studio. He was up all night, more eighteen-hour days, but this time he believed absolutely in what he was doing. In the *rightness* of it. Married with two small boys and a coworker so in love with him she would do anything he asked, it was a hell of a life. There were times he had never been more certain of his power. Exhausted, frightened, scrambling for money, not sure how he was going to pull it off, he had never felt more alive: He was on the path.

"It's not by accident in many cases that people are put through 'the thrills of deprivation,'" he insists. "I think there is a certain type of—plan, that nobody can write the formula for, or shouldn't, that's out there. To me, that is the essence of what we're all about."

IN LATE SUMMER OF 1953, having graduated from Humes the past spring, Elvis Presley walked into that simple entryway sick with nerves, dreaming things he could barely speak of. Can we imagine him? He is alone, and gawky—just under six feet tall, rail thin with greasy light brown hair, bad skin, and longing eyes. Like most teenagers, there was something ridiculous about him; still, his need compels. He was so vulnerable, so aching that you wanted to soothe his raw edges.

He wanted to sing, to express what was inside of him. He wanted to move people, raise them up like Sunday morning. He wanted to break your goddamn heart. There was no air-conditioning and the little anteroom was hot. It was a Saturday in August and the Tennessee sun beat across the venetian blinds that did little to calm the heat. He knew what he wanted, but had no idea how to get there. The woman behind the typewriter looked so cool and collected. The dream began to take shape. He had a goal in mind: 706 Union Avenue. How often he had driven by making sure it was still there, finally working up the courage to go in. God willing, he would sing in that little two-bit room in Memphis.

Who knew where it might lead?

"Ma'am?" He closed the door gently behind him. He had a soft country accent. Like Gatsby, he realized people liked him when he smiled. He—he wanted to make a record for his mother's birthday. Of course, Gladys was born on April 25, her birthday was months ago, so there was no small measure of deliberation behind his canny innocence.

While they waited for Sam to set things up in the control room, Elvis began, tentatively . . . "If you know anyone that needs a singer . . ."

"What kind of a singer are you?" Marion wondered.

"I sing all kinds."

"Who do you sound like?"

"I don't sound like nobody."

Uh-oh, she thought—one of those. From the looks of him, she guessed hillbilly.

"I sing hillbilly."

She tried again, "Well, who do you *sound* like in hillbilly?"

"I don't sound like nobody," he insisted quietly.

SAM—THE SAM PHILLIPS he had read about in the newspaper—motioned to him from behind the glass. He was ready.

Hands shaking, Elvis walked to the middle of the room. He looked at Mr. Phillips, now? Sam nodded. Now.

He sang a song he had been practicing at the Courts for months, "My Happiness," which had been a hit for Jon and Sandra Steele in 1948. Marion listened at her desk. He was right, he didn't sound like anyone else.

Accompanied by his guitar, his voice was tentative at first with nerves and uncertainty. He was so alone he sounded almost like a little boy. Toward the end, dipping into the chorus, came the fuller-voiced Elvis we know. Still, it was a simple ballad. There was no hint of any black influence, of the stalking power of rock and roll to come. What struck Marion most was the emotion that came through his performance, and the calm expectation he held at its center, as if: *There are no accidents.* This was meant to happen. When he finished, he began another, "That's When Your Heartaches Begin," a pop ballad the Ink Spots had recorded in 1941. Here, he was not so successful, running out of time or interest, declaring, "That's the end," at the conclusion of the tape.

He took a step back and looked up at Mr. Phillips.

Sam said he was an "interesting" singer and that "we might give you a call sometime." Out in the front office, Marion made a note of the boy's name, misspelling it and adding, "Good ballad singer. Hold."

Elvis paid his $3.95 and hung around a bit, hoping Sam might come out to say good-bye, but he was too busy. Finally, not wanting to take up any more of Miss Keisker's time, he walked out of 706 Union with his acetate in his hand, convinced that now, finally, he was on his way.

He wasn't.

For months, there was nothing. Elvis would stop by the studio and make small talk with Miss Keisker, seeing if anything was up. Nothing ever was. He did not want to be a bother, but he also did not know what else to do. Marion did what she could to encourage the boy. Long after his success, his impression of neediness, of longing, stayed with her a long time. Through the fall and the winter he came by, hoping to see Mr. Phillips, but he was busy. Mr. Phillips was always busy, he was running a recording studio—he had real work to do.

Elvis' relationship with Sun, if you could call it that, was like having a terrible crush on a woman totally out of his league. Sun, and by extension Mr. Phillips, did not give him the time of day. Bit by bit, he came by less often.

In January 1954, he recorded another little record, with no mention of anyone's birthday this time, Joni James' "I'll Never Stand in Your Way" and an old Jimmy Wakely tune, "It Wouldn't Be the Same Without You." This time, his insecurity betrayed him and he sounded abrupt, off track. For a singer, for any artist, confidence is everything.

Elvis was at an impasse, not knowing what else to do to bring his dream to fruition. Would he just be some anonymous guy driving a damn truck the rest of his life? Marion, who felt almost maternal about him by this time, thought that in the end, it would work out for him. "He was," she says, "so ingenious there was no way he could go wrong."

STILL, THINGS WEREN'T ALL BAD for Elvis. He took stock of his situation: He was nineteen years old, a high school graduate, and he had a weekly paycheck coming in. Now that he had recorded four songs (okay, so they were singles that he paid for) and got a couple of shirts from Lansky, what he needed was a girlfriend.

Elvis and Dixie Locke met cute, as they say in Hollywood—at church. In January 1954, Elvis started attending church regularly, at the Assembly of God church in south Memphis. There, he met Dixie Locke, fifteen and a sophomore at South Side High. She first noticed him in the half hour before the girls and boys split up into their religious study classes, how could she not? He was dressed so oddly in pink and black with his greased hair and fidgety manner. "He was just so different, all the other guys were like replicas of their dads," she recalls.

The other girls thought him peculiar, but the new boy was so serious about his Bible study, and so transparent in his wanting to *belong*.

And yet to Dixie, even at fifteen, he was different in another way: "To watch him you would think, even then, he was really shy. What was so strange was that he would do anything to call attention to himself, but I think he was doing it to prove something to himself more than to the people around him. Inside, even then, I think he knew he was different. I knew the first time I met him that he was not like other people."

For their first date, they went out to the Rainbow Rollerdome just outside the city limits. Well, Elvis did not actually call Dixie up and ask her out or anything like that; Dixie just made a point of talking loudly in the vicinity of Elvis—about how she and all her girlfriends would be there, and hoped he might overhear.

He did.

When she arrived at the roller rink with her girlfriends, wearing her black corduroy skating skirt with white satin lining, Elvis was there, leaning against the rail all by himself with his skates on, trying to look engaged and nonchalant at the same time. He was wearing "kind of a bolero outfit—short black bullfighter's jacket, ruffled shirt, black pegged pants with a pale pink stripe down the side."

Dixie took one look at him—a bolero outfit!—and realized with a start: He can't skate.

Eventually, Dixie took pity on him and went over and introduced herself. "Yeah, I know," he said, looking down and tossing his hair back. They decided, mercifully, to walk over to the snack area and get a Coke.

For someone so shy in public, Elvis talked and talked. It was as if he had been waiting his whole life to unburden himself to someone he could trust. They stayed for the second session. Dixie was supposed to go home with friends, but she sent them on along without her. It was well past ten when he suggested they go to K's on Crump Boulevard for a hamburger and a milk shake. Dixie made a pretend call to her parents (she was too embarrassed to let him know that they did not have a telephone in their house) and rattled on about the nice boy from church she had met, and how she would be home late.

She had never done anything like this in her life. They went to K's in Elvis' borrowed Lincoln. She snuck in the door after midnight, certain her father was going to kill her, not caring in the least. Elvis had whispered that he would call her next week—Wednesday, or Thursday, definitely—about going out the following weekend. She was in love.

He called her neighbor's phone the next day and they went to the movies, and again on Wednesday night. Finally, after running out of excuses, it was time for Elvis to meet her parents and in particular, her father. All the boys she and her sisters had brought to the house were intimidated by Mr. Locke. Big (six foot two) and impassive, he was such a quiet force that everyone in the house did pretty much anything he told them to; that's just the way it was.

Dixie had tried to prepare everyone for Elvis—he was a good boy from a nice family, she stressed, they had met in church, please don't judge him by the way he looks—but even though she was in love with him, she was unprepared for the actual sight of him in her family's living room. There was the Elvis in her heart, and there was another Elvis mumbling "Yes, sir" and "No, sir" to her father. She had forgotten how *different* he looked. She had forgotten about his hair and his dress, and she had forgotten about the effect he had on others.

In the kitchen, her mother read her the riot act: How could she go out with a boy like that? Her sister was perfectly polite to Elvis, but behind his back raised her eyebrows to Dixie, as if to say: *What is with this guy?* The next day, her uncle came over and offered two dollars if the boy would get his hair cut.

The Lockes found Dixie's new beau hilarious. For Dixie, and for Elvis, none of this mattered. Elvis had given her his ring—they were in love and would be together forever.

THAT SPRING, guitarist Scotty Moore, who was working at his brother's dry cleaning shop blocking hats when he wasn't playing in his country band, the Starlite Wranglers, stopped by Sun to see if there was anything he could do to give his record a boost. ("We had six guys in the band, and that's about how many records we sold," he admits.) Since Scotty and Sam Phillips were closer in age, background, and ambition, Sam took the time to sit a spell and talk with him.

Settling into Sun's conference room (actually, the third table back by the window at Mrs. Dell Taylor's restaurant next door), Sam started telling Scotty about a young ballad singer he'd been keeping an eye on. He was interested in maybe trying him out on a new song he had picked up last week in Nashville.

"What's his name?" Scotty wondered.

Elvis Presley.

That sounds like something out of science fiction, thought Scotty. But he did not want to block hats the rest of his life—or play in a hillbilly band, for that matter. Sticking close with Sam Phillips was the best chance, the *only* chance, he had. "Give me his number, I'll look him up," he promised.

"Just give him a listen, kind of feel him out," was Sam's advice.

On Sunday, July 4, Elvis showed up at Scotty's house like he was about to go onstage wearing a Lansky special—black shirt, pink pants with a thin black stripe, white shoes, and his greasy ducktail. After some small talk, the bass player, Bill Black, came by and they got down to work. Elvis picked up his guitar and riffed bits and pieces of seemingly every song he knew—the Ink Spots' "If I Didn't Care," Hank Snow's "I Don't Hurt Anymore," Eddie Arnold's latest hit, "I Really Don't Want to Know," Billy Eckstine's "I Apologize," some Roy Hamilton, and a Dean

Martin–style version of "You Belong to Me." They were ballads, all sung in the same quavery voice that he had attempted with "My Happiness."

They tried small talk but Elvis was so nervous his hands shook. Finally, they called it a day and Elvis went off trailing clouds of oily smoke behind him in his tired Lincoln. "What'd you think?" Scotty wanted to know as soon as Presley walked out the door.

"Well, he didn't impress me too damn much," said Bill, who liked everyone. "Snotty-nosed kid coming in here with those wild clothes and everything."

Forget the fashion critique, what did you think of his *singing*? Scotty wanted to know. Oh, the singing—"Man, he's all right, he knocked me out."

He hated to admit it, but Scotty thought the same thing. It was obvious that Elvis had a good voice, good range, but with that material, he wasn't going to push Eddy Arnold out of the box anytime soon.

Later, he called Sam to offer his opinion. It was the least he could do, since he seemed so keen on the boy. Maybe there was something Scotty was missing. He told Sam what he thought: "The boy's got a good voice."

Sam thought he would have them all come down to the studio tomorrow night to see how they sounded on tape. You never know.

"You want the whole band?" Scotty wanted to know.

"Naw—just you and Bill for rhythm, no sense making a big deal out of it. Let's keep it small and see what happens."

THE NEXT NIGHT everyone assembled at 706 Union Avenue. They mucked around just like they had done in Scotty's living room—scraps of songs Elvis knew, with the boys following along the best they could. *Was there one song that this kid knew all the words to?* It looked as if it was going to be another lost evening. There was something about the kid's sound that got your attention, he was different for sure, but the gig wasn't going anywhere so they figured they'd call it a night. Bill started packing up his gear when Elvis, out of nowhere, started riffing strong and fast on a tune they all knew.

In the control room Sam was angry—they were supposed to be working up some new material, and all they could come up with was an old blues song by Arthur "Big Boy" Crudup? Now what was the damn sense—

Phillips stopped. He had never heard anything like it.

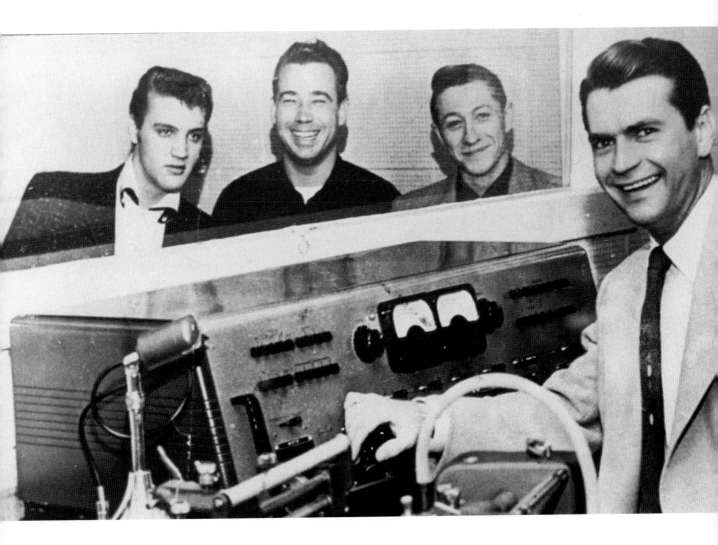

Elvis' voice, his *being*—pulled him up short. Je-sus! What the hell was that? It felt, he said, "like someone stuck me in the rear end with a brand-new super sharp pitchfork." Scotty picked up his guitar and rambled along in three-quarter time, following Elvis' lead. Sam told Bill to stop packing up the damn bass and get in there—the session wasn't over yet.

For Sam, blues was the total effect of a man's experience in life, but where was this damn sound coming from? "The blues can be joyous, if you're looking back on it and things are all right now," he believed. "But if you're looking back on it and they're still bad, the blues can be a little soulful and sorrowful and sad." This kid was eighteen, nineteen years old. Sure, his daddy didn't work and money was tight, but he knew nothing about the world. Nothing. But that voice sure as hell did; that voice was centuries old. "Rock and roll," Sam felt, "is the blues with a mania."

Mania. He didn't know what they were doing out there, but man, it sounded fresh. Elvis gained more confidence with every take. Finally—a song they knew all the way through! "Well—that's all right mama, that's all right for you, that's all right mama . . . " Where was the kid hearing this from? He sang along, chin boppin' free and loose with Scotty's jangly guitar chorus—"da dee de de, de de de deee."

The dream, the dream. "If I could find a white man with a Negro sound," he had told Marion time and again, "I could make a billion dollars."

NOW THAT SAM had the record, there was one man to call, Dewey Phillips— the most happening deejay in Memphis. Dewey (no relation to Sam) had the magic touch. From 9:00 P.M. to 12:00 P.M. every night, he ran *Red, Hot, and Blue*, the radio program every young person in Memphis, including Elvis, listened to.

Dewey stopped by Sun after midnight; for him, this was as good a time as noon. Sam greeted him with a couple of beers and a bottle of Jack Daniel's; he had a song by a new kid he wanted him to hear. Dewey opened a Falstaff and put some salt in it, listening to the tape Sam played. He knew "That's All Right," of course, everybody knew Arthur "Big Boy" Crudup's version. He had played it on his show many times. But this, Jesus—this was *different*. He took another swig, thoughtful now, his feet up on the console, and nodded to Sam to play it again from beginning to end. Then one more time. Again.

Sam cued the rewind button and hit Play. He was too scared to think, too scared to say anything. *Was he nuts, or was this the greatest thing he had ever heard?* The two men listened in silence as Scotty's jangly guitar bounced off the walls with Elvis' voice chasing it.

There was not much conversation as the two men listened, wondering what the other thought. "He was reticent, and I was glad that he was," said Sam. "If he hadn't been reticent, it would have scared me to death. If he had said, 'Hey, man— this is a hit!' I would have thought Dewey was just trying to make me feel good. What I was thinking was: 'Where are you going to go with this?' It's not black, it's not white, it's not pop, it's not country. And I think Dewey was the same way.

"He was fascinated by it. There was no question about that, I mean, he loved the damn record, but it was a question of where do we go from here?"

Where indeed.

Sam and Dewey stayed up late, drinking and listening, talking in relatively muted tones until 2:00 or 3:00 in the morning. Nothing was settled, nothing was decided about what to *do* with the damn record, or with the kid for that matter. Finally, they both went home to their respective beds.

Early the next morning (for all the Jack and beer they had consumed), the phone rang and it was Dewey.

"I didn't sleep well last night," he announced with the sudden ardor of a man who has fallen in love.

"Man, you should have slept pretty good." Sam chuckled, thinking of all the alcohol they had consumed.

No—Dewey said he couldn't sleep because he had been thinking of that record, the joyous guitar and that kid's voice cutting through his brain. "I want two copies for the show tonight, and we ain't letting anybody know," he announced, with the imperiousness of a musical Wizard of Oz behind the curtain. His uncertainty was over.

Sam cut the acetates and brought them down to the station. He called Elvis after work and told him Dewey would probably be playing it on the station that night. He didn't want to get his hopes up, but it looked good.

ON JULY 8, 1954, at about 9:30 P.M., Dewey played "That's All Right." Listening at home, Gladys could not believe that the announcer said Elvis' name at the beginning of the song. The switchboard lit up as Phillips played the song again and again. He called the house, looking for Elvis, but he was not home, he was at the theater. "Mrs. Presley, you just get that cotton-picking son of yours down to the station. I played that record of his, and them birdbrain phones haven't stopped ringing since." Gladys and Vernon went to the theater, walking up and down the aisles in the dark, looking for their son. Finally, they found him and brought him to the station.

Later, he was asked why he had hightailed it out to the theater. "I thought people would laugh at me. Some did, and some are still laughing at me today, I guess."

A YEAR LATER in Germany, in 1955, while serving in the RAF, future Rolling Stones guitarist Bill Wyman heard "That's All Right" on the jukebox at the local dancehall, Zum Grünen Wald, and was entranced. He drew Elvis on the back of his sleeveless leather coat and soon everyone in the camp started calling him "Elvis."

NOW THAT HE HAD A HIT, SAM KNEW the real work would begin. He began booking the boys in hillbilly and gospel shows around the area. Playing at the Bon Air Club in Memphis, where Scotty's band, the Starlite Wranglers, had a regular slot, Elvis, Scotty, and Bill played the only two songs they knew well enough to play in front of an audience, "That's All Right" and "Blue Moon of Kentucky."

By mid October, the boys had so much work that Scotty and Elvis quit their full-time jobs to concentrate on the band. Vernon did not know about this. He had seen a lot of people who played guitar and stuff and didn't work, so he told Elvis straight out: "You should make up your mind either about being an electrician or playing a guitar. I never saw a guitar player worth a damn."

Just before he went on the road, Elvis got a five hundred dollar royalty check from Sun, but not having a checking account, he went to the First National Bank of Lansky.

"Mr. Lansky!" he started, pulling the check out of his pocket. Magic money.

"*Bernard.*" Lansky corrected him yet again, smiling. "Mr. Lansky is my father—I'm Bernard." He was fooling with the kid, who was as polite as a preacher's son. Elvis handed the check over to Mr. Lansky—Bernard—and wondered if he could cash it for him, he'd like to buy some clothes. Bernard turned it over. Five hundred bucks—was this for real? He said, "Sure, son," and tucked the check in his shirt pocket.

SO ELVIS AND THE BOYS hit the road. Forty-five years before MTV and (God forbid) *American Idol*, they played anywhere that would have them—high school auditoriums, community centers, little places in west Texas where they strung chicken wire in front of the bandstand.

Elvis loved being on the road, creating himself as he went along. Talking to someone he might not know well, he was shy, inarticulate. But singing, onstage, he reached people. Talked to their souls. Scotty saw how he set the audience off with his movement. "Most singers, if they play the guitar, would stand flat-footed and play and pat the foot. Elvis kind of stood on the balls of his feet, and if you remember back in those days, the big-legged breeches that everybody was wearing, and when he'd stand on the balls of his feet and play, well his leg would, he was still trying to keep time but he was doing it with his leg and the britches would start shaking. It was natural, it wasn't made-up. It was just a natural thing."

IN THE BEGINNING, Elvis did not expect the wild response he got from the crowd, but then, after the same thing happened a few times, he played with it. Played with them. They loved him, all of them, at once. *Goddamn*—he was happy onstage. He loved being onstage. He would live onstage if he could.

IN MARCH 1955 ALONE, the boys played Newport, Arkansas; the Louisiana Hayride in Shreveport; the City Auditorium in Paris, Texas; the Catholic Club in Helena, Arkansas; the Armory in Poplar Bluff, Mississippi; the City Auditorium in Clarksdale, Mississippi; and Jimmy Thompson's Arena in Alexandria, Louisiana. Then it was back to the Hayride, on to the Ruffin Theater in Covington, Tennessee, and from there, Texas.

On Wednesday, March 23, in what was almost certainly his first airplane ride, Elvis traveled to New York City with Scotty, Bill, and Bob Neal, to audition for *The Arthur Godfrey Show*. The talent scouts showed no interest whatsoever.

From there, they played the Dermott High School in Dermott, Arkansas; the Hayride; the Big Creek High School gym in Big Creek, Mississippi (sponsored by a very prescient senior class, who clearly saw more than the bookers for the *Godfrey Show*); the high school in Tocopola, Mississippi (sponsored, this time, by the junior class); the El Dorado high school auditorium in El Dorado, Arkansas; and finally, on March 31, the Reo Palm Isle in Longview, Texas.

And on and on it went. On May 5, not having been home since a few days in January (much to his mother's consternation), Elvis was chased across a football field by a pack of screaming girls.

When he wasn't singing, Elvis was always nervous. He never could sleep through the night. He was sensitive and quick to take offense where none was meant. In his wildly patterned Lansky jacket, loose black pants, 32-inch waist, and two-tone shoes, his shyness and bravado were right alongside each other, with one perhaps covering up the other. Elvis sensed things—it was almost as if he picked up electricity, currents, plucked what was coming next out of the air. His very presence created the next generation. This is the genius that Sam Phillips gave him the confidence to express. This is the genius he passed on to his audience.

Onstage, backed by Scotty, Bill, and a new member, D. J. Fontana, Elvis offered teenagers—his tribe—a new way to live, a new way to navigate the life you imagined for yourself. A new way to *be*. Onstage (a dozen years before Mick

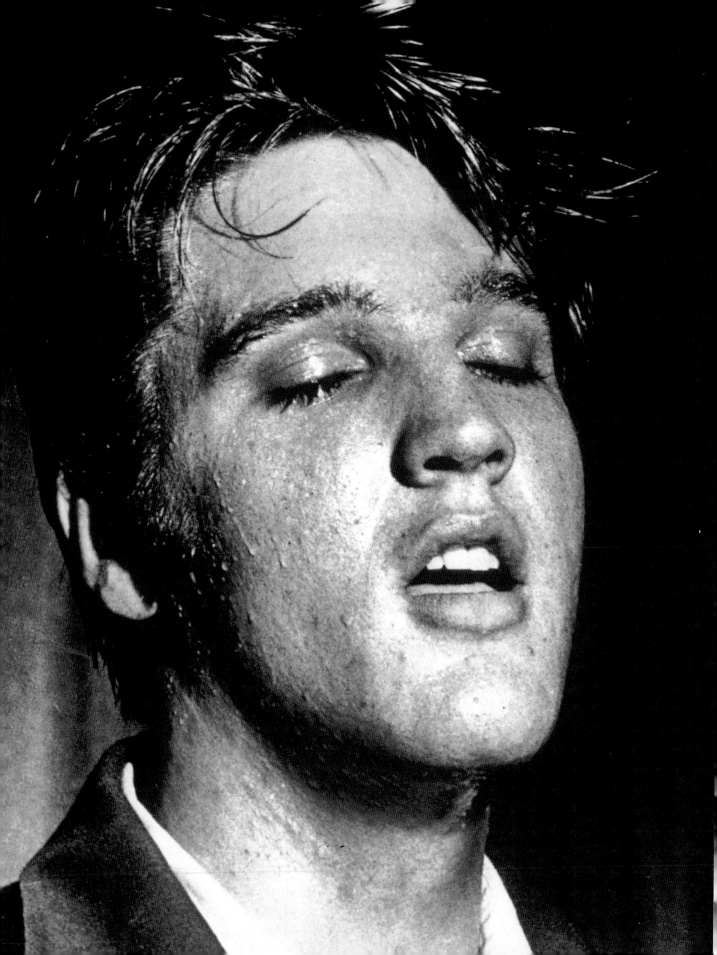

Jagger or Jim Morrison), Elvis was not afraid to work it, in a way no white male performer would dare. Drummer D. J. Fontana had played in strip joints in Shreveport, and this came in handy when he started backing up Elvis. Working with Presley allowed Fontana to use licks he had learned while drumming for burlesque shows, in which the women performers expected him to "catch their leg movements, their tassel movements, their rear end movements." Fontana used the beat to accentuate Presley's whims. "I just played an accent wherever his legs were or wherever his rear end was, and I learned to catch all that by watching those girls strip," he said.

Rock and roll and Elvis' music in particular unhinged women—both black and white, and this made men (their dates, their fathers, religious leaders, Steve Allen) *very* nervous. When Presley came onstage, if he so much as lifted his forefinger and wiggled it to the crowd with that knowing grin of his, they howled like banshees—their decorum, their class, their upbringing, and all the constraints society placed upon them forgotten. Fucking *howled*. It was fearsome, it was the dawn of the modern era, it was impressive to watch.

The boys knew that they were strictly backup—the kids were there to see *Elvis*. As D. J. says, "They come to see Elvis, period. We could have not even played. They couldn't care less. The background singers could have stayed home as far as the kids were concerned."

To make it even more nerve-wracking, the guys in the band never knew what Elvis would do in front of the crowd. One minute he would be standing in the center of the stage, and the next, he would be on the other side, dancing all over the place. He worked purely by instinct—what he was *feeling* right then and there. Nothing was planned; he never gave the same show twice. It was his own personal spontaneous combustion.

By the spring of 1956, Elvis was a wild sensation, and Scotty Moore recalls that the crowd grew so out of control, the musicians could no longer hear the music; instead they had to watch Presley's movement to figure out what chord to hit next. The whole thing was crazy. "We were the only band in history directed by an ass," said Scotty. "It was like being in a sea of sound."

LIKE HIS PROMISCUOUS TASTE in music, from itinerant sharecroppers to Mario Lanza, Elvis picked up bits and pieces of what worked for him stylistically along the way. Along with the wild-man truckers, the late-night sharks on Beale, and Tony Curtis (from whom he picked up the movie habit of wearing mascara), Little Richard was another early influence for Elvis. Only Little Richard was so far out there, he made Presley look like a choirboy. To begin with, Little Richard was openly gay, and by the time he made his first record in 1951 (as an eighteen-year-old named Richard Penniman), he had been performing in women's dresses for several years. In the rural South, stage shows, minstrel shows, and snake-oil salesmen often hired gay performers to entertain the crowd. This lushly sybaritic world coexisted alongside fiery preachers and harsh Bible Belt intolerance. Coming from a religious background like Elvis', Little Richard felt the tension of Saturday night versus Sunday morning. He, like Jerry Lee Lewis, another Presley contemporary, alternated between secular ecstasy and religious guilt and repentance. While this inner tension might be difficult to live with and reconcile on a personal level, it made for compelling creative energy.

ON MAY 13, 1955, at the new baseball park in Jacksonville, Florida, Elvis said to the crowd of fourteen thousand at the end of the performance, "Girls, I'll see you backstage." Well—that was all they needed. A good portion of them thought *Elvis must mean me,* and a full-scale riot ensued with fans pursuing Elvis into his dressing room, tearing at his clothes and shoes. It was at this point that Colonel Tom Parker, who had been sniffing around Elvis since January, saw that Elvis had staying power, and he began seriously seeking to represent him.

"Son," he told him, "you've got a million dollars' worth of talent. By the time we're through, you'll have a million dollars." Because Elvis was not yet twenty-one, he needed the approval of his parents to sign the contract.

His mother was a very protective woman who distrusted the Colonel on sight and she advised her son not to sign the contract, but Elvis and his father went for it hook, line, and sinker, and Elvis began a lifelong relationship with the Colonel.

IN LITTLE OVER A YEAR, Elvis had gone from absolute anonymity to the verge of success. Marion Keisker, who took down Elvis' name and gave him his first shot at becoming a singer, had more than passing insight into what made Elvis *Elvis.* "My total image of Elvis was as a child," she said. "He never said a wrong thing from the very first night he appeared on Dewey Phillips' show. He was like a mirror in a way, whatever you were looking for, you were going to find in him. It was not in him to lie or say anything malicious. He had all the intricacy of the very simple."

Elvis had a dream: to sing in front of the people. Sam Phillips had a dream, to find a singer that sounded like this country. Colonel Tom Parker had a dream, too—to make a hell of a lot of money and personally ensure that he *always* got the best of any deal he entered into. If he had to rip somebody else off, or step on some toes along the way—hey, he wasn't a choirboy, he was a carny. Not the best karma, perhaps, and certainly not art, but there it was. On November 21, 1955, in a deal engineered by the Colonel, Elvis' Sun contract was sold to RCA for $35,000.

For the rest of his life, people would ask Sam, "Are you sorry you sold Elvis?"

"Listen," he says, "as much as I would have loved to have had all the money that Elvis made, or I could have made . . . absolutely not. You're talking about somebody that grabbed at $35,000 like it was all the money in the world—gosh, to give me a little relief here, while I create other things or try to. It was the greatest blessing that ever happened to me."

In 1955, it took an entire family working steady about seven years to earn $35,000. With this windfall, Phillips was able to get in on the ground floor of the Holiday Inn hotel chain, just being started by his friend Kemmons Wilson (who advised him to sell Presley—"The boy isn't even a professional").

Besides, whatever the situation, Sam Phillips was still Sam Phillips—founder of Sun Records and the man who first recorded Elvis. No one could take that from him. And the Colonel, well, he had to go through life being the Colonel. When the cards were counted, Sam Phillips figured he came out okay.

706 union avenue

IF ROCK AND ROLL has a birthplace, it is the little Sun Recording Studio, on Union Avenue in Memphis, Tennessee. Sam Phillips recorded practically any able-bodied person who could sing and pluck a guitar. And many others who could do far more than that. In time, Phillips recorded B. B. King, Rufus Thomas, the Prisonaires, Junior Parker, Ike Turner, Howlin' Wolf—a virtual who's who of African-American performers, most of whom had grown up within a 150-mile radius of Memphis. Anyone could walk into Sam's place and make a demo. And word got out, mostly among the black performers, that here was a man who took them seriously, who would give them a fair shake or, at the very least, not take undue advantage of them.

From there, wild country boys who had no interest in staying down on the farm found their way to Union. Johnny Cash, Carl Perkins, and Charlie Rich all made their first recordings at Sun under Phillips' tutelage. In October 1957, Jerry Lee Lewis pounded out "Great Balls of Fire" on the battered upright piano against the wall.

But Sun, for all its fame, was not the only game in Memphis. During the late sixties and early seventies, Stax Records offered the primary soul alternative to Detroit's dominant Motown sound. And while Motown was a highly orchestrated event geared to a white audience, Stax was raw, rooted firmly in blues and gospel. Sam and Dave's "Hold On, I'm Comin'," the Staple Singers'

"Respect Yourself," Otis Redding's "Sittin' On the Dock of the Bay," and Isaac Hayes' "Shaft" were all recorded there.

Was it something in the water in Memphis? Over at Hi Records (a former movie theater on South Lauderdale Avenue), Al Green was laying down "Let's Stay Together," as well as "You Ought to Be with Me" and "Tired of Being Alone." In 1969, former gospel singer Ann Peebles came to Memphis from her home in St. Louis and with her husband, Don Bryant, wrote and recorded "I Can't Stand the Rain." John Lennon called it "the best record I've heard in two years." Fifteen years later, Tina Turner covered it on her *Private Dancer* album. In 1975, Syl Johnson had his biggest hit with "Take Me to the River." Three years later, the Talking Heads took it to the Top 30.

Elvis is great. We love Elvis, but if you want to explore some of his early influences, as well as the music that followed him, check out the Memphis sound.

We being poor have only our dreams. Be careful
where you walk for you tread on them.

—W. B. YEATS

shakey town

IT WAS ALL THERE IN THE BEGINNING: his love of gospel, the freedom he felt when he sang, the love of his mama, his tugging sense of inferiority. Elvis was two years old, sitting in her lap at the Assembly of God Church on Adams Street in Tupelo, Mississippi, waving his arms at the joyous sound. Gladys liked to tell the story about how "he would slide down off my lap, run into the aisle and scramble up to the platform. There he would stand looking at the choir and trying to sing with them. He was too little to know the words, but he could carry a tune and he would watch their faces and try to do as they did."

"That music became such a part of my life," he later recalled, "that it was as natural as dancing. It was a way to escape from problems, and my way of release." It was good he'd found gospel because Elvis, perhaps more than other young boys his age, had much to escape.

ELVIS AND HIS TWIN BROTHER, Jessie, were born on January 8, 1935, in East Tupelo, Mississippi, a town so volatile, so religious, so prone to fighting, so *Southern* that it had nine bootleggers in its small community, and the rest of "proper" Tupelo was terrified to set foot there.

Jessie, the older, was stillborn. Elvis was born about thirty-five minutes later in the Presleys' shotgun shack (so called because you could stand in the front door and shoot a shotgun out the back door without hitting anything) that could practically fit in the living room of his future home, Graceland. If it was not exactly Abraham Lincoln's log cabin, it was close. There was a tiny bedroom where Elvis was born and his twin brother died in front, the kitchen in back, and that was all.

In the region's way, their middle names were intended to match, Jessie Garon and Elvis Aaron (pronounced with a long *a* and the emphasis on the first syllable). Jessie was named for Vernon's father, and Elvis was Vernon's unused middle name. Although his middle name shifted through the years, depending on who was doing the spelling, Aaron was for Vernon's friend, Aaron Kennedy. But *Elvis* was such an unusual name, then and now. As he grew older, Elvis asked his father if it had any special meaning.

"You got me, son," Vernon replied in his folksy way. "I just took what they gave me."

For someone who did not experience one living moment on earth, Jessie exerted an enormous influence on Elvis and his parents. Since they could not afford a headstone, he was buried in a makeshift coffin, a cardboard box, in an unmarked grave next to a tree at Priceville Cemetery just outside town. Unable to have any more children, Gladys' maternal devotion to her surviving twin was interwoven with her love for her first son, lost but not forgotten.

Elvis was an unusually sensitive child and as a small boy was haunted by the thought that Jessie had died because of something he had done. "From the moment I realized I was a twin, I had a feeling my brother would have lived if it hadn't been for me," he once said. "I was plagued by the thought that I may have hurt him in some way, or wrapped my arms or legs around him so he couldn't breathe when we were in our mom's womb together."

IT HAS BEEN SAID that the Presleys came to America (with the spelling of "Pressley") from either Scotland or Ireland in the mid-1700s. But in truth, this may be wishful thinking, because according to the archivists at Graceland, it is not known *where* they came from, since no definitive genealogy has ever been written about either side of Elvis' family.

Both his parents could sing, but there were no musicians or, God forbid, entertainers in Elvis' family tree. The Presleys lived anonymous lives of sharecroppers and hard-luck farmers, with the occasional moonshiner added for good measure. "We were poor about as far back as I can remember," said Elvis. There was nothing in Elvis' past to indicate the remarkable direction his life would take. And no one would come after him to take his place. Practically coming up out of the dirt, Elvis was *sui generis*.

THE TWO DOMINANT FORCES in Elvis' formative years were poverty and faith. They influenced Gladys and, through her, played a big part in Elvis' considerable work ethic and his love of music. As he grew up, his doting mother made sure Elvis had good manners. They might be poor, but no one would accuse them of being white trash, and manners made the difference. Gladys taught him to stand when adults entered the room, not to argue or interrupt, and to respond with "yes, sir" and "no, ma'am" when addressed. As he grew older, there was an easy grace with which Elvis treated everyone. To the Presleys, putting yourself above others, that was the gravest sin, something a Yankee might do.

"There were times we had nothing to eat but corn bread and water," recalled Vernon not long before he died. "But we always had compassion for people. Poor we were, I'll not deny that. But trash we weren't. We never had any prejudice. We never put anybody down. Neither did Elvis."

Elvis, a much loved, gentle little boy, was highly sensitive and occasionally suffered from sleepwalking. He and his mother were unusually close, everyone agreed on that. Knowing how nervous she was, he did everything he could to make her happy—if he was off playing with one of his friends and she said she wanted him home by one o'clock, just after noon he would begin glancing nervously at the sky, and say "I 'spect we'd better get back now. . . ." Nobody loved him like his mama. And what did Gladys and Elvis do together? In keeping with that time and place, their social life revolved around the church. Gladys took him there practically every day from the time he was one month old. In the spring, they also went to camp revival meetings.

Meanwhile, Vernon struggled to make ends meet the best he could. At various times, he worked as a milkman on a farm, truck driver, lumberyard man, and painter. Gladys was employed as a sewing-machine operator for the Tupelo Garment Company and later at Reed's Department Store. With a family income of $1,232.88 in 1943, the Presleys were about as poor as white people could be.

But everybody the Presleys knew came up the same way; things were tough all around. In this sense they were united. They had their faith in God and some occasional small thought that tomorrow might be better to carry them through. But in those days in East Tupelo, nobody was on easy street. Sam Phillips, who grew up on a farm in Alabama, recalled, "Things were tough back in those days. Real tough. I mean, just to physically eke out an existence. You worked all the time you wasn't in school. I worked every day except Sundays when I went to church."

In addition to poverty, faith was another strong, and constant, component of Elvis' life. For Elvis, for his mama and daddy, God was not a distant figure up in the sky, but someone walking beside him each and every day. Someone who understood his secret thoughts, someone to lift his earthly burdens. Elvis and his parents were (like Little Richard and Jerry Lee Lewis) Pentecostal, an active faith where speaking in tongues was not uncommon. "Language from heaven," they called it. On Sunday morning, the choir sang "All things are possible, if you only believe." And Elvis, well, he might not come from much, but he had faith. For him, God— and His place in his life—was very real.

For Elvis, heaven was not a concept but a destination, and he took his path there seriously. When he was touring and on *The Ed Sullivan Show* in 1955 and '56, and the parents and preachers protested his exuberant ways, he declared, "My Bible tells me that what he sows he will also reap, and if I'm sowing evil and wickedness it will catch up with me. If I did think I was bad for people, I would go back to driving a truck." He had no doubt that at the end of the day, after his struggles and his solitude, he would be reunited with Jessie, whom he had missed all those years.

Elvis associated gospel with a feeling of peace, of all being right in the world. When he was frantic with nervous energy after performing in Vegas and had trouble calming down, he would stay up until dawn, singing "Peace in the Valley" or "How Great Thou Art," songs that reminded him of little storefront churches in Tupelo and Memphis. When he sang gospel, it was something Elvis did for himself. It brought him back to a time when his mother was alive, and Daddy was there, too: that perfect dream of home he carried in his heart. "We were always happy when we were together," he said.

THEY MAY HAVE BEEN HAPPY, but things were often tough. Although they did not know it, 1937 would be an even darker year for the Presleys. Gladys' mother, Doll, died in June. In constant financial difficulties, Vernon (along with Gladys' brother Travis and a man named Lether Gable) made an ill-conceived decision to alter and then cash a $4 check that their landlord, Orville Bean, had made out to Vernon to pay for a hog. Although there is some dispute about whether the $4 check was changed to $14 or $40, there is no question that on May 25, 1938, Vernon and his two friends were sentenced to three years in Parchman Farm State Penitentiary, a penal "farm" that featured chain gang labor. It was the South and

Vernon was a common laborer, not some Wall Street hotshot with friends in high places. A Mississippi chain gang in 1938 was hard days. Hard, hard days.

NONE OF HIS FAMILY and neighbors held the forgery thing against Vernon, since everyone makes mistakes. Besides, everybody knew that Bean wanted to make an example of Vernon and his friends—sentenced to three years in a Mississippi prison, he sure as hell did—and that Vernon was a good man, except for this one slipup. But his time in prison radically shaped Vernon, and the Presleys' view of the world. No longer, if it ever had been, would the world be seen as a benevolent place. Outsiders were regarded with suspicion. "Though we had friends and relatives, including my parents," Vernon recalled, "the three of us formed our own private world." Vernon became even more taciturn and "dry" as the expression went, not saying much, not trusting anyone, keeping his thoughts to himself. It seemed that he gave up hope and turned his back on the world, too, rarely employed, always between jobs; things just stopped working out for him.

Vernon's feelings of low self-esteem, of not being good enough, must have, on some level, permeated their home, because for all his son's later success, they followed Elvis and limited him, to some degree, the rest of his life. Sam Phillips thought that Elvis was almost like a black man in his self-regard. "He tried not to show it, but he felt so inferior. He reminded me of a black person in that way."

With Vernon gone, Elvis spent even more time with his mother. She clung fiercely to her towheaded child, the rare jewel in her bleak life, putting all her hopes and fears into him. As if things could not get any worse, Gladys and three-year-old Elvis were evicted from their home for nonpayment of their mortgage by Orville Bean, Vernon's boss and mortgage holder, the man who had ensured that he was sent to prison in the first place.

Vernon served only eight months, but to his family it might as well have been eight years. Gladys moved in with her in-laws, but there was no love lost between them. For a time, she lived with her cousins Frank and Leona Richards and got a job in the Mid-South Laundry. With Vernon gone, Gladys, who had been so animated, the spark in the marriage, became more and more nervous. Their little world, precarious to begin with, fell apart. Leona vividly recalled Elvis "sitting on the porch crying his eyes out because his daddy was away." On weekends, the bereft couple, Gladys and Elvis, frequently rode the Greyhound bus five hours each way to visit Vernon.

IN TUPELO, Vernon hacked around, doing the best he could to provide for his family, but nothing really took. Finally, he decided opportunities would be better in Memphis. According to Gladys, "One day we just made up our minds. We sold off our furniture, loaded our clothes into this old car we had, and just set out." They packed up their '39 Plymouth and left in November 1948, on a Saturday so Elvis would not miss a day of school. Their friends were surprised but not shocked; people like the Presleys moved all the time. As Elvis later recalled, "We were broke, man, broke . . . And we left Tupelo overnight. We just headed for Memphis. Things had to be better."

In Memphis, after a few stopovers at various rooming houses, the Presleys ended up at Lauderdale Courts, on September 20, 1949, during Elvis' freshman year at his new school, Humes High School. The rent was $35 a month, about what they paid for the rooming house they had been staying at on Poplar Avenue, but for the first time, the Presleys had a real home—two bedrooms, a living room, a kitchen, and a bathroom of their own.

Lauderdale Courts was an ambitious and largely successful project headed by the Memphis Housing Authority, whose aim was to enable people to go from "slums to public housing to private ownership" in a single generation. For the 433 families that lived in the Courts, there was a $2,500 annual cap on family income, and the units were inspected at frequent but unspecified times. No matter. Mrs. Presley was so proud of their new home, you could have eaten off the floor.

For the Presleys, Lauderdale Courts was a real step up as a family. For some who lived there, it was the first time they had had indoor plumbing or taken a real bath.

AS A TEENAGER, Elvis' main style influences—which is to say, his way of escaping—were music (mostly gospel and blues), Beale Street, movies, and comic books. Like a lot of creative kids with a chaotic home life, Elvis created his own world inside his head. He read comic books and was drawn to Superman, Batman, Captain Marvel, and, most of all, Captain Marvel Jr. Unlike the sidekicks of other superheroes (like Robin to Batman), Captain Marvel Jr. was not totally subservient to his master, and, in fact, had his own comic books and story lines. Around the age of twelve, Elvis discovered Captain Marvel Jr. and quickly became almost obsessed with him.

FROM THE COURTS, Elvis walked the ten blocks down Jackson to Manassas to Humes High School each day. It was here that he began to create himself.

When he arrived at Humes, Elvis was a skinny, awkward thirteen-year-old—shy, eccentric, and living mostly in his own head. Being an outcast, he wasn't a slave to high school pressure (the worst kind there is), since his peers already considered him an outsider anyway. Perhaps having been born a twin, or being the much-loved only son, gave him the presence of will to do things his way. Since he was never going to get the approval of society, he might as well keep doing what he wanted. When everyone else wore crew cuts, Elvis had long hair by those days' standards. He had no way of knowing it then, but this rebuff gave him tremendous freedom to do whatever he wanted, since his way of dealing with teenage rejection was to stop caring, or do a good job of pretending not to care.

For a boy who was already the target of schoolyard taunts to set himself further apart shows what a stubborn sense of individuality he possessed. Some of the boys, the guys on the football team, mostly, called him Miss Elvis. His theatrics made them nervous—who did he think he was, anyway? For such a shy goober, it was like he wanted them to look at him. They wanted to take him down a notch or two for his individuality, for the fact that all the girls liked him so. He ignored them.

By sixteen, Elvis was used to being called names, anyway. "Had pretty long hair for that time and I tell you it got pretty weird," he recalled. "They used to see me comin' down the street and they'd say, 'Hot dang, let's get him, he's a squirrel, get him, he just come down outta the trees.'"

Of course Elvis wanted to belong, but on his terms, not anyone else's. Perhaps through force of will, he would create his own world, his own vision of what the world, *his* world, might be. It was a daunting thought, this kid from nowhere, with nothing to his name. Was it possible to create a world based largely on his style, his belief, and his talent? Well, hell, he might as well try. He could see it so clearly in his mind. "When I was a child I was a dreamer," he said. "I read comic books, and I was the hero of the comic book. I saw movies, and I was the hero in every movie."

Years later, he would say that "every dream that I ever dreamed has come true a hundred times." But for now, all he had were his dreams. For now, not knowing how he would get to where he wanted to be, they were enough. A high school friend said that Elvis walked as if he were a gunslinger in a Western movie.

DIXIE LOCKE DID NOT KNOW if she thought Elvis' family situation was odd, so much as different. She loved Gladys, a warm and bubbly woman who, like her, adored Elvis. Their shared interest in him was almost inexhaustible; they could—and did—spend hours talking about what a wonderful boy he was.

But Dixie had never seen a grown-up like Elvis' father, Vernon. Unlike her own father, who ran the show at her house, he was unusually passive. He did not behave decisively or confidently like the other men she knew, her uncles or other friends' fathers. She did not recall seeing him work; he said he suffered from a bad back. Every Friday without fail, Elvis handed over his forty-dollar paycheck from Crown Electric like *he* was the breadwinner, and no one in the Presley family found this unusual, unlike Dixie. Elvis explained to her that his parents were getting on in years, and it was up to him to take care of them; that's just the way it was. At the time, Vernon was thirty-eight years old.

"I never saw him be unkind. I never saw him drink or be unruly. I'm sure he was a very loving husband and devoted to the family, and it probably had to do with his self-esteem—but he was like an outsider, really, he wasn't part of Elvis and Mrs. Presley's group." She knew it must sound strange, but "They had such a strong love and respect for each other, and I don't think there was a lot of respect for him during that time." Elvis would kill her if he ever heard her talk like this, but it was almost, she said, "like Elvis was the father and his dad was just the little boy."

Although it did not make any sense, Elvis always believed that someday things would get better. "He always knew he was going to do something," said Vernon, as if he and Gladys had ever doubted the immutable superiority of their son. "When we didn't have a dime, he used to sit on the doorstep and say, 'One of these days it'll be different.'"

FOR HIS ELEVENTH BIRTHDAY, Elvis had wanted a bicycle but was given a six string guitar instead. Now, living in Memphis and a teenager, Elvis defined himself *to* himself, as someone who sang. He carried his guitar everywhere, taking care to keep it out of the rain.

Although he was painfully shy, singing was the first thing that allowed Elvis to step outside of himself. "I wasn't popular in high school," he admitted. "I wasn't dating anybody [there]. I failed music—only thing I ever failed. And then they entered me in this talent show and I came out and did my first number, ' 'Til I Waltz Again with You,' by Teresa Brewer. And when I came onstage I heard people kinda rumbling and whispering and so forth, 'cause nobody knew I even sang. It was amazing how popular I became after that."

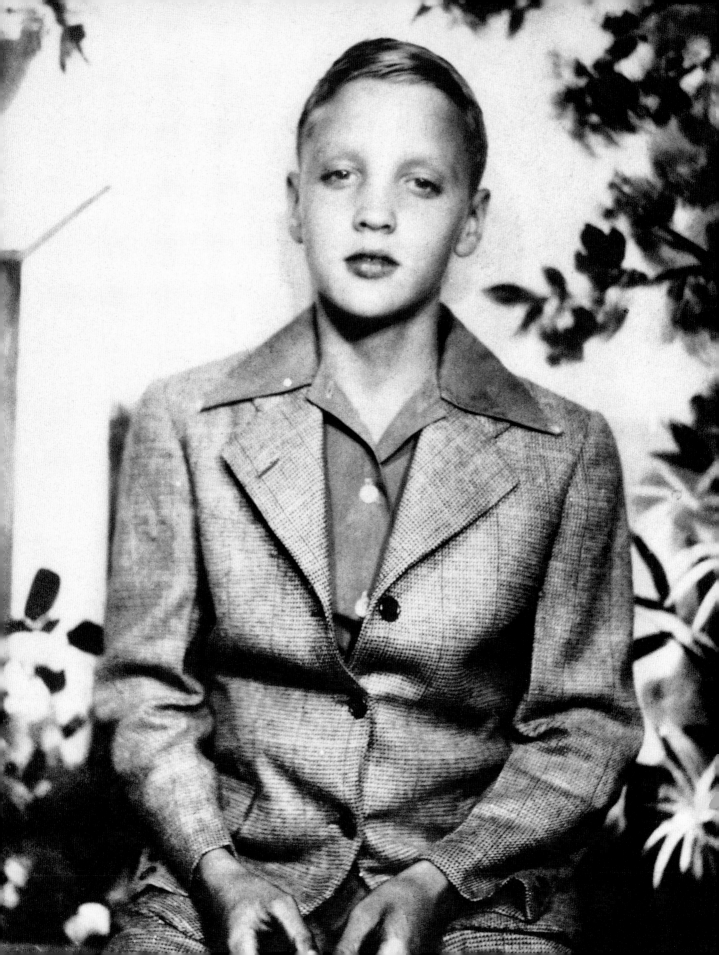

ELVIS LOVED THE DREAMS in his head because they were like when he sang: perfect. When he sang, his mama's worries and daddy's helplessness fell away from his mind. He no longer puzzled about how he would make everything all right, about the fact that Jessie was not there. As a skinny mama's boy from the Courts, Elvis had no power, but when he sang, he was powerful. He was no longer alone. People loved him and, more important, he loved himself. He wanted to take that feeling with him everywhere. He wanted to live in that feeling all the time.

Elvis would sit on the steps outside the apartment building at night. He loved the dark. In the shadows his rawboned face was almost handsome. In the dark, he had the courage to be more completely who he wanted to be. Fingering his guitar, his voice barely above a murmur, he sang love songs, mostly. He sang Eddy Arnold's "Molly Darling," Bing and Gary Crosby's "Moonlight Bay." A crowd would gather, neighbors who might have passed him by and not given him a second glance in the daytime. He sang a Kay Starr tune, "Harbor Lights," but his voice trailed off, he didn't know all the words. His audience, quiet and companionable now, did not move, waiting for him to continue. At night no one laughed at the way he looked, the acne he was so embarrassed by. His ungainly adolescent features took on an almost delicate beauty.

Most of the crowd that gathered around him those summer nights were women. Elvis preferred them. He loved to be around women of all ages—teenagers, their mothers or grandmothers. They reminded him of Gladys. He was more comfortable with them, more himself. He didn't have to put up a front or compete, the way he did with boys. They didn't make fun of his hair or his clothes; they accepted him the way he was.

That wasn't something he would admit to his friends, Buzzy and Farley and Paul. It was something he probably could not even admit to himself, since it was his secret wish to be accepted by the cool boys, the guys on the football team. Until his success, he wouldn't be.

His aunt Lillian noticed, though. "Elvis got out there at night with the girls and he just sang his head off. He was different with the girls. I'm embarrassed to tell, but he'd rather have a whole bunch of girls around him than the boys—he didn't give a thing about the boys." For his whole life, starting with his mama, women seemed to sense something within Elvis, an aching sort of vulnerability, a still sort of yearning, that made them want to soothe him with their presence.

Marion Keisker picked up on this when he walked in the door of Sun. In just a few years, millions of young girls and women would connect with his unabashed emotional openness. For now, though, he was just an aching skinny kid, singing in the dark at the Courts.

BY THE TIME he graduated from high school, the essential Elvis was in place.

Elvis' parents loved him. His twin brother was dead. But no matter what happened, they would always be together in his heart. That was all, really, that he cared about.

There was nothing holding him back. He was bound by no one and nothing except his dreams. Walking down the street, he had his own sound track in his head. Ever since he had reached the age of reason, he was the star of his own damn movie. Since he lived outside "proper" society and would never be accepted by it anyway, Elvis was not bound by its precepts. Instead he had tremendous freedom to create his own world. His own vision. And this, hell, this was worth any college education, any desk job working for the man—Sam Phillips could tell you that.

Elvis had remarkable intuitive instincts and was able to synthesize—in a way no Southern woman would socially be able to—what was coming up off the streets, what was in the air on Beale. He could barely articulate it to himself. But man, he knew what it was. He felt the change. He channeled it and *became* the change.

This possibility, the new order coming up just over the horizon, became his style.

JERRY SCHILLING, future Memphis Mafia member, met Elvis in July 1954, when he was twelve years old, two days after Dewey Phillips played "That's All Right" on the radio. They had both grown up in north Memphis, which, as he recalls today, "was the poor section of town." There was a little park a couple of blocks away, and Jerry had walked by and saw some older guys just out of high school trying to get up a football game. One of them, Red West, knew Jerry's older brother and knew Jerry could play pretty well. He called out and asked if he would like to join them.

Jerry hustled over, he wasn't doing anything in particular.

Jerry's mom had died when he was a year old, and he was raised by his grandmother and aunts and uncles. He didn't have much—well, not any less than anyone

else — but music was the stable thing in his life. He was only twelve, but he had been listening to *Red, Hot, and Blue* on the radio for close to two years. He'd go down to Beale with his older friends to buy records because that was the only place you could get black music at the time.

Two nights before, Dewey had played "That's All Right" for the first time on the radio, and that's all the kids could talk about. "This is a boy from Humes High," he said by way of introduction. Jerry's older cousins and his brother went there, so he knew about Humes. Dewey played the record, it sounded wild, and Jerry thought, God — a boy from Humes?

They went to the huddle to start the game, and Jerry looked over at Elvis and realized, Oh my God, that's the guy on the radio. "I just *knew*," Schilling recalled.

"He had this coolness about him. It's not that he was dressed that different for a Sunday afternoon. It's not like he came out dressed in a pink shirt to play football, he couldn't afford it, for one thing.

"I think he had on jeans and a white T-shirt. His hair was longer. It was cool as hell, like something out of *Blackboard Jungle*. What I noticed about him though, he was so different it was like—even without him accomplishing anything at this point, you wouldn't just go up and slap him on the back. You kind of let him come to you on his terms. You had to kind of build up a respect with him. He was so cool, almost unapproachable, and then he'd give you this little smile that would be the warmest smile you'd ever experienced in your life. He was like this lovable rebel."

That day, Jerry played with the older guys and just started hanging out with them. That was how their friendship began, simple as that. In later years, when they ruled Vegas, or meeting Nixon in the White House, he would smile to himself, re-membering how unpopular, how *alone* Elvis was in the beginning—"He couldn't get six people to play football. I'm not talking six on a side, I mean six people!"

In those days, Jerry was extremely shy. In addition to being the youngest in the group and not wanting to impose himself, he wanted to be careful not to pre-sume friendship, like practically everyone else in Memphis, who now claimed to be Elvis' best, best friend. Still, he was a very good football player, and Elvis started looking out for him.

With Elvis' success—the Dorsey Brothers, the Opry, Sullivan, and all of that, going to the park on Sunday afternoon became the cool thing to do in Memphis. The whole town practically showed up. Eventually they had real teams with seven, ten guys on a side. So many girls and kids came to watch and hang out, it became a real social event. The sidelines got so crowded it almost embarrassed Jerry. He would never run out and get a T-shirt to make sure he got in the game like some of the pushier guys. But Elvis always put aside a T-shirt for him. Jerry thought his friend must have remembered that he thought Elvis was cool before everyone else did. No matter who else showed up, Jerry Schilling always got to play.

And what kind of an athlete was Elvis? According to Jerry, Elvis' playing ability was another expression of his style. "Elvis could throw the ball very well. I wouldn't call Elvis a natural football player, but what he didn't have he far exceeded with determination." Eventually, it worked out that it was Elvis and his guys against whoever showed up to play on the other side. One time, a couple of ex-professional football players, real bruisers, arrived and you could tell they thought, Who the hell does this guy think he is?

They took it upon themselves to take down the pretty boy singer and knocked him on his butt pretty good. Red went back to the huddle, cursing, and said, "I'll take them this time, Elvis!" And Elvis would say, "No, no, man, it's okay. . . ." They went back out and they'd knock him down again. And Red and some of the guys got really upset, and Elvis said, "Leave it alone, it's all right." By the third time he came out of the huddle, they had such respect for him, for taking it like a man. By the end of the game, they said, "Elvis, can we bring our wives over to introduce them to you?"

If he was your friend, Elvis had a real kindness to him. And a great sense of humor. People would ask him, "Elvis, how did you start?" "As a child . . . ," he would say, with that smile of his. In all the years Jerry worked in show business, Elvis was the only person he knew with that kind of charismatic style. And he had it before he had hit records and movies, when he was trying to scrounge up a touch football game on Sunday afternoon in Memphis, Tennessee.

Jerry recalled, "Over the time I spent with Elvis, I would hear people—'Ah, I don't care for him!' I never met anyone who felt that way *after* they met him. I think sometimes when you meet people that you admire, your opinion of them drops. I think with Elvis it was the opposite. At nineteen years old, Elvis was a star. He couldn't get five guys together to play football, nobody knew who he was! But he was a star, just by himself."

jessie garon

PEOPLE ARE FASCINATED with twins, one of the strongest, most inexplicable bonds between two people; for there are some loves that go beyond luck or mere attraction, standing outside the world and all it asks of us. Imagine: someone you've known forever. Holding hands, listening to your secrets. The first voice you hear and also, quite possibly, the last. Someone who understands your need and your fear, your ambition, your jokes, the ticking of your psyche because he shares so precisely the same inclinations.

A twin—someone to care about more than anyone you will ever know. It is almost a dream, isn't it? That perfect love to shut out the world.

But where there is love, there is fear. And the death of a twin, or worse, having to be the surviving partner, is every twin's greatest nightmare.

Jessie Garon, Elvis' older twin, was stillborn. The only sibling of one of the most recognized men in the world was buried in a pauper's grave in Priceville Cemetery, Mississippi, without a headstone, so the Presleys were never sure, exactly, where he rested. With his sure sense of the dramatic, Elvis decided he and Jessie *had* to have been identical—alike in every way, as opposed to fraternal twins; although in 1935, in that very rudimentary two-room house, this could never be tested or confirmed.

Elvis loved the idea of being a twin. It was his secret against the world. Perhaps along with his voice, his charisma, or his remarkable rise to fame, this was something else that set him apart from others. Like the son of a king

who is temporarily a pauper, he carried this *specialness*, this perception of himself, the rest of his life. He loved daydreaming about Jessie, a boy—and later a man—with his walk, the sound of his voice. Someone he has known forever. Someone who understands him even better than he understands himself.

For us, trying to conjure up a twin of Elvis—a man so singular, so absolute in his talent and the way he viewed the world, we almost can't perceive it. It is unimaginable that there could be another one of him. His friend Liberace also had a twin who died at birth; perhaps—along with stagecraft—they discussed this when they met in Vegas. Imagine two Liberaces: all that gilt, all those candelabras.

Was Elvis "obsessed" with Jessie, as the common press would have us believe? When he was out in California making movies, one of the tabloids concocted a story that he had long conversations with Jessie, and this hurt him deeply. His boyhood friend Jerry Schilling said that Elvis never spoke of his brother. Ever. "I think all that stuff's bullshit." His wife, Priscilla, says the same thing, "Elvis hardly ever spoke about Jessie." In 1964, Larry Geller, a friend with twin sisters, had long conversations with Elvis about his deceased brother. Perhaps the truth, like most truths, lay somewhere in between. One of Elvis' great gifts, after all, was always being able to read his audience.

Did he feel guilty that he was the surviving twin? Did he ever wonder why he was here, with his ridiculous success—greater, perhaps, than anything he had ever imagined—and Jessie was not? "I always felt a bit lonely when I was little. I suppose it might have been

different if my brother had lived. A lot of things might have been different," he mused. "But he didn't live and I grew up alone."

Elvis never looked in his brother's eyes, heard his voice, or held his hand. With Jessie dead at birth, he did not even have a picture of him. For Elvis, and for us, too, Jessie was a myth, an idea in his mind. Still, from this loss he held one thought: He knew what it was to love, and to lose that love. This loss, it was said, haunted him his whole life. He searched for that love, that connection—in Priscilla, in women, in his audience—always.

And yet, in an odd way, Jessie was always with him. His mother believed and told Elvis that "when one twin died, the one that lived got all the strength of both"—a devilish burden that would roil the calmest psyche, almost guaranteeing a future spot on *Oprah*. But in his quiet way, Elvis carried Jessie's energy—his

imagined love, his concern for his well-being. That voice he never knew.

In the end, Elvis' twin was a ghost. A phantom. Having died before he lived, Jessie was perfect. He would never grow old or make his way in this flawed world of ours. Instead he was consigned, forever, to the benign grace of Elvis' heart.

As someone whose faith was as strong as his voice, Elvis never had any doubt that he would see Jessie in heaven. Part of his life was here—with his new RCA contract and Colonel Tom Parker, his mama's pink Cadillac, the girls, and all the rest—but part of it was attuned to the world after this one, where he would surely see Jessie again.

There were many mysteries in Elvis' life, and for him, Jessie was just another one. Further along we'll know more about it. Further along, we'll understand why.

All I've got is a red guitar,
three chords, and the truth.

— BONO

1956

DURING THE WEEK OF September 8, 1956, twenty-one-year-old Elvis Presley was on the cover of *TV Guide* wearing a favorite gray striped Lansky blazer and nubby white shirt with the collar outside the jacket. He was singing into a microphone, his hair a bit disheveled off to the side. "The Plain Truth About Elvis Presley," the fifteen-cent magazine trumpeted and then, hilariously because it was still necessary, "Elvis Presley" is identified in small type on the bottom left for those in Middle America—and apparently there were many, who did not know who he was.

Inside, stories about television, about what people watched and did not watch that second week in September, tell us much about our nascent media age. Its paternalism is vast and certain. What is striking, now, is how *earnest* television was. Its belief in the viewer's betterment, and how it might contribute to this process, is touching and certainly defies our current reality-television, oversaturated imagination. On Tuesday, September 11, the *Kaiser Aluminum Hour* presented *Antigone* by Sophocles with Claude Rains and Marisa Pavan ("Creon is reluctant to punish the young girl, but he must, and in doing so, he himself becomes a victim of the tragedy").

On Saturday, after conjugating Latin infinitives, one could catch *Renaissance on TV* in which Aldous Huxley led "a discussion of the Renaissance philosophy of life, when men stopped thinking only of the next world and started living in this one." Or at 2:00 P.M., take in *Long Before Shakespeare*, where NYU professor Lionel Casson discussed "Euripides, the Innovator," the most versatile of the Greek playwrights.

As Holden Caulfield would say, what a bunch of goddam phonies. In September 1956, prime-time television was more pretentious than a Civ. class in New Haven.

In the mid-fifties, what passed for American culture was devoutly, unapologetically East Coast (read: New York)–centric. Antigone, Euripides, mezzo-soprano Mildred Miller singing selections from Bizet's opera *Carmen*—do you think there was a chance that Sam Phillips, Bernard Lansky, or Vernon Presley would watch any of this? No wonder they preferred tomcatting on Beale Street.

Of course there was also something delightfully non-PC about much of television at this time. About life, for that matter. For starters, everyone presented in the media looks alike (with the exception of Elvis, obviously). The men pictured within are all stable, solid seeming. Think Doctor Kildare. All of the women are blond, shapely, and extremely pale with blood red lips. Even if they have dark hair they give off an impression of impeccable coolness. In *TV Guide* and elsewhere, cigarettes and Rheingold beer are enthusiastically promoted with optimistic, brightly colored ads. There is zero concern about what smoking and drinking all that stuff might actually *do* to you.

When we imagine the innocence of the sock hop era, there is also the fabulous sense, from watching television, that nothing anyone did had any consequences—seatbelt laws, the Surgeon General's Warning on Smoking, the importance of doing well on the SATs, none of these things are even remotely on the horizon. One morning on the *Today* show, Dave Garroway and the cast are at the Kentucky Fair, giving us a view of the various shows and exhibits: "There is a film profile of Louisville and a tour of a cigarette factory"—Hey, why not?

In addition to Elvis making his debut on *The Ed Sullivan Show*, the week brought the first appearance of *Popeye*. ("Our muscle man will go into action from the afterdeck of the specially constructed S.S. *Popeye*. Ray Heatherton emcees.") And there are old reliables like *Lassie* ("Jeff and Porky decide to enter a beehive contest . . . a marauding raccoon threatens their project") and many, many Westerns.

Finally, on Sunday, September 9, at 8:00 on Channel 2, we get the *Ed Sullivan* lineup (accompanied by a sketch that makes Presley look like Jay Leno with a guitar). "Elvis Presley, controversial rock 'n' roll singer who is presently the idol of the teenage world, headlines tonight's show." Also appearing were the Vagabonds, a novelty quartet; singer Dorothy Sarnoff; the Amen Brothers, Egyptian tumblers; Conn and Mann, a tap-dance team; and Amru Sani, Indian vocal star of the Broadway show *New Faces of 1956*.

Don't laugh—this stuff is good for you!

FOR ELVIS, everything good happened in 1956. On January 28, he made his first television appearance on the Dorsey Brothers' *Stage Show* in New York City, taped at the CBS studios on Broadway and Fifty-third Street. For rehearsal, he wore a dark suit, black shirt, and no tie. He was far more conservatively dressed than the wild plaid blazers he wore for the roadhouses.

Elvis wanted something special—he was going to be on the Dorsey Brothers and had to look sharp as a tack. But he wanted different, man, different. Mr. Lansky

knew that, didn't he? He didn't want to look like he worked in a bank or nothin', they were going to New York City, the big time. Bernard pulled at the racks, selecting a few things. The boy was going to be on Dorsey—they were taking Beale Street uptown. No man knows another like his tailor, and for Elvis and Mr. Lansky, this was true. Just under six feet tall, Presley wore a 40-inch suit with a 32-inch waist. He had a 31-inch inseam, and a size 12 shoe. Bernard held up a jacket for him to try.

"What do you think?"

"I like it—I like it."

Like Elvis, Lansky was a man who knew his clothes. When you like something, it's like a woman—you know right away. You got it covered like dew on the ground.

Elvis was quickly becoming Lansky's best PR. They did his wardrobe for *Ed Sullivan*, Tommy and Jimmy Dorsey, the Louisiana Hayride. Every gig he had, he'd come right back to 126 Beale; he always wanted something sharp, something fresh.

Elvis liked to make a statement on stage. He was the headliner, after all, the man they came to see. At the time, blazers were in. Lansky had them made up with velvet cuffs and collars. You turn up the collar and look real sharp. The first colors were pink and black. But then Elvis decided that was too Humes, not sophisticated enough for the man he was becoming. He was an entertainer now. He graduated to striped blazers, he liked patterns on them, or maybe an orange raw silk number with an ivory button blouson cuff—a man's got to make a statement, after all. He wore them with black pants, like the blues players, and a thin leather belt, the silver buckle pushed to the left side. Elvis had no damn interest in any Ivy League look.

A man and his tailor: Lansky could read Elvis like a book. He wanted to be different, always different. "Don't worry about it, Elvis," he assured him, smoothing his jacket at his shoulders, kid looked like a million damn bucks already. "I got you covered like dew on the ground."

THE DORSEYS' STAGE SHOW opened with a big MGM-type production number—there was a giant pit orchestra in the back, then a dozen pretty women in little tap dance outfits came out playing the xylophone, two more tap guys in tuxedos entered stage left, then three men playing the horn. The men danced among the Xylophone Women. It's kind of touching, actually, that someone went to the effort to think this extravaganza up, and that people stayed home to watch it. It was not meant ironically at all.

You watch it now, all the gloss and pseudo splendor, knowing what is about to break, and you think: Man, they are going to *freak* when they see Elvis.

Here he is and your heart's in your throat. Seeing him on television for the first time, you feel the way Dixie Locke must have when she saw him in her living room meeting her family—protective and a bit stunned. Out among regular people, you forget how gorgeous, how wild looking Elvis is. He wears mascara, accentuating his remarkable eyes. God, he looks nervous. Wearing a nubby jacket, black shirt, and white tie, he's singing something about rattle those pots and pans. Still, for all his youth, inexperience in front of the camera, and general Greek god factor, he is a total actor.

By his fifth and sixth appearance on the Dorsey show in the spring of 1956, Elvis was fully conscious of the way he presented himself to the audience. Dressed in a sophisticated, well-fitted gray suit, he launches into "Blue Suede Shoes." Comfortable enough onstage, now, to tweak his image further—is he a smooth showman? A handsome country boy?—his guitar is artfully tied with a piece of knotted rope like Blind Lemon Jefferson, or some old blues guy on the chitlin circuit, and you smile to yourself. Typical Elvis: He knows exactly what he is doing. That homespun string against that perfect city suit and polished shoes is not there by accident.

Wearing shirts and ties, Scotty and Bill are close by, supporting his effort. Everything about Presley is different. He's doing a beat and it's like the stage can't contain him. He takes a step back, banging his guitar, flailing his hips, arms, and shoulders at the same time, lost in the music. "I said, ah-shake, rattle and roll! Ah-shake rattle and roll!" They all sing together now. Bill Black is banging on the bass, straddling it, flapping his arms in the air. Elvis has so much energy, it's almost hard to understand his rockabilly phrasing. "I got so many women I don't know which way to jump!"

Unless you were fifteen, no one knew what to make of Elvis at first. The 1950s Eisenhower era was a time of such devout conformity in American life that Elvis' shake, rattle, and whatever had nothing to do with "Que Sera Sera," or other white bread platitudes being offered up on the *Hit Parade* in 1956.

A week later, on February 4, Elvis was back on the Dorsey show. Over on NBC, Perry Como sang his current hit, "Hot Diggity, Dog Diggity" while Elvis ripped into "Baby Let's Play House." So you've got Perry Como in a button-down sweater singing with all these clean-cut singers in the background: "Hot diggity, dog diggity, oh what you do to me, when you're holding me tight . . ." It's all very Harvard Glee Club, very

Wellesley '56. Then over on CBS, Elvis stalked onto the stage loose hipped, guitar at his side, covering it like dew on the ground. He wore a patterned jacket with a dark tie and white shirt. He was extraordinary looking.

"Baby baby baby baby bab-ie, bababababababy, babababbaba, babababba, abababababba come back baby, I wanna play house a-with you . . ."

There is a close-up of Elvis' face—his eyes as beautiful as any woman's, his full lips. It is thrilling the way he throws his voice around, growling, instinctive. It's pretty obvious: If you're playing house with Elvis, there is just one room he is interested in.

He's a real country guy, rough around the edges, fascinating. Again, the mike is in front and he steps back into the arms of the band—"Come on, let's hit it! Hit it!"—and goes nuts. Flailing away on the guitar, moving his hips and everything, it's a long way from Perry Como and his tight-ass sidekicks.

Elvis looks off to the side smiling like a dark angel; he's having a great time. Bill Black chews gum as he plays the bass. "Yeah—let's go, let's go." Elvis is dancing around, but it's really tight, tight. All those months out on the road have made them. The band is right with Elvis, his voice another instrument in the group.

"Listen to me, baby, try to understand—I'd rather see you dead than with another man." Elvis was shocking, the way he presented himself onstage, what he sang about—hey, what happened to the Xylophone Gals? No one knows it yet, but Elvis has just knocked down the door for a new world order: the Rolling Stones, Altamont, the Vietnam War, the heartbreak of the 1960s. America will never be the same.

It's a long way from "How Much Is That Doggie in the Window."

The song over, Elvis stops singing as if jerked by an invisible force. He takes a step back and wipes his mouth with the sleeve of his right hand, then walks off, leaving the audience to recover.

IN MARCH 1956, Philadelphian Grace Kelly, by then Princess Grace of Monaco, visited America. Pregnant with her first child, a newsman asked if she had a name picked out. Her shortish prince piped up—"We've decided what *not* to name it . . . I will never name the child Elvis."

BETWEEN TV APPEARANCES (and getting dissed by foreign principalities), Elvis and the boys continued to tour furiously. In 1956, there was no MTV, no national radio stations, no *Rolling Stone* magazine, no internet, no email, no IM, no cell phones, no *American Idol.* If you wanted to reach the people, you got in your car and drove.

The Colonel mapped out a breakneck series of one-nighters—Richmond, Sarasota, Greensboro, a swing through east Texas. Scottie Moore was on guitar, Bill Black on doghouse bass, and D. J. Fontana on drums. They all looked so young, like the Beatles in Hamburg when they were just starting out. Crazy nights: running away from boyfriends who wanted to beat Elvis to a pulp. Girls leaving mash notes all over the front window of the car. Gladys worried about Elvis' eating properly, getting enough sleep. "Look after my boy," she would plead with Red West. Forget it, they were having the time of their lives. Half the time they hardly knew where they were. Elvis barely had time to *breathe.* They never slept. There was no tomorrow, no next year. There was only the road, the next town, the next gig.

Things were crazy on the road, crazy. If Mrs. Presley only knew. Bill used to goad Elvis to toss his belt into the audience. Elvis would do anything to get a rise from the crowd. He just wanted a reaction. One time he threw his shoe out and hit an old lady in the head. He didn't mean to. "We had to clear out fast after that one," recalls Scotty.

Elvis owned a 1954 Cadillac convertible and a 1955 Cadillac Fleetwood. It was estimated that the two Cadillacs would be driven 100,000 miles in the next year, divided between Scotty Moore (30,000 miles), Bill Black, D. J. Fontana, and Red West (20,000 each), and Elvis the remainder.

On Wednesday, April 11, in El Paso, Elvis' car (with 32,581 miles on the odometer) was serviced at the Lone Star Motor Company. He paid $58 for the replacement of the left rear window glass, new wiper blades, a new outside rearview mirror, and a radio aerial. The lube and the oil order was crossed out with the notation "no time."

"We were working near every day," said Scotty. "We'd pull into some town, go to the hotel room, and get washed up or go right to the auditorium or movie house, and after we played our shows, we'd get back in the cars and start driving to the next town. We never saw newspapers . . . And we didn't hear much radio, because it was drive all night, sleep all day. All we knew was drive, drive, drive." It was, said D. J., like being in a fog.

On the road, they couldn't possibly feel the rumblings of the earthquake they'd created. When they returned to New York on March 24 for their sixth and final Dorsey appearance, "Heartbreak Hotel" (a strangely morbid song Elvis

recorded about a hotel, a heartbreak hotel, where the desk clerk was dressed in black) was racing up the charts to the number one spot.

"We-e-ll, since my baby left me . . . " This time, the guys were set back on the stage; they were no longer on top of each other. Bill Black was no longer riding the bass, flapping his arms in the air like a giant hyena. There was less of a crazed, on-the-road feeling; the Colonel had spoken to the boys and let them know who's boss. Elvis was calmly in the spotlight, accepting it as his due. Even his hair had calmed down. It was more sculpted, less manic. Now he played to the camera, not a rowdy drunken audience. He had a suit on, a black shirt. He still had the guitar, but he was making much less of an attempt to actually play it; now, it was more of a prop. "I'll be so lonesome I could cry . . ."

Elvis was much more assured, expecting the audience's interest in him. He did not need to toss his shoe to hold their attention. Slowed down without nerves and fear running through him, you can't take your eyes off him.

HOLLYWOOD WAS THE FLIP SIDE of Elvis' dream. Ever since he was a fifteen-year-old usher at the Loews State Theater he had watched screen idols like Robert Mitchum and Tony Curtis and fantasized about being a movie star. More than anything, he wanted to be a serious actor like the late James Dean. He worshipped the star who had tragically died in a car crash just four months earlier. He had seen *Rebel Without a Cause* no less than a dozen times, and memorized every one of Dean's lines.

On March 7, 1956, William Morris agent Harry Kalcheim forwarded the script of *The Rainmaker*, which was to be used for Elvis' screen test. The Colonel passed the script along to Elvis and implored him not to tell anyone. He should study it well, but keep it to himself, don't share it with anyone or leave it lying around. "You can show it to your parents but don't show it to anyone else because this is a private matter. . . . *Do not discuss this matter with anyone—not the boys in the band, the people at the Hayride, anyone, because this is private.*"

Aw hell, what fun was that?

On March 26, 1956, Elvis had a screen test for the legendary producer Hal Wallis. Allan Weiss, who worked for Wallis, was there. "Hal Wallis had an eye. He signed people before they got famous. Sign them to a long contract, and then he wouldn't have to pay them very much. But what an eye."

Of Presley's film tryout, "No one had any expectations," Weiss recalled. "He was such a strange, quiet fellow—so completely foreign. But he sang, and read a scene from *The Rainmaker*, and answered questions asked from off-screen—and it was phenomenal. It was an amazing experience to be there. One of those life-changing experiences." (By the way, Weiss is convinced that Presley's screen test is still knocking around in a Paramount vault somewhere.) Hal Kanter, who worked for Wallis when he wrote and directed *Loving You* and *Blue Hawaii*, was there, too. He noted that Elvis "was charming and witty and completely unafraid of the camera."

Immediately recognizing his potential, Wallis decided to loan Elvis out to another studio for a Debra Paget, Richard Egan Western called *The Reno Brothers* (later retitled *Love Me Tender*). Shooting would begin in August.

Of his upcoming stint in Hollywood, Elvis said, "It's a dream come true, you know? I've had people ask me, was I going to sing in the movies? I'm not. I mean . . . not as far as I know. I took a straight acting test. And actually, I wouldn't care too much about singing in the movies."

ONE NIGHT, back home in Memphis, Elvis stopped by Lansky's to pick up some clothes. Red West went into the store and left Presley in the car.

"Where's E?" they wondered, in that nice Southern way.

"In the car reading his script," said Red with no small importance, like this was an everyday occurrence in Memphis. In the car, hell—boy can't come inside and say hello? Bernard walked to the curb to see what was up. Elvis was in the passenger seat reading his script, making sure everyone saw him.

"Hey, Elvis, what are you reading?" asked Bernard, although he knew.

"I'm doing my first movie."

"Aw, man, you know you cain't read—now what you looking at?"

Elvis looked up and started laughing. In the shop, they called it his shit-eating grin. "I'm gonna be in a movie."

"Man, that's fantastic, Elvis—give me my ticket now," Lansky said, laughing.

"LADIES AND GENTLEMEN, Elvis Presley."

On May 4, Elvis and the boys played Vegas for the first time. Inexplicably, the Colonel promoted him as "The Atomic Powered Singer." They played two shows, at 8:00 P.M. and midnight at the Venus Room of the New Frontier Hotel, on the same bill as Freddie Martin and His Orchestra, and comedian Shecky Green.

He launches into "Blue Suede Shoes," which had been such a hit on Dorsey. "Well, it's a—one for the money, a two for the show, three to get ready, now go cat, go!"—but is greeted with ominous silence. The women in the mostly elderly audience wear little fur capes, their hair in tight permanents. They regard Elvis with dull, pinched faces, as if he is keeping them from the slots. Or church. The men beside them wear safe gray suits, eyeglasses glinting, their faces impassive. They give him nothing. *Entertain me*, they defy him. *Move me*. Clearly, this is not the Rat Pack. They sit in their seats, their hands folded in their laps. Nobody's feeling the love. The Atomic Powered nothing drops like a lead balloon and gets off the stage, fast.

Shaken by their response, Elvis recalled, "I went outside and walked around in the dark. It was awful . . . I wasn't getting across to the audience." Was this whole thing—the Colonel, his number one records, the house he just bought his parents on Audubon Drive, a fluke? Everything was happening so fast. "I'm scared," he admitted to a reporter. "You know, I could go out like a light, just like I came on."

Variety agreed with Elvis' assessment. Reviewing the Vegas gig they said: "For teenagers he's a whiz; for the average Vegas spender, he's a fizz."

Beyond the dullard audiences, though, Elvis loved the lifestyle of Vegas, a city without parents; the action, the night-for-day schedule, the sense that you can do anything you want. But Elvis got something out of Vegas other than a bruised ego and some showgirls' phone numbers: "Hound Dog." One night, he and the boys catch another show on the strip, Freddie Bell and the Bellboys, whose novelty performance of Big Mama Thornton's rhythm-and-blues hit "Hound Dog" impresses him as a potential show-stopper. "When we go to New York, we'll cut it," he assures D. J.

A month later, in Hollywood for his second appearance on *The Milton Berle Show*, Elvis unveiled his version of "Hound Dog." He played it like a stripper on stage, shaking his shoulders on the backbeat, not caring what anyone else thought. He was really connecting with the audience, much more controlled. He wasn't jumping around like a crazy kid anymore. Like the best seducer, he had learned: Hold your ground and make them come to you.

He went back, mildly kicking his feet, but he was much more aware of himself, an actor. He did a side burlesque thing, smiled over at Scotty. Almost ironic, a bit mocking of the audience and perhaps of himself for the effect he had on them, he withheld himself. It was all a bit of a goof. Elvis was totally, utterly conscious of the effect he had on others.

As soon as he did "Hound Dog" on Uncle Miltie, the vultures descended. No longer singing in a south Texas bar with chicken wire strung up in front of the bandstand, television and newspaper critics took notice of Elvis and his raunchy ways, with the emphasis on critical. Descriptions of his singing style ranged from "highly erotic" to "downright revolting." Jack Gould, *The New York Times'* television commentator, was typical: "He might possibly be classified as an entertainer, or, perhaps, just as easily, as an assignment for a sociologist."

"His body," wrote wiseass Ivy League sweatshop *Time* magazine, "takes on a frantic quiver, as if he had swallowed a jackhammer."

There is nothing the media likes more than an obvious scandal. Everyone piled on—Elvis Presley was such a slow moving target it was impossible not to take a crack at him. A December cover story in *Cosmopolitan* magazine wondered, "What is an Elvis Presley?" *TV World* asked simply: "Singer or Sexpot?" A typical newspaper article began, "Elvis Presley, who was driving a truck in Memphis two years ago . . ." The truck driver comment gives it away. The subtext being, of course, two years ago he was a redneck hick, definitely Not Our Kind, Dear—and where *is* Memphis, anyway?

It was beyond unfair—Elvis was such an easy mark. Innocent, charismatic, a small-town boy only mildly aware of the effect he had on others. First, the preachers warned against him from the pulpit. Then the parents. Now, *The New York Times.* The "Elvis the Pelvis" chorus persisted.

"If he did that on the street," said a Los Angeles policeman, "we'd arrest him."

It was pretty obvious that the Eastern Establishment that, up until then, set the cultural tone of the country did not Get Elvis. They never would.

Averell Harriman—*Mr.* Eastern Establishment who, along with Bob McNamara, was one of the great proponents of the Vietnam War—once said that "Americans just want to go to the movies and drink Coke." He meant it dismissively but he also happened to be describing two of Presley's favorite pastimes.

ON JUNE 24, at the Municipal Auditorium Arena in Kansas City, Missouri, there was a riot in which D. J.'s drums and Bill's stand-up bass were smashed and

D. J. was thrown into the orchestra pit. The headline in the paper the next day reported, ELVIS PRESLEY FLEES TO CAR AFTER 20 MINUTES ON STAGE. He flew out of Kansas City at 4:35 A.M. for Detroit.

AFTER MILTON BERLE, Steve Allen decided he had to get in on the act.

Steve Allen was everything that Elvis, and the rest of the country, feared about those smart-aleck city folks. Condescending and chummy behind a bland everyman exterior, Steve Allen was like a passive aggressive ex-boyfriend who does something really mean and says, "Hey—it's just a joke." As if that made everything okay. Capitalizing on the whole Demon Elvis thing, he and his cronies cooked up a number where Elvis comes out dressed in white tie and tails, with an orchestra in the background, and—get this—sings "Hound Dog" to an actual hound dog.

Oh, and then there was a mock Western skit where Elvis plays "Tumbleweed" Presley, a cowboy who sings a ditty about "Don't step on my blue suede boots."

Introducing Elvis, Allen says, "Some viewers interpret it one way, and some viewers interpret it another." *Passive aggressive alert.* "Naturally, it's our intention to do nothing but a good show—" We hear an offstage bark. "Heh, heh, someone's barking back there. . . . We want to do a show the whole family can watch and enjoy and we always do, and tonight we're presenting Elvis Presley—heh, heh, what you might call his first comeback—this time it gives me extreme pleasure to introduce the new Elvis Presley!"

Elvis comes out and starts singing to a basset hound perched on a white pedestal. "You ain't nothin' but a hound dog—c-cryin' all the time . . ." The dog looks away and Elvis takes hold of his chin to sing directly into his eyes. Boy, if anyone can pull this off, he can. "You ain't nothin' but a hound a dog . . ."

Wearing a tuxedo, Elvis, of course, looked fabulous—but he counted this as the most ridiculous performance of his entire career. He did a pretty good job of it, considering. He started smiling a bit because he was trying to sing without moving, and still keep the dog's attention. He was an incredibly good sport about it.

In later years, he would recall how angry and embarrassed he was by the whole spectacle. Well, whatever, he had done the best he could and now it was over. Back in his dressing room, his tails were piled in a heap on a chair.

After *The Steve Allen Show,* an exhausted Elvis spoke to *Herald Tribune* columnist Hy Gardner on his televised talk show *Hy Gardner Calling!* It was late at night and Elvis was wiped out, tired and overwhelmed at all that was asked of him. He looks incredible, though. His eyes are heavy lidded, extraordinary. He has the profile of a Greek statue. He speaks in a soft Southern accent, at odds with his androgynous beauty.

"Did you have fun tonight on *The Steve Allen Show?*" Gardner wondered.

"Yes, sir, I really enjoyed it."

"First time you ever worked in tux and tails?"

"First time I ever had one on, period."

"What do you keep in mind most, some of the songs you're going to do? Or some of your plans, or what? What goes through your mind?"

"Well, everything's happening to me so fast in the last year and a half, uh, I'm all mixed up—I can't keep up with everything that's happening, and uh . . ." His hand flutters across his forehead. He rubs his eyes. He sounds a little dazed here, lost.

"They predict that Elvis Presley will be another James Dean, now have you heard that?"

"I heard something about it, but, uh, I would never compare myself in any way to James Dean, because James Dean is really a genius. I've seen his uh . . . I sure would like to, I guess there are a lot of actors in Hollywood who would like to have the ability that James Dean had. I would never compare myself with James Dean in any way."

"Now, if you had your choice, would you prefer to be an actor than to be a singing entertainer?"

"If I were a good actor—although, uh, if I ever break into the acting completely, I'll still continue my singing, I'll still continue making records—"

Gardner cuts him off. He's made his point, time to wrap things up. "Uh huh, uh huh, yeah," barely listening. "That's always a very, very good side line. . . . I want to tell you it's just a thrill talking to you and you make a lot of sense. Give my best to the Colonel, now."

"I sure will . . ."

Steve Allen, Imogene Coca, Hy Gardner, and Middle America may have found Elvis' performance with the top hat and the hound dog cute, but Sam Phillips of Memphis, Tennessee, was having none of it, that's for damn sure. Right after the show he called Elvis long distance in New York City, apoplectic: "You better call home and get straight, boy. What you doing in that monkey suit? Where's your guitar?"

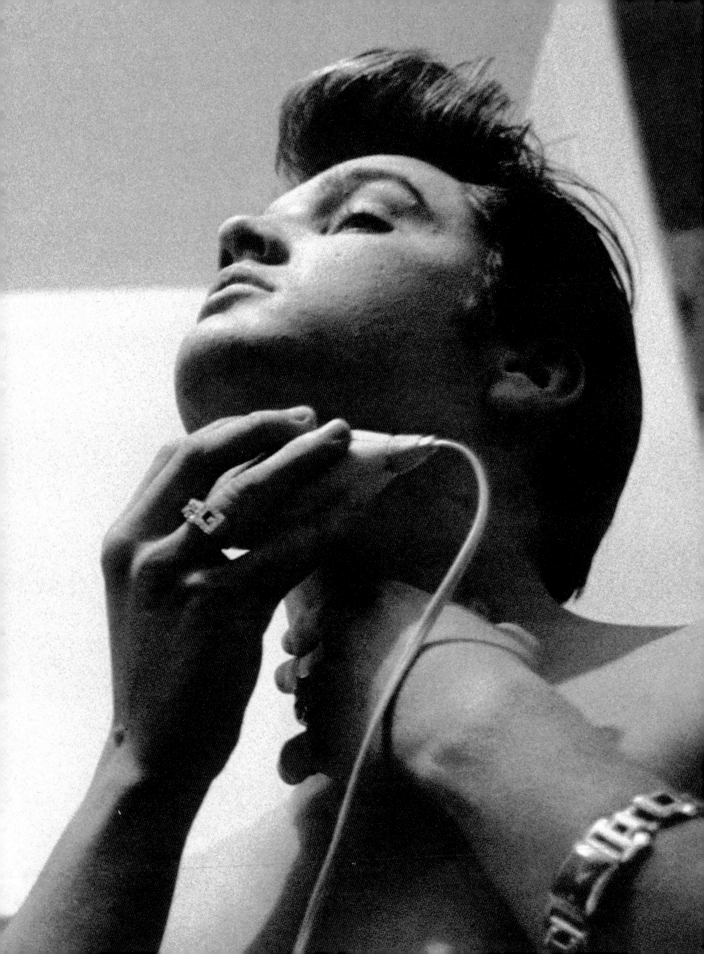

SO THEY DIDN'T LIKE HIM in New York—so what? He didn't like himself in that damn monkey suit either. The day after the whole ridiculous hound dog thing, Elvis went into a studio and over the next seven hours recorded "Hound Dog," "Don't Be Cruel," and "Any Way You Want Me." This is the first time he has taken over a recording session.

Alfred Wertheimer, a young New York City freelance photographer, had been following Elvis around for the past few days. RCA was not sure about the future of their latest acquisition, so they had advised Wertheimer to shoot him with black-and-white film. Although Anne Fulchino, the publicist for the Pop Record Division of RCA Victor, supported Presley, there were some who did not think he would last six months. If Presley was just going to be a flash in the pan, they did not want to waste good money on color film.

Wertheimer had been trailing Elvis since his third Dorsey appearance in March, down to a riotous concert he gave in Richmond before *The Steve Allen Show*, then the *Allen* show itself. He had seen Elvis shaving, walking anonymously around Times Square, falling asleep in his room at the Warwick Hotel on a couch amid his torn-up fan mail, making out with a pretty blonde just before he had to step onstage in Richmond. Elvis did not mind being trailed at all; he was so open, so unself-conscious about it, that there were times Wertheimer was more uncomfortable than he was. Wertheimer found Elvis the perfect subject for a photographer, "unafraid and uncaring, oblivious to the invasion of my camera."

The boys were tuning up when Wertheimer arrived at the recording studio. Elvis greeted him warmly; he was used to him by now.

"How ya feel?"

"A little tired," Wertheimer admitted. Living on coffee, Viceroy cigarettes, and vending machine snacks, he felt like he had not been home for a week. "It should be a good session." Al didn't know what made him say that. He just felt that way about the kid.

Elvis was more at home in a recording studio than practically anywhere. He surveyed the room like John Wayne preparing for a cattle drive, and replied, "Well, I hope so."

Steve Sholes, the engineer running the operation, suggested they try "Hound Dog" first. The engineer set the levels.

As Wertheimer explains, recording in 1956 was a laborious, exacting process with no room for error. Artists did not enjoy the luxury of twenty-four-track tape recorders and post-recording mixes. "Modern artists can add or subtract instruments, overdub, change levels, and electronically alter the sound with so much range that the final product may barely resemble what was heard at the original session." In 1956, you had to play the song all the way through—and what you heard was what you got. If the drums were too heavy, if the singer flubbed a line, if anything went wrong, it was back to the beginning to try it again from the top.

They started in on "Hound Dog."

Take one, take two, take three. By take four they managed to get past the opening and Elvis was bopping to the beat, feeling it, but Steve interrupted him, walking out of the control room. "You were off mike," he told him quietly. It seemed this was something he had spoken with him about before.

Elvis started up again. His voice cracked, D. J. screwed up the drums, someone hit a microphone, he went off mike again.

At around take fourteen, Wertheimer stopped taking pictures. "The humor that had started the session was fading and people began glancing to Elvis to check his mood. He wasn't happy. Out of seventeen takes, maybe four were complete." Wertheimer had been in recording studios before and right about now was when the talent starts blaming the photographer—anybody—for throwing off his concentration. Wertheimer crouched in the corner like a piece of furniture.

For the flubs and missed marks, though, the recording session was all Elvis'. He was unique, thought Wertheimer. "In his own reserved manner he kept control, he made himself responsible. When somebody else made a mistake, he sang off-key. The offender picked up the cue. He never criticized anyone, never got mad at anyone but himself. He'd just say, 'Okay fellas, I goofed.'"

At take eighteen, the boys got their groove on. Elvis grabbed the mike and rolled into the lyrics, Scotty's guitar bouncing and sharp with Bill's bass right behind. Elvis looked so joyous, what the Greeks call *telesis*—man working with his highest power toward his greatest good. On the afternoon of July 2, 1956, at the RCA studios on 155 East Twenty-fourth Street in New York City, Elvis Presley was in his moment, what Mihaly Csikszentmihalyi describes as "flow." He knew this feeling onstage, or when he declared his love for a woman. He had felt it with Sam Phillips at Sun.

Elvis was in his moment, doing what he was meant to be doing. Take eighteen: There was no mistaking it this time.

Everyone thought they had it, but Elvis wanted to try it again. At take thirty-one—*thirty-one!*—Steve thought they had it but Elvis wanted a few more. He got them, but inspiration had left, mistakes began creeping in. Sholes was sure they had it in the can. Clearly, it was time to take a break.

According to Wertheimer, "The recording had taken over two hours and without the air conditioner turned on (the mikes would have picked up the noise), the air in the room hung low and close. The double doors were opened, admitting cool air, the noise of the vending machines and visitors with glowing compliments." Elvis drank the Pepsi offered to him by his cousin and shrugged in reply to comments about how good the music was.

"Would you like to hear a playback?" Steve wondered.

"Now's as good a time as any," he said.

Elvis sat cross-legged on the floor in front of the speaker the size of a refrigerator, his head in his hands, concentrating absolutely. Hearing his efforts, he winced, chewed his fingernails, and looked at the floor. He was so caught up in the moment, it seemed he did not know whether it was a good take or not.

Sholes cued up take eighteen.

Elvis moved to a folding chair, sat astride it backward, and draped his arms across it, staring at the floor, his gray-striped Lansky jacket on the whole time. At the end of the take, he looked up and smiled, unable to hide his joy. That was it— the best one yet.

Still, he wanted to hear take thirty-one. This time, he went and crouched on the floor, as if hearing it from a different angle would alter his response. Again, he went into deep concentration. Wertheimer realized that in all the time they had spent together, this was the first time he had seen him still and motionless. Take thirty-one. At the end of it Elvis rose from his half crouch, turned to the room, and said with a wide grin, "This is the one."

That settled it then.

HIS WORK IN THE CITY WAS DONE. The next day, he caught the 11:30 A.M. train for Memphis, a twenty-seven-hour ride leaving from Pennsylvania Station. Clearly, it was time to go home.

When they finally reached the outskirts of Memphis, Elvis got off early at a small signal stop called White Station. The Colonel told him to make sure to give his regards to his mother, who distrusted him as no one else did. Elvis promised he would. Carrying his radio that looked like a briefcase with knobs, and wearing the same proud suit and white knit tie he had on in New York, he made his way across an empty field like he was walking into Richmond's Jefferson Hotel. He asked a woman passing by for directions to Audubon Drive and with a wave and a smile that could be seen for a hundred yards, Elvis walked home alone. His cousin Junior would take care of the bags like he always did.

ON WEDNESDAY, JULY 4, his first night home, Elvis gave a concert at Russwood Park in Memphis. Dressed all in black save for red socks and a red tie he and his father had picked out just before the show, all he ever wanted was to be well thought of by the folks back home. These days, he moved between controlling television studios that shot his image out to a million people and the open air concerts where he played his heart out for thousands. Elvis loved being onstage. He would live onstage if he could.

Elvis strode out raising his arm in salute, the returning emperor. The crowd roared their approval. He could not read a note of music—then, or ever—but singing, he knew how he wanted the words to come out. He bent sound to his will, dominating it like a woman, then casually tossed it aside, bored already, looking for the next moment, the next phrase, the next possibility. Everything was happening so fast: It was a life he could barely share with anyone. In time, where he went, others followed.

Still, Elvis was becoming the thing every man dreams of: He was becoming more himself.

"I just sing. I let the audience do the work," Elvis confided, but he was being disingenuous. By Russwood, he knew precisely what he was doing. After *Steve Allen* he would never let anyone dictate what he could or could not do onstage again. During the show he told 14,000 cheering hometown fans, "You know those people in New York are not going to change me none. I'm gonna show you what the real Elvis is like tonight."

For sixteen-year-old Jack Baker, who had lived next door to Elvis just nine months ago, "There was this keening sound, this shrill, wailing, keening response, and I remember thinking, That's an amazing sound, and then I realized I was making it too."

Elvis opened with "Heartbreak Hotel," threw in "Mystery Train" and "I Got a Woman," brought out the Jordanaires for "I Want You, I Need You, I Love You"

and "I Was the One," roared back with "Blue Suede Shoes" and "Long Tall Sally," and ended the set with the one good thing to come out of Vegas, "Hound Dog."

Slowing down to one-quarter time, his right arm whirling in the air, up on his toes now, hips grinding sideways to the beat, Elvis barely knew where he was. This loss, this absence of self, was what terrified his mother. "You ain't no-thin' but-a-houn-dog . . . c-cryin' all the time . . ." Then slower still, a burlesque, growling, driving it home in case anybody missed his point: "You ain't a nothin' but a houn-dog"—the girls howled like banshees. Like some ancient Greek rite, they wanted to rip him to shreds. Elvis was black and white, country and rock, male and female. Beyond definition, he brought to the light what others saved for the dark.

And he was going to take you with him, or he was going to die trying.

ELVIS BEGAN DATING June Juanico of Biloxi, Mississippi, in July. Over the next few months, they shared magical times, deep-sea fishing, horseback riding, waterskiing on Lake Pontchartrain. June was young, energetic, and, like Elvis, full of good-natured earthiness. Gladys loved her and envisioned her and Elvis giving her the "blue-eyed grandbabies" she had dreamed of. June also introduced him to Kahlil Gibran's *The Prophet*, a book she had gotten for her high school graduation. Elvis would refer to it again and again, for the rest of his life.

Still, if you were going to date Elvis, there were a few things a girl had to know: It was always his schedule, you had to keep your calendar entirely free at all times, and you could not ever, *ever* call him.

For no matter how much she loved Elvis, June quickly learned that being his steady girlfriend (which meant simply that you were the first among many) was not for the faint of heart. You might not hear from him for two or three weeks at a time, and this was after he had brought up marriage. In 1956, there were no answering machines, no call waiting, no cell phones, so waiting for Elvis to call meant, literally, sitting by the phone waiting for it to ring. He might miss your birthday (yes, this happened to June), you might read about his having showgirls out to the house, he might miss Christmas and then you would hear from him the next day. "I tried to call, baby, but the circuits were busy."

Having fallen in love, they discussed marriage, although the Colonel objected. Big time. "Am I in love?" Elvis asked rhetorically during a late-night television interview in New York City after *The Steve Allen Show*. "No. I thought I've been in love but I guess I wasn't, it just passed over. I guess I haven't met the girl yet . . ." At one point, the newspapers were full of rumors that June and Elvis were engaged. Now, he's called three times in the past five months—and she keeps reading about all the showgirls he is dating, Natalie Wood being invited to Memphis. Clearly, the relationship was losing momentum.

Whatever. It was his show, and if all else failed, he could always blame it on the Colonel.

LATER THAT MONTH, the Italian liner *Andrea Doria* sank off the coast of Nantucket after it was rammed by the Swedish liner *Stockholm*. Unfortunately, songwriter Mike Stoller happened to be on board. A talented kid on a winning streak, he had a couple of rhythm-and-blues hits, made some money, and was feeling on top of the world, well, until the damn ship turtled. Pop culture might have suffered a greater loss if a passing rescue freighter had not picked him up.

When he landed in New York, his songwriting partner, Jerry Leiber, was pacing the dock, unconcerned about his partner's near death experience, just ecstatic.

"Hey—we got a smash hit!" The one thing that really mattered.

And Mike was bobbing around in the Atlantic. It figures. "You're kidding, which one?" Stoller wondered.

"Hound Dog."

"Big Mama Thornton?" Stoller was puzzled. Her version had topped the R&B charts three years ago.

"No—some white kid named Elvis Presley."

Boy, did that name not ring a bell. "Elvis Presley?"

THE GREAT STONE FACE was worried. He, Ed Sullivan, may have been the nation's stiff Nixonian uncle, but he was no fool. And given the ratings of his rival Steve Allen, he could not ignore what was happening with this Presley kid. He had vowed never to have Elvis on his show, but the sheer power of his popularity forced him to change his mind.

In 1955 and 1956, Ed Sullivan, a Broadway newspaper columnist, was at the height of his power as the host of the first national variety show in the nation. Broadcast at 8:00 P.M. every Sunday night, Sullivan was America's Minister of Culture. For a performer, appearing on *Sullivan* was the big time, and every important entertainer in the country vied to be on his show. Sullivan took his role seriously, making sure *The Toast of the Town* was a program—inoffensive, broad-based, culturally uplifting, just the way America imagined herself to be—the whole family could watch.

Sullivan's popularity was all the more remarkable because he was so unlikable in print and on the air. A staid, humorless, mildly puritanical man, there was no way he would ever understand Elvis. Unlike most performers, Sullivan made no attempt to warm up to the camera. He was almost completely expressionless; his voice, sharp and high pitched. Television critic John Crosby wrote as early as December 1948, "One of the small but vexing questions confronting anyone in this area with a television set is: 'Why is Ed Sullivan on every night?'"

Sullivan was obviously uncomfortable interacting with others, and ripe for parody. *And now, for a really big shew. . . .* Once, famously, after Sergio Franchi sang the Lord's Prayer on his show, Sullivan turned to the audience and said, "Let's hear it for the Lord's Prayer." Comedian Jack Paar observed, "Who can bring to a simple English sentence suspense and mystery and drama?"

Mystified by the criticism of her highly paid husband (about $250,000 in 1956 dollars), Mrs. Sullivan once tried to mollify his critics with an article for *Collier's* entitled "I'm Married to the Great Stone Face." In it, she debunked rumors that he seemed so stiff because he had a serious war wound or that he had been hit on the head with a golf club. Jack Paar could not have said it better himself.

If he could, Sullivan would have preferred not to have this crazy Southern kid on at all—couldn't they book Greg Peck reenacting scenes from *Moby Dick* again? But Presley's ratings were through the roof. Sullivan sighed, Get the Colonel on the phone. Let's give the kid a shot.

ON SEPTEMBER 9, 1956, Ed Sullivan was laid up from an auto accident, so actor Charles Laughton substituted as host for him in New York, with Elvis performing in Hollywood.

Wearing a plaid jacket, open-necked patterned shirt, black pants, and black shoes, Elvis bopped instantly into his latest hit, "Don't Be Cruel." His voice was silly, goofy, going low and then up a notch to make Scotty and the audience crack up. He was totally self-aware of the camera and how he presented himself. "If you cain't come around, at-least, please uh tely-phone," with a funny dip in his voice. It was a long way from his manic first appearance on the Dorsey Brothers eight months ago.

In the television world, nothing succeeds like success (as the Colonel could have told him), and Sullivan's ratings skyrocketed after Elvis' appearance. He had him on again on October 28, 1956, and January 6, 1957. The third time he appeared, Sullivan made one last desperate attempt to censor Elvis by photographing him from the waist up but it didn't matter. His fierce charisma overrode the camera. To the band, he said "Here we go" and went into his moves as the camera cut away, the audience squealing in the background. Presley wound up as he knew he must, for the big finale: "Weeeeelllllllll—I don't want no other love—baby, it's just you I'm thin-king offffffff!"

Elvis announced that he was going to sing a brand-new song, "it's completely different from anything we've ever done. This is the title of our brand-new Twentieth Century Fox movie and also my newest RCA Victor escape—er, release." He shrugged apologetically to the audience's good-natured laughter. Clearly, they were on his side.

Alone in the spotlight, Elvis sang "Love Me Tender," quiet and soft. His obvious vulnerability as well as the sweetness of the love song and warmth of his delivery blunted the edge of public wrath. As the country boy showed his other side, more were converted.

But lest we think Elvis had gone too Lite-FM, he roiled right into "Ready Teddy": "Well, I got a gal that I love so, ready ready ready ready ready ready ready to—rock 'n' roll." He stopped dead for two beats, then started up again. Just like in Spartanburg, Pensacola, or Charlotte, girls screamed in the background.

Now, what was that about not putting the camera on him? Right now, Presley owned Sullivan, he was wiping the floor with him. As a final "I'm the Boss Here" to Stone Face, Elvis closed with his snarling humping favorite, "Hound Dog." "You ain't no-thin' but- a houn' dog." Keeping his back straight and holding his knees precisely apart, he slowly worked his way sideways across the stage, D. J. following his every bump, about as far away from Perry Como as humanly possible.

This was most of young America's introduction to Elvis Presley. Bruce Springsteen was nine years old, sitting in front of the TV, and his mother had *Ed Sullivan* on, and on came Elvis. "I remember right from that time, I looked at her and I said, 'I wanna be just . . . like . . . that.'" In Hope, Arkansas, ten-year-old Billy Clinton and his mom were watching, too.

In all his striptease splendor, the crowd started screaming; they were beside themselves. They could not believe he was doing this *on television*. Only Elvis held himself in check. He straightened up, hit the last note, fell all the way back among the band, lifted his arm in salute, and walked offstage. Acting on the Colonel's advice, he never did encores. "Always leave 'em wanting more," he says.

For Sullivan, the Elvis ratings were phenomenal. Fifty-four million people watched the show—one out of every three Americans. The next day, RCA got 1 million advance orders for "Love Me Tender," and Elvis got his fifth gold record. "I always felt that someday, somehow, something would happen to change everything for me, and I'd daydream about how it would be," Elvis said in the face of his daunting success.

It was happening.

On October 24, *Variety* published a front-page banner headline: ELVIS A MILLIONAIRE IN ONE YEAR. He had sold over ten million singles, a figure representing about two-thirds of RCA's singles for the year. "Hound Dog" sold two million copies and "Don't Be Cruel" sold three million. "Heartbreak Hotel" was number one on the white chart, number one on the country chart, and number five on the rhythm and blues chart. "Don't Be Cruel" and "Hound Dog" were number one on all three charts. To give a sense of the almost unreal trajectory of his success, in 1952, his father earned $2,781.18. In 1956, Elvis earned $282,349.66. In 1958, he brought home $1,001,727.89.

LOVE ME TENDER opens at the Paramount Theater in New York City on November 15, 1956. Some 1,500 fans begin lining up the night before under the forty-foot cutout of Elvis. Reviews are lukewarm, if not condescending, but the Colonel's one piece of advice to theater operators is to be sure to empty the house after every matinee showing.

The two top-grossing films of 1956 are *Giant,* with James Dean, Elizabeth Taylor, and Rock Hudson, and *Love Me Tender.*

NOW, SULLIVAN NEEDED HIM. He had Elvis back on October 28 and again on January 6, 1957, two days before his twenty-second birthday. By January, he was gone in spirit. He did not need the boys in New York anymore. Bigger than television now, he was heading to Hollywood to film *Loving You.*

Averell Harriman, *The New York Times, Time* magazine, and the Eastern Establishment did not get Elvis, but by then, it did not matter. With his *Sullivan* appearance, Elvis wrested popular culture away from the dads and handed it securely over to the teenagers. The bond between the generations was ruptured. Never again would American youth look to the Establishment for anything.

For his final song on the show, Elvis sang the Negro spiritual "Peace in the Valley." Sullivan did not want him to sing it, but he insisted. It was a promise he had made his mother. His voice was pretty and peaceful—no Scotty, Bill, and D. J. in the background, no jumping bass, no sexual mayhem. "Oh well, I'm tired and so weary. But I must go alone. Till the Lord comes and calls, calls me away . . ." This was strictly Sunday morning Elvis. Mama's good boy as he wanted to be perceived. "There will be peace in the valley for me . . . there'll be no sadness, no sorrow . . ." At such a young age, he was singing as if he were eighty-seven years old, looking for peace, dreaming of a quiet time he was not going to have anytime soon. There will be peace in the valley for me.

At the close of it, Sullivan tried to make amends. "This is a real decent, fine boy. . . . We want to say that we've never had a pleasanter experience with a big name than we've had with you." Sullivan had not only thrown down the gauntlet, he had lost the war. Tired, perhaps, of the critics and the New York runaround, this was the last song Elvis would sing on television for twelve years. He had promised his mama, and he had done it.

After the show Elvis took the midnight train to Memphis. The next day he would be home, celebrating his twenty-second birthday. Although he did not know it, he was about to receive his draft notice.

It was the end of an era.

fool for love

SOME MEN LOVE WOMEN. They feel comfortable in their presence, preferring them, almost, to their own sex. (Once, asked what sort of girls he liked, Elvis said, "Female mostly.") Like puppies, women sense this—they sense who can and cannot be trusted and are instinctively drawn to them.

Some of these Men Who Love Women grow up to be president (liberal Democrats, generally). Some grow up to be hairdressers. Some grow up to be movie stars playing hairdressers who dabble in democratic politics (Warren Beatty). But because of the wide swath of his affections—not to mention the

millions of women who fantasize about him even today—Elvis is in a class by himself.

With E, there were famous women, Hollywood starlets, hometown girls, women who claimed to bed him posthumously, unknown women, and women whose names he could not remember, or perhaps never knew. Presley was a Method Lover. In the same way that he threw himself into singing "Hound Dog" or acting in *Harum Scarum* (playing a matinee idol on Cecil B. DeMille's leftover sets from *King of Kings*), Elvis believed. In the moment, it cannot be doubted that he loved every woman he was with. Even the slightest student of Presleyana soon learns that the King did not sleep alone and "Mornin', baby" can cover a lot of bases.

For Elvis, every day was Valentine's Day. He was the Love Potentate and as such, it was fundamentally impossible for him to be monogamous. It's not that he was chronically unfaithful, it is just unfathomable that this might be in the realm of possibility for him. Like Jesus, like Buddha, like George Clooney, E *was* love. And yet conversely, Elvis was a product of his era in that no matter how many women he slept with, he definitely subscribed to the good girl/bad girl theory, except for Ann-Margret—who rode motorcycles, loved her parents, and looked great in skintight pants. She was both Good Girl and Bad Girl.

From a technical standpoint, Elvis was a great kisser, that first "should we or shouldn't we" hurdle, and loved holding hands in the dark. He had the confidence of a much loved son; the eternal circle: One loves and is loved in return.

It is said that you can tell what a man is like in bed by watching him walk across a room. Elvis could dance, certainly. With E, there was no mugging twist. No chasing the backbeat. No embarrassing Earth, Wind & Fire ("Okay people, put your hands together for 'September'"), *here we are at the Greenwich Country Club—get down!* white guy air guitar for him.

But putting aside his physical presence, Elvis wooed women with a dizzying combination of charm, truculence, Southern good manners, underlying sexual tension, and just enough little boy neediness to keep one interested. Whatever it was, it worked. "He always had a playmate," observed Alfred Wertheimer.

Elvis was a definite closer, romance-wise. Women—teenagers, grandmothers, eight-year-olds—*loved* him.

But what was it like to date Elvis? Like Mick Jagger, he had the world's dark magic, and this was a big part of his appeal. "Man is limited only by the bounds of his imagination," said Franklin Roosevelt (granted, about the Depression), but it could apply to Elvis, too. A rock-and-roll star since the age of twenty, E was never in need of a Mrs. Robinson to teach him a thing. In the early days of touring, the boys had to drag Elvis out of bed to get to the next gig. He was, *naturellement,* not alone. "He looked like he'd been beaten up with a blender," recalled Scotty.

A date with Elvis could mean anything. Well, it wouldn't mean a weekend in Paris, since he never returned to Europe after the army, but in later years you could get on the *Lisa Marie* and fly to Vegas for an overnight.

Or just lounge around in matching PJs all day, reading Kahlil Gibran and checking out the security cameras positioned throughout Graceland, then picking up the dinner tray left outside the bedroom door.

Like most men, we see Elvis had his good and his bad points. He knew how to kiss. He looked better than Jim Morrison in black leather pants. His profile reminded some of John Barrymore—or Michelangelo's *David.* On the other hand, he never helped with the carpool, fetched a cup of coffee, or knew how to unload a dishwasher. Still, "Whoever he was with at the time," a friend recalls, "he loved."

> If I say the army made a man of me,
> it would give the impression that I was an idiot
> before I was drafted. I wasn't exactly that.
>
> —EP

euro elvis

ONE OF THE BEST THINGS about Elvis' success was what he could do for his parents. In 1957, he bought Graceland, a grand estate on fourteen acres of land, for $102,500. Vernon was thrilled with his new life. As Elvis' father, he was treated with a newfound respect he quickly grew accustomed to. There was always something to do at Graceland; it was like running a small farm, and Elvis deferred to him on money matters.

But still, the Presley family's extraordinary leap from abject poverty to riches beyond belief (which seemed to occur in the space of about a week and a half) was not without its stress. The whole thing just happened so *quickly*—Elvis being on the radio, then all the other songs he recorded, the RCA deal, Ed Sullivan, being on television, and now, the movies—and all from Elvis' recording a few itty-bitty records at Sam Phillips' place. It was unreal. No less than for anyone else, it was unreal for Elvis, too.

"I just don't know what it is. Only the other day Daddy looked at me and said, 'What happened, El? The last thing I remember is that I was working in a little ol' paint factory and you were driving a truck.'"

In spite of, or perhaps because of, Elvis' success, Gladys was not pleased with the changes in their lives. She had been feeling poorly for some time now and had gained a good deal of weight. There was an inescapable aura of sadness around her that she just could not shake no matter how many gold records Elvis had, or what success the Colonel promised next. Although she might not have been able to articulate it, she felt her life was no longer her own, that things were getting away from them. Her boy was gone more than he was home and when he was home, there

were always strangers rushing in and out. Elvis knew her feelings, but on some level, he wanted it this way. "It's a fast life," he admitted, "I just can't slow down. Seems like I'm hurrying all the time."

Gladys liked things to be simple; she missed her friends from the Courts. Bernard Lansky remembered her as "a real lady. She stayed around the house, she used to wear dusters, not dressed up," and if you came over to visit, she would always ask if she could get you something to eat or drink. "She never did go nowhere after they moved out there," said her sister Lillian. Alan Fortas, a friend of Elvis', recalls Mrs. Presley "sitting by the window in the kitchen, daydreaming, or looking out in the backyard at the chickens." She used to go to the grocery store, but the cook or the housekeeper did that now. Lillian felt that "she never was satisfied after she moved out there, I think the house was too big and she didn't like it. Of course, she never told Elvis that."

Elvis' life—and theirs—was moving so quickly, she had no control over it. With all his crazy running around, Gladys was scared to death that something would happen to Elvis. "I hope I'm in the grave before he is, because I could never stand to see him dead before me," she said.

ON JANUARY 8, 1957, with Elvis celebrating his twenty-second birth-day at home with his parents, the Memphis Draft Board announced that Presley would be classified 1A, meaning that he would most likely be drafted within the next six to eight months.

Think of the biggest star you can imagine at the height of his power—Mick Jagger? John Lennon? Tom Cruise? Eminem? Justin Timberlake? Then imagine the inanity of the government drafting him into the U.S. Army for two years during peacetime. It was unthinkable. Part of the appeal of rock stars, of course, is their debauched omniscience—they routinely do things we would never get away with, living lives we can only imagine, which is why we put them on a pedestal. And now, Elvis was giving all that up? It was unfathomable.

It is one thing to do what is expected of you in the public eye, but when you are about to enter the restricted world of the United States armed forces, well, lesser men have made sure they were taken care of. Seeing what a man is made of when push comes to shove: This, too, is style. All three of the services (except the marines) offered Presley special consideration. The navy wanted to create a specially trained "Elvis Presley company" (which would, what, appear on *The Ed Sullivan Show* and infuriate parents?); the air force wanted him to tour recruitment centers; the army offered a two-year enlistment with a 120-day deferment to allow him to complete his new movie, *King Creole*, which had now been rescheduled for January 1958. Elvis decided to go with the army.

On March 24, 1958, Elvis was drafted into the army. Although he worried about the effect his absence would have on his career, Elvis was philosophical about what was going to happen. "Every able-bodied American boy should go into the service. And I am an able-bodied American boy, so why not?" Most of all, he was determined to prove himself, and to do a good job no matter what the army handed him. "I'm going to be a good soldier or bust," he decided.

Upon receiving a draft notice, most modern Hollywood celebrities—cosseted, vastly entitled, barely able to wait in line at Starbucks—would probably turn tail and get their manager to take care of it. But rather than take the easy way out, which he could have, what Elvis felt mostly was gratitude "for what this country has given me. And now I'm ready to return a little. It's the only adult way to look at it."

For some reason, getting a haircut was almost a bigger deal with the public than his going into the army. Hadn't people been trying to get Elvis to cut his hair since he was sixteen? Now Uncle Sam would do it for him. And although very few people would notice, he had been going to Jim's Barber Shop in downtown Memphis every few weeks before his induction, getting it cut a bit shorter and shorter, so it would not be so drastic when it was officially trimmed the first time. "My hair is my trademark," he said. "I never meant to offend anyone with it, but people have been making such a big to-do about my keeping my hair. I don't want any partiality. I don't want to go into the service and have the rest of the boys in short hair and me in long hair."

In front of the fifty-five reporters and photographers who covered his army induction haircut, he could not help but quip (of course), "Hair today, gone tomorrow," before playfully blowing a handful of it in their direction.

It might sound strange to the Average Joe, but for Elvis, twenty-three, going into the army would almost be a bit of a rest, a way to get away from the endless demands of the public and the Colonel. Only someone who had lived through the highs and lows of his past few years could understand what he had been through. "I look upon my reporting to the army this way: it'll be a relief. It won't be a snap, I know, but it'll give me a chance to unwind, to catch my breath."

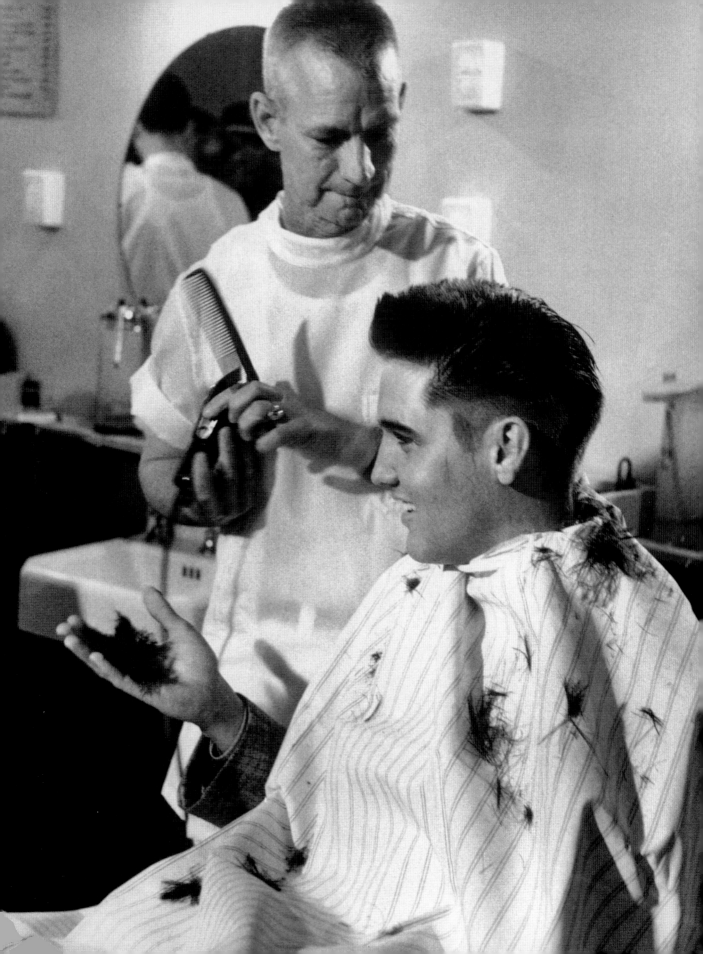

ON THURSDAY, AUGUST 14, at about 3:15 in the morning, Gladys Love Presley died with her husband at her side. Though she had been feeling unwell all through the summer, her death was a shock, and Elvis and his father were inconsolable. At the cemetery Elvis leaned over her grave, crying, and said, "Goodbye, darling, good-bye. I love you so much. You know how much I lived my whole life for you. Oh, God! Everything I have is gone." Elvis' grief was heartrending, beyond imagining. It was terrible to watch.

WHEN MRS. PRESLEY DIED, Bernard Lansky was out at Graceland for a whole week. It was such a terrible time for Elvis and his father. They needed all the help they could get. "I took care of everybody at the house, all his cousins," he recalled. "We took care of all their clothes and everything, made sure they all got dressed. Took 'em to the funeral home and everything, came back, I stayed out there, made sure everything was right. Anything they needed from the grocery store; got into one of Elvis' cars and went to the store."

Bernard always thought Elvis was never the same after his mother died. "To my thinking, they were tight: mother and son. Man, there's nothing like being home. You go home now, the house is empty, there's nobody to talk to. Man, when you come home you want to relax, you want somebody to talk to! Now who you goin' to talk to, Momma is gone. Nobody. You sit up there, you nervous, you walking the floor. Goin' crazy. 'What can I do? Who can I talk to?'"

For Elvis, nobody loved him like his mama. Bernard knew the guys couldn't fulfill that role. "What are you going to talk about to the guys, what they gonna talk about?" he demands to know. "You *already* talked to 'em—you been with 'em for two or three weeks at a time, maybe a month. But you have to go home and get that mother's love."

After the funeral, Elvis' doubts about what he was doing resurfaced. He wished he could just walk away from the life he was leading. In his grief, he asked to see Dixie Locke, his high school girlfriend who was now married. Elvis got rid of the dozens of people hanging around, and they sat in the living room and talked and cried about the old days.

As Dixie recalls, "We talked about his mother and rehashed from the time that I'd met her and all the things that we'd done that were funny and silly. And he expressed how special it was just to be with somebody you knew from those many days back that loved you and accepted you for what you were back then. He said, 'I wonder how many of my friends that are here now would be here if it were five years ago?' He said, 'Not very many, because they are all looking for something from me.'"

He also told Dixie about one of the guys who was singing backup for him, who had really given his heart to the Lord. He had been out in the world and was really messed up, and he told Elvis that he was going to walk away from the life that he had been leading. And Elvis said, "I wish I could do that."

For Dixie, it all seemed so sad, sitting next to Elvis in his beautiful living room, nicer than any hotel she had ever been in. It was like the White House, almost. "Why don't you?" she wondered. "You've already done what you wanted to do. You've been there, so let's just stop at the top and go back."

"It's too late for that," Elvis said. "There are too many people. There are too many people that depend on me. I'm too obligated. I'm in too far to get out."

That was the last time Dixie ever saw Elvis in person. Well, not the last, because she came by Graceland the next night, but by then the house was full of people again. "You know, it was like, this is the way it will always be," she observed. "That was his lifestyle. That was his life. It just reinforced to me that what I was seeing that night was really it. We both realized that. He was in it, and there was no way out."

ELVIS NEVER GOT OVER losing Gladys. "It wasn't only like losing a mother, it was like losing a friend, a companion, someone I could talk to . . ." Years later he recalled, "The bottom dropped out of my life the day my mother died. I thought that I had nothing left. In a way I was right."

EDDIE FISHER, *Eddie Fisher*, that's all the officers could talk about the first few weeks after Elvis arrived at D Company in Freiburg, Germany, Eddie Fisher. Lieutenant Bill Taylor, Elvis' commanding officer, explains. "It was in the background—everybody *knew* he could've pulled an Eddie Fisher, and gotten out of the army. We all wondered, What the hell is this guy doing out here with us in this crap?"

At first, Elvis was assigned as a jeep driver to Captain Russell, the commander of D Company. This lasted for about three weeks. The story was that Elvis had ear problems and couldn't stand the crack of the tank gun over his head. Wrong. What really happened was that Captain Russell couldn't handle it.

One day, First Lieutenant Bill Taylor, a twenty-five-year-old who had been the recon platoon leader ("the best damn job in the army," he says), but had just

been promoted to executive officer of B Company, got a phone call from the battalion commander, asking him to come see him. The battalion commander ran the whole show, so Taylor hustled over there, double time.

"We've got Elvis Presley."

"Yes, sir . . ."

"Captain Russell tells me he's going crazy, he can't handle Presley. The phones are ringing off the hook, reporters from everywhere are at higher headquarters all the time about Presley. Girls climbing over the fence, under the fence, through the fence, going *around* the fence to try to get to Presley."

"Yes, sir," Taylor said, wondering where this conversation was going.

"D Company used to get three bags of mail every day, now they're getting about twenty-five bags of mail a day, and they're all for Elvis Presley. And Fat Daddy Russell can't handle it.

"Now, Bill, I got an idea—what do you think about putting him in your old platoon? Sergeant Jones is the best NCO in the army."

"Sir, you're damn right. Great idea—do it."

"Well, I was going to do it anyway." That's the army for you.

So Elvis went to C Company, the scout platoon of the thirty-second tank battalion. That's thirty-two men, fourteen jeeps, some machine gun jeeps, some scout jeeps without machine guns, but heavy on the radios because scout platoon is the eyes and ears of the battalion. Elvis loved being in scout patrol; they were the cutting edge. Charlie Company was out front, in contact with the enemy all the time.

ELVIS BROUGHT HIS FAMILY and a few buddies with him, in order to make his transition to the army less taxing. Vernon; Vernon's mother, Minnie; and two guys from home, Red West and Lamar Fike (who, at three hundred pounds, tried to join the army with Elvis but was turned down), all join him in Germany.

After a few months at the Hilberts Park Hotel in Bad Nauheim, a restrictive upscale hotel full of pensioners who did not appreciate Elvis and the boys' rowdy Memphis ways, they decamped to a three-story, five-bedroom white stucco house at 14 Goethestrasse, nearby. The landlady, Frau Pieper, charged them an exorbitant rent of $800 a month, while continuing to maintain a room in the house to serve as housekeeper and oversee her famous tenant. At Elvis' suggestion, and to placate the neighbors, a sign was put up on the gate reading: AUTOGRAMME VON 19:30 20:00 [autographs 7:30–8:00 P.M.].

Now that he was in Germany, Elvis embraced the "when in Rome" ethos and bought not one but three different cars. After the bloated appeal of American Cadillacs, he fell in love with the perfection of fine German engineering and bought a sleek black Mercedes sedan. In fairness to Bavarian Motor Works, he also leased a white BMW 507 sports car immediately dubbed *der Elviswagen* by the press, and an old Volkswagen "bug" for the guys to drive around. There was no way they were going to touch the Benz.

Being in the army was the closest thing Elvis had to a day job. He had to keep regular hours, waking up at 5:30 A.M. (an unconscionable hour, he was used to going to bed by then) to get to the base at 6:30 in the Mercedes taxi he hired to take him back and forth. He often came home for lunch, hopping over the wall in back so the fans would not see him, and was home by 6:00 in the evening, except for Friday night, when all the GIs cleaned the barracks for Saturday morning inspection. All in all, it was pretty homey at 14 Goethestrasse. Grandma cooked his favorite burnt bacon, hard eggs, and biscuits for breakfast.

PRESLEY HAD A WONDERFUL WAY of addressing Lieutenant Taylor: "Loo-tenant." With the auspices of rank, Taylor called him "Presley."

When the scout party had aggressor duty, Lieutenant Taylor was always asked to lead some of the aggressor party. "Aggressors" were small patrols that were supposed to penetrate a tank company security perimeter at night. And, as he told Elvis, "There is no tank company security perimeter in the world that cannot be penetrated." And so they'd go out in the pitch black and slide through the mud and climb up hills with their faces darkened, and Elvis *loved* it. He just flat out loved it!

The first time C Company penetrated a tank company's perimeter, they captured the tank company commander and after that was accomplished, there were graders to evaluate how the mission went. Taylor was there, talking to the graders, when out of the corner of his eye he noticed a first lieutenant, a guy he knew, bothering Elvis, giving him a whole bunch of stuff, wanting his autograph, and so on. Taylor knew that when Presley got nervous, he started shuffling his feet and looking down. The guy asking was a lieutenant, so Presley didn't know how to get out of this one.

Taylor walked over. "Now, what's going on?" he drawled.

"All I want to do is get Elvis' autograph."

"Aw, would you leave him the hell alone, please?"

"Who the hell do you think *you* are?"

Taylor decked the son of a bitch right in front of Elvis. "You stay off the guy!" He stepped over him, brushing his hands on his fatigues. That was the end of that damn problem.

Yes sir, Elvis loved the army.

THERE WAS AN EXPRESSION they had in the army, when a man looked sharp in his uniform: *STRAC*. Private First Class Presley definitely looked *strak*. During World War I, F. Scott Fitzgerald and his Princeton cronies had their uniforms tailored at Brooks Brothers. Of course, Elvis being Elvis, he looked fabulous in a uniform. Although his fatigues were army issued, his dress blues were hand tailored, and looked it. He had dozens of extra uniforms, cleaned, pressed, and ready to go at a moment's notice. He special-ordered ten pairs of nonissue tanker boots from the PX at $45 a pair.

Joe Esposito met Elvis in Germany and he always remembered how cool he looked when they met at his house, wearing camouflage pants, a white T-shirt, and his spit-shined boots (Lieutenant Taylor swears he shined them himself) worn unlaced. Joe, an Italian kid from Chicago, thought he was the coolest guy he had ever seen.

After a few weeks on the Continent, Presley's personal style took a decided step forward. He was never one to get stuck in one look in the past, and with the discipline of the army and postwar Germany, he became Euro Elvis. Lansky's flashy duds, perfect for Beale, started to look a little déclassé on the Champs-Élysées. Elvis would never be one of those sweat-suited Americans besmirching Europe—he got with the program with narrow, dark suits, white shirt and tie, and a showgirl on each arm.

AFTER FIVE MONTHS ON BASE, it was time for a road trip. In early March 1959, Elvis, accompanied by Red and Lamar, traveled to Munich where they visited Vera Tschechowa, an eighteen-year-old actress he had met in January doing publicity shots for the March of Dimes. Vera's mom was not impressed with EP and the boys. Actually, she kicked him out of the house. As Vera said, "After he had bothered our animals, canaries, dogs, and cats long enough, my mother said to him, 'Now you better leave—there is the door! Bye!'" But the trip was redeemed by several late nights spent at the Moulin Rouge, the famed striptease club. The next morning Elvis met Vera for breakfast. "He had bits of tinsel everywhere, in his hair and his eyebrows. I asked him what happened and he only said: 'I stayed there.'"

E L V I S   P R E S L E Y   and Priscilla Beaulieu met, yes, when he was twenty-four, and she was fourteen years old. She had just arrived in Wiesbaden with her father, Captain Paul Beaulieu, mother, Ann, and two brothers and a sister, barely a month before, when, as she recalls, "there was a whole group of guys around Elvis at the time, and a man named Cliff Gleaves came up to me, about two weeks after my family and I had moved to Wiesbaden, and asked if I would like to meet Elvis.

"And I said, would I? Well—who wouldn't? Of course I would—who wouldn't? Of course I would have to ask my parents, which I did, and so a few days later, Cliff and his fiancée drove me out to the house to meet Elvis."

The Italians have a phrase when someone falls instantly in love; they speak of lightning striking your heart. For Elvis, meeting Priscilla was like that. It was Sunday, September 13, 1959, and he was sprawled in an armchair in the living room at 14 Goethestrasse, Bad Nauheim, wearing a red sweater and tan slacks, enjoying a cigar, when Cliff brought her over to meet him.

"Elvis, this is Priscilla—" Cliff began, while Priscilla worried about whether she looked okay in her navy and white sailor dress. Elvis jumped out of his chair like he was sitting on a hot plate.

What Elvis was actually responding to, although he could not tell Priscilla this—then, or ever—was how much she resembled Debra Paget, his *Love Me Tender* costar, who had not given him the time of day when he was in Hollywood because her strict parents disapproved of him. Whether she intended to or not, Priscilla had unwittingly mimicked Debra Paget through her hairstyle, facial structure, and delicate porcelain beauty. Joe Esposito confirms this prosaic reality. "He was flipped over Debra. From the stories I was told by him and some other people, he carried a torch for her all during the making of that movie and even after it. But it never happened."

Elvis was a deeply romantic individual. He fell in love quickly, absolutely, and often. (Very often.) So it was with Priscilla that night. When he saw her, Elvis must have felt the universe was giving him another crack at the Paget Saga: Debra Part II. Priscilla barely said a word while Elvis fell over himself trying to impress

her. After chivalrously escorting her to a chair in the living room, he went to the piano and began playing, showing off like a schoolboy.

Priscilla's first impression—like everyone's first impression of Elvis—was how "extremely good-looking" he was, "I mean, he was even better looking than in *Love Me Tender*." But now that they had met, she was definitely not feeling the love on her part, not like Elvis. "No," she acknowledged later. "No—although there was definitely a pull there, the energy was very electric, but not in the sense that this is *it*."

Still, there was the feeling that they were meant to connect. Years later, when Priscilla was fifty, having divorced and buried Elvis, she reflected on their meeting. "I've gone through that night many, many times. It was a setup that was meant to be. It was something that—again, that power, that drawing power—I felt that night. I mean—what are the odds that I would ever meet Elvis Presley—in *Germany*, of all places?"

And so it was: Priscilla and Elvis. On some level, they were going to be together. To what degree and for how long, neither of them could know. But it was a fait accompli; they would be together.

After a short while, Elvis took Priscilla by the hand and led her up to his bedroom.

Priscilla may have been fourteen when they met, and Elvis a world-famous singing star, but in many ways, she was the adult and he was the child. Like Elvis, she, too, possessed great instincts, but instead of music, her forte was in human relationships.

At fourteen, Priscilla Beaulieu's young life was full of secrets. Captain Paul Beaulieu was not Priscilla's true father, but he had adopted her after marrying her mother when she was three. Priscilla's father, Lieutenant James Wagner, was a navy pilot who had died in a plane crash when she was six months old. Her mother had never told her the truth and she found out the worst way possible— after coming across a picture of herself and her parents and a folded American flag traditionally given to families of servicemen killed in action. She questioned her mother, frantic for information. Her mother told her and then, inexplicably, asked that she not let Beaulieu or her other brothers and sister know that she knew. It was a terrible burden for a young girl.

Any infantryman can tell you, you really see what a man is made of, spending weeks out on maneuvers. One time, the scout platoon was out in the field and Elvis said to Taylor, "Hey, sir, they tell me your middle name is Jessie."

"That's right, Presley," the lieutenant said, wondering how he had learned a thing like that.

"You know, my brother's name is Jessie."

Really? Taylor didn't know he had a brother.

"Well, he died when we were born," Presley said simply. "But that was his name, Jessie."

Taylor thinks that Elvis, being far from home, thought a lot about his family, about his past, and where he had come from.

Since they got along so well in a professional capacity, did Lieutenant Taylor ever visit Elvis in Bad Nauheim?

"No." Taylor is adamant on this one. "I never visited him there. I never wanted to get privately into his life. Officers don't do that. I don't have a single photograph of him. I would never do it, I would never ask for an autograph, neither would Sergeant Jones. No, officers don't do that. It wouldn't have been good for him, or me, or anything."

IN SOME WAYS, in spite of her youth, Priscilla was far more worldly than Elvis. She had not grown up in a simple, loving home like he did. But in her own way she was clever. She had the nerves of a gambler. She did what she had to do to survive. At an early age she smiled, watching the angles, adjusting herself to suit others' opinions of her. In 1959, this was how a pretty girl got by. She was an officer's daughter consorting with a GI. She was a fourteen-year-old being romanced by the most famous man in the world. Secrets upon secrets. Because of her background Priscilla was not unfamiliar with secrets. They calmed her, they gave her strength.

Soon, Priscilla was coming to Bad Nauheim several nights a week whenever Presley summoned her. At school, she became known as Elvis' girl.

Because of her instincts, Priscilla had remarkable self-possession for such a young girl and knew not to discuss Elvis with anyone. Her tendency to draw an imaginary line between herself and others, the aura of mystery she possessed even as a child, "got worse after I met Elvis," she said. "Where most girls would probably exploit it and would probably be giddy, I protected it passionately. And why, I do not know. I don't know why I was so protective of it."

Robbie Jones, a friend who met her the next summer, said that Priscilla was very guarded, even then. When asked a question about Elvis, "she would specifically answer that question and drop it." In their way, Priscilla and Elvis insulated each other. He embraced the little girl who had lost her real father and was expected to conceal it. She honored his trust in her by guarding his privacy. As provocative as sex, their secrets bound them.

Reflecting on their relationship, Priscilla believes that "I think Elvis and I connected because he knew, on some level, that he could trust me. Yes, I was a young girl, but he was so lonely during that time in Germany—he was so far away from home in strange surroundings, and mourning the death of his mother, and I think he connected with me. He could talk to me about what he was feeling. And he knew I wasn't going to tell anyone. For some reason, I felt very protective of him."

Like all lovers, Priscilla and Elvis created their own world, magical, sexual, distinct. Those nights in his bedroom in Bad Nauheim bonded them forever. He told her about his mother, his fears that his career might be over, the pressure of fulfilling others' expectations for him. Emotionally, she gave herself to him absolutely. She lived for their moments together. There was nothing she would not do for him. Nothing he could ask she would not give. She stood before him stunned, mute with love. He allowed everything. Those hours were some of the most devout they would ever know. At the end of the night, Priscilla dreaded to hear "Goodnight, My Love," the closing song of the armed forces radio station, which meant it was time for Lamar or Mr. Presley to drive her home.

Attraction often takes place on a subconscious level, and Elvis and Priscilla's union can only be construed as karmic. It was meant to happen. For Elvis, deep in the throes of grief, Priscilla represented the adored mother he had just lost. Priscilla's resemblance to Debra Paget linked her to Gladys Presley. For Priscilla, young as she was, perhaps because she *was* young, Elvis was a beautiful, black-haired soldier who would be her guardian angel and protector.

Of course, the person Priscilla Beaulieu really resembled was Elvis himself; with their dark hair and sparkling eyes, they were opposite-sex versions of each other. This may have been the unspoken attraction, because Elvis, like all surviving twins, still grieved the death of his brother. On a subconscious level, finding Priscilla may have symbolized a reunion with Jessie, and thus, himself.

C COMPANY HAD A Private First Class Garcia from New Mexico, who was notified through the Red Cross that his family had been killed in an accident. His mom, dad, and two sisters were dead. The army and the Red Cross would pay to send him home and bring him back, but that was all they would do.

About a month after he got back from the funerals, Garcia told the story of how Elvis came to see him alone in the barracks and said, "Garcia, I'm so sorry. I wish I could do something real big to help you." Elvis handed him $2,500 cash in an envelope, to help with the expenses. In 1959, people made that in a year.

Elvis never told anyone what he had done, and the guys never said anything either.

"Elvis didn't want attention as Elvis Presley, superstar," says Taylor. "He wanted to be part of the platoon and how do I tell you? The guys in the platoon

loved him because of the way he was. He told everybody, 'I'm here and I'm serving in the army—I'm on the fighting edge.'"

He rarely performed. The guys would get him in the barracks area—*come on, Elvis, for god's sake, sing something!* Army life was hard on the grunts, so far from home with few diversions in a very grim postwar Germany. Elvis knew this. And he'd sit down on a foot locker at the end of a bunk and strum a few, and they loved him because of it.

LIKE ANYONE IN LOVE, Priscilla began living a double life: going to high school during the day, where she dozed through class, and the life in her head where she was dreaming, dreaming, always of *him*. Almost as if to prove they had been together, she began collecting small memories of Elvis in a treasure box—cigar bands, little notes he had written her. She even had a piece of windshield glass from when Elvis had been in a car accident.

After a few weeks, school became intolerable. After rising at seven o'clock on less than five hours' sleep, it became impossible to stay awake. But Priscilla knew that if she complained, her parents would end her nocturnal visits to Bad Nauheim. Not surprisingly her grades, never stellar to begin with, suffered. She was failing algebra and German and barely passing history and English. At the end of the fall semester, she altered the D-minus grade on her report card to a B-plus, praying her father would not find out. He didn't.

One night, waiting for Elvis to finish his karate class, Priscilla fell asleep downstairs. When Elvis saw how exhausted she was, he asked how many hours of sleep she was getting.

"About four or five hours a night—but I'll be fine," she assured him quickly. She was just a little tired because of extra tests they were having at school.

Elvis thought a moment and said, "Come upstairs a minute. I have something for you." He led her to his room, where he placed a handful of small white pills in her hand. "I want you to take these, they'll help you stay awake during the day. Just take one when you feel a little drowsy, no more than one, though, or you'll be doing handstands down the hallway."

"What are they?" Priscilla wondered.

"You don't need to know what they are. They give them to us when we go out on maneuvers. If I didn't have them, I'd never make it through the day myself. But it's okay, they're safe," he assured her. "Put them away and don't tell anyone you have them, and don't take them every day. Just when you need a little more energy."

They were Dexedrine, of course. The beginning of a long hard road for Elvis. And neither of them knew a damn thing about them.

As Priscilla recalls, "Elvis honestly thought he was doing me a favor by giving me the pills, and I'm sure the thought never entered his mind that they could be harmful to him or me." Later, she learned that a sergeant had given them to him and a few of the other guys, to help them stay awake when they pulled guard duty. Elvis, a night owl who despised waking before dawn, began taking them when they were out on maneuvers at Grafenwöhr.

If they weren't so dangerous, it was almost touching, Elvis' faith in the tiny white pills: mother's little helper. For a while, it seemed all the guys were on them—they were fantastic! They gave you energy, you could eat whatever you wanted and never gain weight. They were like magic. As he told his friend Rex Mansfield, "They will give you more strength and energy than you can imagine." It was better to take them with coffee, he advised, because caffeine made the pills work quicker. Elvis told him that they were completely harmless, and that if you ate anything, the effects of the pills would be gone immediately. He also informed Rex that they were appetite suppressants prescribed by doctors to millions of overweight people every day. Rex gladly got his own little bottle of amphetamines from Elvis' supply.

With her vast reserves of innate self-preservation, Priscilla never took the pills. Instead, she kept them in her little box with the rest of Elvis' treasures.

ACCORDING TO TAYLOR, "Elvis was a *competitor* with a capital 'C.'" He wanted to be the best with everything that came along with the job. And that meant being good on jeep maintenance. He wanted to read a map better than anybody else. He wanted to be the best shooter of a .45 pistol or an M1 carbine. "He wasn't all that good a shooter," admits Taylor. "He made marksman, not expert. He was a good map reader."

Elvis wanted to compete physically. Every morning they had PT, physical training, right after reveille, which was about 6:30 in the morning. They'd do push-ups, squat thrusts, jumping jacks, and then run. Elvis wanted to outrun Taylor so badly, and he couldn't do it. He couldn't outrun the lieutenant, couldn't do more push-ups. But Taylor recalled, "There did come a day, and I swear I never told him this, I let him beat me on a run. Never told him. Never told anybody.

"On the one hand," says Taylor, "he was a really serious young guy—I'm going to do my duty, I'm going to do it better than anybody else can do it. A competitor. Somebody devoted to his nation, red, white, and blue. On the other hand, he was a *fun* guy!"

One Saturday afternoon, Lieutenant Taylor, who was with his wife and two small children, ran into Presley at the PX. (Elvis loved the children. Taylor recalls him meeting his one-and-a-half-year-old son, who took Elvis' cap off his head and started chewing on the bill.) On their way out, Elvis wondered, "Sir, what are you doing this afternoon?"

"Well, I'm tuning up my damn car."

"That's that 1952 with a '48 Caddy in it?"

"Yup."

"Really, you gonna work on it this afternoon? Can I help?"

"Sure," said Taylor. He liked the kid. "Come on over in about two hours. I'll be putting in points, plugs, and condensers . . ." Elvis came over and they worked on it—replaced the points and the plugs, got it so everything was set and sounded good. "Okay," said the lieutenant, "let's take it out for a test. Presley, you drive."

They drove out to the autobahn and Presley turned to Taylor and said, "Sir, let's see what it can do."

Well, says Taylor, "he put that thing down and this 1952 Ford with a 1948 Cadillac engine in it with special equipment, it just—man, it was moving! We're over a hundred miles an hour and *moving*—I said, 'Hey, Presley—we've got to slow down.'"

He slowed down. In a couple of minutes, a white BMW with the top down was about to pass them. In it were two German girls, hair flowing in the wind. Now they were down to about sixty miles an hour. The girls went past, then they slowed down and got abreast of the Ford and started looking. *It's der Presley on the autobahn!* And the lieutenant said, "Now, what the hell are they looking at, Presley?"

Elvis grinned, keeping his eye on the road. "I don't think it's you, sir."

ELVIS MAY HAVE fallen madly in love with Priscilla Beaulieu, but let's face it, he was still Elvis Presley, and there were lots of other girls hanging around 14 Goethestrasse. There was Heli Priemel, a fifteen-year-old German beauty nicknamed

"Legs." Elvis also occasionally romanced his German secretary Elizabeth Stefaniak, whom he thought looked just like "BB" (Brigitte Bardot), and he was known to have a steady girlfriend back in Memphis, Anita Wood. The competition for Elvis' attention was keen, and Priscilla showed that she intended to win.

The Duchess of Windsor (who, after all, got King Edward VIII to give up the throne for her) thought a woman should always weigh lightly on a man, and in her own way, Priscilla took the duchess' advice to heart. Priscilla's basic romantic game plan was to be whatever Elvis wanted her to be, his own personal tabula rasa.

From her brief time visiting Goethestrasse, she had already deduced that Elvis liked his girls to be quiet and submissive. If he wanted an intellectual hotshot, he'd date a damn Vassar girl. Don't curse, don't smoke, don't take exception to anything he says, especially in front of the guys. Don't make a big deal about how you love all his records and movies, he hates talking about that stuff. After her first night with Elvis, Priscilla knew to get in the game sexually, don't talk about anything that goes on at 14 Goethestrasse, and whatever you do, don't hassle Elvis, he's got enough to worry about.

Delicate, quiet, beautiful, and utterly self-possessed, Priscilla allowed Elvis to project whatever he wanted onto her—and he did.

IN APRIL OF 1959, the scout platoon had a going-away party for Sergeant Jones, and Lieutenant Taylor was asked to be there. It was a hell-raising time. At one point, a bus came up with girls that Elvis had somehow or other arranged for the unmarried guys. It was a blast! There was lots of beer drinking going on, lots of dancing, whatever. (Taylor hastens to add that Elvis never smoked or drank— "Although I did both, a *lot*.") The guys asked Elvis to get up and sing, and he did. And at one point, he pointed to Taylor in the smoky crowd, by this time as wild as any Southern honky-tonk, and said, "Loootenant—I wanna dedicate a song to you!"

"You ain't nothin' but a hound dog!" he roared. Ah, man, that Presley was a great guy.

Afterward, Taylor went outside for a cigarette, and Elvis came out and said, "Lieutenant, I want to thank you for everything."

"Presley, you don't have anything to thank me for. I've just been around, just doing my job, same as you and the rest of the boys."

"Well, but I just want to thank you, sir."

It was good of him to say it, with that quiet grace he had around those he trusted. It was good, and that was the last time the lieutenant saw Presley. But he loved the kid.

For Christmas 1959, Elvis (adroitly playing both sides of the fence) arranged to have a French poodle delivered to Anita Wood for Christmas and threw a Christmas party at Goethestrasse for family and friends. Priscilla gave him a set of bongo drums.

ON APRIL 29, 1960, as Elvis prepared to leave Germany—and the army—*Billboard* reported that he had sold eighteen million singles to date, a feat accomplished by no other recording artist in history. For his part, Elvis just wanted to get back home to Memphis.

The next day, the army held a press conference just before Elvis' departure from Germany, with over one hundred reporters and photographers in attendance at the enlisted men's club in Freiburg. Also there was Marion Keisker, who had encouraged him when he first walked into Sun Records a lifetime ago. Serving her tour of duty in Europe as army Captain MacInness (her married name), she had not seen Elvis since she enlisted in 1957. Spotting her in the crowd, he said excitedly, "I don't know whether to salute you or kiss you . . ."

"In that order," she said.

FINALLY, ON MARCH 2, 1960, it was time for Elvis to fly back to America and get discharged from the army. His two years were up and he was ecstatic at the thought of going home. Priscilla had far less positive feelings. Wearing a scarf, poodle skirt, and a suede jacket, she did not tell her principal why she wanted to be excused from class, only that she was seeing a friend off at the airport.

It was a cold misty afternoon, to match her mood. As Priscilla recalls, "When he left, the car ride was extremely painful. I didn't know if that was the last time I was going to see him, if he would ever call. It was always in my head, you know, why would he even call me? He was going back to Hollywood, and his days would be filled, where I'd be at home, I'd be at school, thinking of nothing but him, writing his name down on a piece of paper every day like a kid."

Now that he was leaving, Priscilla found it hard to believe that *any* of it had been real. "Was it infatuation? Was it illusion? At the time it was very real for me. I was in love, and these were the first deep emotions that I had ever felt. I wasn't sure if it was a good feeling or not, in a way I didn't like these feelings because I couldn't control them, I just knew they were very painful and very real."

Like a high school football player, Elvis gave Priscilla his army jacket, "to show that you belong to me." Elvis kissed her and got out of the car to board a bus that would take him to his plane. Priscilla headed for the airport, "numb." After six months together, she could not believe that he was leaving. She thought she would never see him again.

At the airport, she was surrounded by fans and news photographers, who now knew who she was. With her sharply defined features and dark curls peeking out from under her scarf, she looked heartbroken and achingly beautiful. At the door to the airplane, Elvis saw her and broke into a grin. He waved.

Then he was gone, off on his own adventure—back to America.

DAMN, ELVIS WAS GLAD to be home in Memphis. It was almost unreal, two years away, and now here he was back at Graceland. "I just can't get it in my mind that I'm here," he said, slightly amazed, almost as if the whole thing were a dream. "I'm hungry, but I haven't taken time to eat. I just keep walking around and looking." The day of his return, the Colonel arranged a press conference in the little office behind Graceland that his father maintained. Elvis was dressed all in black, the Continental male now, his light brown hair dramatically upswept.

"Now, gentlemen," he began from behind his father's simple metal desk, "I have called you here to discuss a very important matter." Some of the reporters picked up on the allusion to President Eisenhower's televised press conferences. Then the questions began, fast and furious, as inane as ever. Had he chosen his first single yet? What had he learned from army life? Was his music going to change, and the ever-important, why had he changed his hairstyle?

"It's like a car you've driven in for a couple of years," Elvis replied, as good-natured as ever. "It's just time for a change." But mostly, he just wanted to get one thing across: "I've learned one thing in this man's army—man, coming home is the greatest!"

"Do you plan to reenlist?" a reporter wondered.

"Good Lord, no. My manager would probably cut my throat."

He probably would. Now that he was home, Elvis was anxious about his career; that is, if he even *had* a career anymore. He had been away two years, and in spite of the Colonel's incessant scheming, would they even remember him? "I hope I'll be able to take up my career where I left off. That is, if my fans want it that way."

On Sunday, March 20, having been home less than two weeks, Elvis secretly arrived in Nashville at RCA's Studio B to record his first post-army single. Working from 8:00 in the evening until 7:00 in the morning, he recorded "Stuck on You" and "Fame and Fortune," which would be pressed and shipped within two days. Without waiting for orders, RCA shipped more than one million copies directly to the stores. "Stuck on You" debuted at number eighty-four on *Billboard*'s chart for April 10, reaching the number one position three weeks later.

Elvis need not have worried about his career, and about the fans. Having been away for two years, it was as if he had barely left.

AT ONE TIME, Frank Sinatra dismissed rock and roll as music for "cretinous goons." Ouch! In the early 1960s, the tables were turned, and it was Sinatra who now needed Elvis' bona fide young person's props. Like Ed Sullivan, he was prepared to eat a bit of crow to align himself with Presley. First, his daughter Nancy met Elvis as he walked off the plane from Germany with a peace offering from her father—a box of dress shirts from his own Hollywood tailor, Sy Devore. Welcome back to civilian life and Rat Pack clothes! Then, Elvis returned the favor by taking the train to Miami for Frank's TV special, taped on Saturday, March 26, in the Grand Ballroom of the Fontainebleau Hotel, where Sinatra assured the press with the artfulness of a politician, "The kid's been away for two years, and I get the feeling he really believes in what he's doing."

Far more important, Sinatra realized that a dose of Elvis' sexiness with the kids could inflate his own sagging ratings. Presley came out about forty minutes into the show, smooth as silk, totally *STRAC*, baby, looking impossibly elegant in his perfectly draped tuxedo. All those memorable nights with the Folies-Bergère must have imbued him with some Continental charm. Even his hair looked hipper.

As he launched into his new single, "Stuck on You," Elvis was almost practicing a modified Elvis: With intimation rather than a direct assault, he drew the audience to him, then launched into a lovely duet with Sinatra, "Witchcraft," which was artful and subdued. It was great to have Elvis back again, his voice, once again, reminding us why we loved him. They closed with the last lines of "Love Me Tender," harmonizing with the big band in the background.

"Man, that's pretty," said Sinatra.

what would jackie do?

AS A MATTER of sociological study, it is intriguing to compare the dating techniques of two twentieth-century It Girls (granted, in totally different social strata), Priscilla Presley and Jacqueline Bouvier Kennedy Onassis.

Priscilla, we know, captured Elvis' heart by being whatever he wanted her to be. If he wanted her to cut his meat for him (which he did), consider it done. If he wanted her to wear goofy, sexy clothes from a place called (ahem) Suzy Creamcheese in Las Vegas, fine. If he wanted to haul out the Polaroid camera . . . you get the idea.

Jackie took the opposite tack. Even before *The Rules*, she was an original Rules Girl. Jackie attended Vassar, where blowing off Harvard guys is, along with tea served every afternoon in the Rose Parlor, practically a core requirement. (The basic rule of thumb is that if they don't call by Wednesday, the entire weekend—that's drinks, dinner, and dancing, often with three separate dates, is gone gone gone.)

Jackie blew hot and cold. By caring, and then appearing not to care, she left the men she knew in a constant state of emotional upheaval. "All men are rats," her father, "Black Jack" Bouvier, the original Wall Street roué, counseled her. Jackie was not obviously sexy, like Priscilla, but she read everything, sat at the best dinner tables, and—from her father and JFK—knew how to hold a man's interest.

She had a subversive wit totally at odds with her upper-class demeanor. She dressed exquisitely, like Audrey Hepburn, and would then lean over and say something wildly risqué to make her dinner partner's eyes (generally men like Nikita Khrushchev) pop. Jackie's sure combination of charm, beauty, the occasional well-timed sulk, and "Would you like me to translate your appeasement speech?" worked.

"She had more men per square inch than any woman I've met in my entire life," recalled her Vassar chum and White House assistant Letitia Baldrige. Like her husband, John F. Kennedy, Jackie had the *über*-WASP ability to compartmentalize, big time. If something bothered her (say, her husband's vast infidelities), she ignored it. Or spent more than her husband's salary his first year in the White House on French couture and "incidentals." Or disappeared to the Mellons' Virginia estate and went horseback riding when she was supposed to be hosting— oh, some boring congressional wives' thing back at the Maison Blanche.

Jackie was very much her husband's intellectual equal and kept him on his toes by doing whatever the hell she wanted. JFK, it should be noted, liked a challenge.

IN GERMANY, Priscilla learned about Elvis' Memphis girlfriend, Anita Wood, and anguished over what to do. There were times, she later told a magazine, that she felt "cheap and unloved" (very 1950s, no?). But she persevered with a determination that would do the marines proud and continued sleeping with him while not dreaming of telling Elvis what he could or could not do; i.e., break up with all the other women he was seeing.

For all her Hussar determination, Priscilla developed a surprisingly Zen approach to dating Elvis. She had to, otherwise she would probably have had a nervous breakdown. "All I knew was that the time I spent with him was totally devoted to him. And that's all I could do. I couldn't change his mind. So if it was meant to be, it was meant to be." In other words (and you know this from yoga class)—*release expectations.*

Priscilla's full-bore approach was radically different from Jackie's, who once gave Joan Kennedy the advice that "men can sense desperation." In recalling their "spasmodic courtship" (now there's a girl who gives her man a lot of rope), Jackie kept JFK, perhaps the most eligible bachelor in the United States, off balance by rarely returning his phone calls, staying engaged to stockbroker John Husted for months longer than she probably should have ("Don't believe all those silly rumors you hear about me and Jack Kennedy," she assured him), and occasionally disappearing on weekends and not telling Kennedy where she was going. (So maybe it was only up to Newport to visit her stepbrother, Yusha Auchincloss, he didn't need to know that, did he?)

Priscilla, on the other hand, studied Anita's love letters to more fully fashion herself into the woman Elvis wanted. "All those things that he would say, I internalized: you know, he didn't *trust* Anita anymore . . . so I knew that was important to him." Kind of scary, no? Not to Priscilla. "You have to remember," she admitted years later, "it wasn't difficult to behave like that. I knew that he loved feminine girls. I knew that he loved small girls . . . I knew his thoughts. I knew what he liked. I knew what he was attracted to. So what was I going to do? *Become* whatever it was."

But before you think, "paging Anita Bryant," Priscilla did manage to close the deal and marry Elvis after a mind-numbing eight-year courtship, so in the end it worked out.

For a while, at any rate.

Moving away from their early affairs of the heart, Priscilla ensured that her former husband's memory was kept alive by being the guiding figure in the development of Elvis Presley Enterprises, and opening Graceland to the public. Jacqueline Kennedy Onassis kept this country together during three harrowing days in November 1963, raised her children, maintained her discretion, and gracefully passed into history. In their youth, neither could imagine what fate had in store for them.

I never feel like I'm really home
until I get back to Graceland.

— E P

mansion over the hilltop

WITH HIS FIRST SERIOUS MONEY, Elvis, like the rap and sports stars who would follow him, bought two things—a car and a house. One of his early purchases was a Cadillac, a pink 1955 Fleetwood Series 60 Special Sedan, bought for his mother, who did not drive. The house was Graceland, bought in 1957 when he was twenty-two years old. Located several miles south of downtown Memphis in the Shelby County township of Whitehaven, Graceland was an eighteen-room mansion built by Dr. Thomas Moore, who named it in honor of his wife's aunt, Grace. Built in 1939, the same year *Gone With the Wind* was released, it was Elvis' own Tara.

Fresh from shooting *Loving You*, Elvis and his parents went to see the mansion and decided on the spot to buy the fourteen-acre estate for $102,500. Within the first six months of his occupancy, however, he spent half that amount on improvements, including an eight-foot-high fieldstone wall erected to keep Elvis' always zealous fans from overrunning the place.

Graceland was a beautiful house, impressive as hell. Faced with Mississippi fieldstone, it boasted the archetypical symbol of a Southern mansion—the classic white-columned portico. It was worlds, worlds away from a two-room shanty in Tupelo, Mississippi. Owning Graceland told the world: Elvis had arrived.

IN HIS CARS, his clothes, and now, his home, Elvis had a keen, untutored, and completely instinctive visual sense. Much the way he saw himself onstage in his wild Lansky jackets, or the way he hiked his collars up, Elvis knew in an instant the way he wanted Graceland to look. While Jacqueline Kennedy chose Sister Parish (and secretly René Boudin) to redecorate the White House, and the Duchess of Windsor favored

Boudin as well as Englishman John Fowler, Elvis' stylistic influence for Graceland was a middlebrow comedian. "This is going to be a lot nicer than Red Skelton's house when I get it like I want it," he promised the day he bought Graceland.

When Elvis visited Hollywood, the house he admired more than any other was Skelton's five-acre Bel Air estate. His Georgian house was refined and dignified, a real showplace. The grounds included an eleven-car garage and a mile-long driveway that meandered through formal French gardens to the vine-covered red brick mansion. But in the privacy of his proper Georgian establishment, Skelton, one of the highest-paid TV comics, betrayed a childlike sensibility Elvis appreciated. Like a true connoisseur, Skelton had the aesthetic confidence to mix high and low. He kept a stuffed gorilla in the shower room next to a 35,000-gallon swimming pool. The manicured lawns were peppered not with Henry Moore sculptures, but circus relics. And to really annoy the neighbors, the owner hinted at plans to line the drive (already lit up like an airport runway after dark, a detail Elvis would similarly rig at Graceland) with life-size statues of saints.

Like Elvis (who earned $1,001,727.89 in 1958), Skelton's $750,000 a year salary was cited in the newspapers with mingled envy and amazement, at a time when a white-collar professional earned $10,000 a year. More than any distinguished actor of the day, this homely man, with his stock of sentimental, vulgar routines, symbolized the ascent of everyman in the prosperous 1950s. On the coffee table in his living room, Skelton kept a doll representing a sad tramp (the character figuring in one of his better-known TV sketches) to remind him just how far he had come. Like Elvis, there was a private undercurrent of sorrow to the comedian. In a pink art studio in the back garden he painted picture after picture of the father he had never known, a clown with the Hagenbeck and Wallace Circus.

ELVIS HAD NO INTEREST in the old, which, to him, equaled poverty, not status. "I had enough antiques when we lived in the Courts," he proclaimed with enough sincerity to disarm any Sotheby's know-it-all. Provenance meant nothing to Elvis. For him, history was just a sack of old stories. His own history, the history of the Presley family, was so discordant and sad—no money, Jessie dead, Mama worried all the time—why would he want to be reminded of that?

Like the most authentic of artists, Elvis created himself as he went along. He liked color, lots of it. He wanted his home to look new, jazzy, to reflect his status as a young rock-and-roller and, now, Hollywood guy. And he knew precisely how he wanted things to look. Before he headed off to shoot *Jailhouse Rock*, he told his mama, who enlisted the decorators from Goldsmith's department store to help out, that he wanted the downstairs painted purple, with clouds and twinkling lights on the ceiling of the foyer just like at Loews Theater, every piece of molding in the whole place gilded, and white corduroy curtains. Subtlety was the mark of a lesser man, not EP. He wanted his home to be youthful! Fun! Impressive as hell!

On the train back from Los Angeles, he could not wait to see how it had turned out, so he got off the eastbound sleeper in Lafayette, Louisiana, rented a car, and raced back to Memphis, bounding up the front steps at about midnight, his mama and daddy in the front hallway, waiting for him.

Inside, the first stages were done. Even though Gladys knew that young people liked rich, dark colors, you could not have purple in the main downstairs rooms of this great house. She chose a deep Dresden blue with soft gray undertones. Blue was calmer, more restful, more possible to live with in the day to day. While bright, the rooms were still subtle and commanding. And after all those years of working in the curtain factory, Mama knew her drapes as surely as John Fowler. Corduroy would never hang right, it was too stiff, too bulky. Instead, Gladys ordered ivory brocade, edged in white satin tassels, with blue for the cold winter months. Although the colors and fabrics were not exactly what Elvis had requested, the overall effect was the same. Even half finished, Graceland was full of energy and mystery, giving off the message: A bold man lives here.

Final decisions on the furnishings still had to be worked out, but fortunately, decorator George Golden was coming in the morning.

Golden was Sam Phillips' man, so Elvis knew he had to be all right. Phillips had done so well with the sale of Elvis' contract and other recording projects that he had moved to the more fashionable east side of Memphis, and hired Golden, a flamboyant, forty-three-year-old former Lipton iced tea salesman, to spruce the place up. Golden was talented, sure, but he also advertised his services by having several fully decorated flatbed trucks driving around Memphis day and night, decked out with illuminated three-foot-wide miniature rooms, built to scale, complete with carpet, wallpaper, and a two-foot sofa, upholstered in chartreuse satin. *Day and night*, Elvis mused—you had to love a man who would dream up a scheme like that; it sounded like something the Colonel would do.

After Phillips moved on up, he had Golden decorate his home not in boring old Louis *quinze,* or whatever, but in a lush, free-spirited modern way that few of his more hidebound neighbors would have risked. This open-minded effect and even better, the response it evoked, appealed to Elvis, big time. He decided he wanted the same for Graceland, only XL.

First Phillips, now Elvis, hiring a *decorator*—made them all sound like god-damn Liberace. Who knew what would happen next?

The next day Golden came over with sketches and a few unifying ideas, but Elvis did not have time for sketches. Do it yesterday, he commanded, with the imperiousness of a Georgetown grande dame. For his bedroom, he envisioned an eight-foot-square bed, the walls painted "the darkest blue there is . . . with a mirror that will cover one side of the room. I will probably have a black bedroom suite, trimmed in white leather with a white llama rug," just like Sam's. According to Golden, two requests came through most strongly—"one was that he had the most beautiful bedroom in Memphis for his mother, and number two, he wanted a soda fountain, a real soda fountain with Coke and an ice cream thing, so his young friends could sit and have a soda."

With Golden and his mother looking on, Elvis moved quickly through the fabric samples, turning aside all but the most sumptuous material, the most inventive schemes. Just as he knew the sound he wanted in the recording studio, at Graceland he saw what he wanted with the snap of his fingers, like that. Right off the bat, he knew he needed a white, fifteen-foot custom-built sofa anchoring the living room, a monstrously sized coffee table in front of it, black wood consoles, and tall lamps with rubbed gold on the shades. There would be no English country, no safe Pierre Deux Provençal look for Elvis. *Bring it on!* he wanted his rooms to say.

Golden explained to him about samples, fabric runs, material that might take weeks to order, the innate diceyness of custom-made anything. Elvis shook his head politely. He had just come from Hollywood, the dream factory. He knew what was possible. How it was done, he did not care, he had little time to waste—tomorrow, he was off to Biloxi with the boys for some R&R. Got to keep the show moving, after all.

His mother sighed. She had hoped this home and their decorating project would keep her son more securely by her side, and even more secretly (although she hesitated to ever mention this to Elvis or Vernon), she dreamed he might give up the whole singing thing for good and stay in Memphis, maybe open up a furniture store, he was so good with putting a room together.

But that wasn't the way it was going to be no matter what Mama wanted. See, Elvis had to be gone, man, gone—he had miles to go before he slept. He told them what he wanted, impressing once again upon Mr. Golden the blend of grandeur and down-home chic he envisioned for Graceland, and that he wanted it done now—then left the details to his mother, Goldsmith's, and the decorator with the flatbed truck.

TOLSTOY BELIEVED one way to judge art was whether it evoked a response, either good *or* bad. Without ever having read Tolstoy (probably without ever having heard of Tolstoy), Elvis agreed. The worst sin, according to him, was to be *boring*, to pass through life unnoticed. You're here, make a damn statement. With its sure presentation of one man's vision (does anyplace else in the world look like it?), Graceland certainly did.

Still, the decoration of Elvis' home, like his hair, his singing, and his stage presentation, just got on some people's nerves for some reason. Perhaps they were put off by the chicken coop in the backyard, the ducks in the pool, or the peacock that strutted up and down the driveway, pecking the finish off his black Rolls-Royce. Perhaps they were secretly riled that a simple country boy could afford practically the biggest house in the entire state and do whatever he wanted with it.

Elvis knew that some people put down the house he was so rightly proud of. About a week after Gladys died, Elvis' dentist, Lester Hofman, and his wife, Sterling, went to Graceland to pay their respects. They did not know what they should do—send flowers? A card? All of Memphis knew how broken up Elvis was over her death. He had received over 100,000 cards and letters, 500 telegrams, and 200 floral arrangements in sympathy over his loss. The police even took Elvis for a ride on a helicopter to try to take his mind off his sorrow. Then the Hofmans got a call asking them to please come out to the house, Elvis would like to see them.

After they got there, Elvis came down and cleared the room of his buddies, so it was just him and the Hofmans. They said how sorry they were, and Elvis turned to Sterling, and said, "Mrs. Hofman, I don't know if this is the right time, but the newspapers have made my house sound so laughable, I would love to have your opinion of my home."

"Laughable," that was the word he used. It broke your heart that the boy should have it on his mind at a time like this. Mrs. Hofman was somewhat taken aback. "Elvis, I really didn't come here to go through your home. We came here to be with you."

He insisted, "I want your opinion."

The three of them went through the house, room by room, with Elvis pointing out one feature or another. As Dr. Hofman recalled, "It was very attractive, it all fit. There was a modern sculpture on the chimney over the fireplace, and I had the same sculpture in my office. It was called *Rhythm.*"

"What do you think?" Elvis wanted to know.

"If you give me the key, I'll swap with you," Sterling said, and she meant it. "I won't even move a dish." Then, as an afterthought, she could not help but wonder: "Did you ever think, one day, you might have all of this? It's just so beautiful."

"Mrs. Hofman, I never thought I'd get out of Humes High."

AFTER MAMA DIED, everything changed. When he returned to Memphis after two years in the army, a reporter asked him, did he think he would sell Graceland? *Sell Graceland?* Elvis would go back to driving a truck before he sold Graceland. "It would be foolish to sell it now that it was completed," he replied steadily, realizing that the reporter had no idea how important the place was to him, how it symbolized how far they, as a family, had traveled. "And I don't think my mother would like it," he said finally.

For Elvis, Graceland (pronounced the soft Southern way, Grace-*len*) was not just his mother's house, although it surely was that (when he went into the army, everyone was left with strict instructions not to touch *anything*). After his father married Dee Stanley, a divorced woman with three sons whom he had met in Germany, Dee took it upon herself to make some decorating changes at Graceland. Big mistake. Big, big mistake. As soon as Elvis found out, her bags were packed and she was out on the front lawn that afternoon, with the truck from Goldsmith's racing up the driveway to repair the damage.

Graceland was also the physical manifestation of all that Elvis had accomplished. Like the great nineteenth-century robber barons—Carnegie, Rockefeller, Jay Gould, J. P. Morgan, with their gilded Newport "cottages" and sprawling Fifth Avenue domiciles—Graceland was Elvis' own (as the gospel song goes) mansion over the hilltop. A house as beautiful as Graceland was surely a sign that God loved him—even if he was not sure of the source of his talent, or why he was chosen to lead this life he had been given. How could he explain any of this to a reporter? He barely understood it himself. "I am going to keep Graceland as long as I possibly can," he said simply.

But beyond this, Graceland was, finally, his respite from the outside world and all it demanded of him. According to Joe Esposito, life at Graceland was whatever Elvis wanted it to be; which could change from day to day, or minute to minute, depending on his whim. Days generally began at 4:00 in the afternoon and ended at dawn. Dinner was served at 9:00 P.M., with Elvis and the boys hitting the town at midnight. It was a topsy-turvy life with few rules, time rarely spent alone, and little structure.

In a way, the thought was fabulous—to do whatever you wanted, but sometimes the reality could be odd and lonely. Even the ultimate bachelor seraglio gets tiresome at some point. With his mother gone and his father recently remarried, there was no one to provide any sense of a prevailing maternal instinct in the house. Elvis was a young twenty-six-year-old who liked to be babied, and let's face it, nobody loves you like your mama.

Life at Graceland soon took on its owner's innate rhythms. As Esposito recalls, "Elvis woke up at about four in the afternoon, that's what he wanted it to be. He liked to go to bed when the sun came up. We were vampires." In the great Southern Pentecostal tradition, there was Sunday Morning Elvis versus Saturday Night Elvis. When the sun went down, anything was possible; people were looser, more themselves, that's just the way it was. At night, with the good people home asleep in bed, things just *happened*. To a journalist who came to interview him at Graceland in 1965, Elvis said, "It's after eight and the night's pretty outside. The sun's down and the moon's pretty—it's time to ramble."

MEANWHILE, BACK IN WIESBADEN, Priscilla was not rambling, but pining away. Elvis called when he thought of it, but in those days, getting a phone call from the States was like hearing from the man on the moon—you might call if there was an emergency or if someone died, but there was a lot of static and God only knows what it cost. After he left her at the airport, Elvis phoned three heart-stopping weeks later.

Was their romance real, or not? Priscilla would not dream of asking Elvis what was going on with them; in 1958, no girl would. The ball was in his court. In the interim, her little bedroom was a shrine to Elvis. Debbie Ross, a friend whose family lived across the hall from the Beaulieus, recalls going into her bedroom and seeing Elvis' combat jacket nailed to her bedroom wall, as if she needed further proof of their time together.

She wrote him letters care of Joe Esposito (now working for Elvis) on pink stationery, so he would know it was from her. Elvis sent her 45s from the States, "songs that identified with our relationship," Priscilla recalled. "Sealed with a Kiss" was one. "Hey, Paula" another. He even sent her a copy of "Good Night, My Love," the song that signed off the broadcast they listened to in his bedroom. "So many reminders," as she put it. As if she needed any more.

BACK AT GRACELAND, with three cooks manning the stove in 24/7 shifts to feed the house full of people with different schedules, Elvis liked simple Southern fare, food Mama made—fried chicken, mashed potatoes with gravy,

burnt bacon, steak cooked through and through. To drink, there was Pepsi and icy
bottles of Mountain Valley water.

     According to the rules of the house, breakfast was served at about 3:00 or 4:00
in the afternoon. As Esposito recalls, "For breakfast a lot of times he'd have eggs
and bacon. Biscuits. He didn't eat grits. Eggs, bacon, home-fried potatoes, and then
sometimes pancakes. But he liked applesauce on his pancakes instead of maple
syrup, and melted butter. Bacon, he loved bacon. Had to be burnt, burnt, burnt,
burnt. Just crisp. That was basically what he had for breakfast. He didn't eat

omelettes, he didn't eat eggs Benedict. That's what he was raised on, and as we know, the South in those days was all fried food—everything! All the greens were fried, everything you could eat was butter and fried and grease."

Did Elvis ever have fruit or vegetables?

There is a telling pause as Esposito thinks. Then thinks some more. He can probably come up with the last ten names of Elvis' girlfriends (and put them in alphabetical order) with greater ease. "Ahhhhhhhh, *sometimes.*" He sounds exceedingly doubtful, forgetting the party line for the moment.

Much has been made of Elvis' habit of eating the same meal over and over again. (One thinks of the memorable eight-month meatloaf-for-dinner repeat.) But actually, this is fairly common among people who lead compelling public lives—it's like they have enough going on, they can't take any more excitement on their plate.

In the White House, in spite of the French chef his wife had imported from Le Pavilion, JFK's favorite meal was tomato soup and a grilled-cheese sandwich, accompanied by the occasional Heineken with Louis Sherry vanilla ice cream for dessert. Diana Vreeland, the visionary editor of *Vogue* who coined the phrase "Pink is the navy blue of India," had very particular ideas about what she would and would not eat. She was determined to keep her famous sylphlike figure. Every morning, after yoga-type exercises she invented herself, she had oatmeal for breakfast, the idea being that "one needs to coat the stomach."

At the office she never went out for lunch—too much time away, but, instead, ate at her desk. Every day, after consulting a diagram as to where to place Vreeland's drink, food, ashtray, and No. 2 Black Bear pencils, her assistant arranged a peanut butter and marmalade sandwich on whole wheat with a shot of scotch and the inevitable Pall Mall cigarettes.

ELVIS' INSTINCT TOWARD GENEROSITY, another element of his style, was with him always, even when he had nothing. He wanted to share what he had, to make life better first for his parents, and then others. His mother recalled, "He would hear us worrying about our debts, being out of work, and sickness, and he'd say, 'Don't worry none, baby. When I grow up, I'm going to buy you a fine house and pay for everything you owe at the grocery store and get two Cadillacs— one for you and Daddy, and one for me.'" Vernon, perhaps the worldliest of the lot of them, said dryly, "I just didn't want him to have to steal one."

Roland Tindall, a friend in seventh grade, recalls that at Christmastime, Elvis gave him and another friend a little truck of his. "I remember that impressed me, that he wanted to do something so badly that he would give us one of his own toys when he couldn't afford anything else."

In Germany, Elvis would secretly make a contribution to the staff sergeant to pass on to the guys in his company who could not afford to go on leave. Joe Esposito recalls him handing out $100 bills to total strangers, just to see their reaction. Given the astonishing, almost unreal trajectory of his own life, the 1950s television show *The Millionaire* really struck a chord with Elvis—he loved the magical possibility that money could be used for good, especially when given to a total stranger. He loved to see the expression on people's faces when he gave them a totally unexpected gift—a car, jewelry, even a house. That was the best part of all.

When Joe first met Elvis, he thought his bursts of generosity were a way to shake off loneliness. Now, he thinks differently. "Elvis didn't pass out money just to massage his ego. He got a genuine thrill from making people happy, and he was always a bit amazed at the public's reaction to his presence." So much so that he couldn't resist testing it once in a while, just to shake things up, to get a response. "Elvis wanted to make a difference in people's lives, especially to his fans, to whom he was always grateful," Esposito recalled. "He often said that if it weren't for them, he'd be driving a truck."

Elvis' identification with his fans was so absolute that he was almost their alter ego. He once told Joe, "My fans expect me to do the things they wish they could do— if they'd had the breaks I had." Elvis connected with his fans because he knew what it was like to be just folk. "A lot of my fans have a rough life. They see me as someone who was lifted from poverty and dropped into a world of glamour and excitement. My job is to share that glamour and excitement with them. When I'm onstage, I want to create excitement. I want each person to feel I'm performing for him or her, and even when I'm offstage, the show goes on. The clothes I wear, the cars I drive, my style of living—they're all part of what my fans expect from me.

"Most people get kicked around in life," he continued. "They just don't get the breaks. I love the idea of overwhelming a total stranger with a gift of a new car, just because they happened to be nearby. It's an incredible kick. No drug can get you as high. It's the same thing I feel when I'm onstage and every eye is on me. I'm giving it all I've got and they're loving every move, every sound. Man—there's nothing better!"

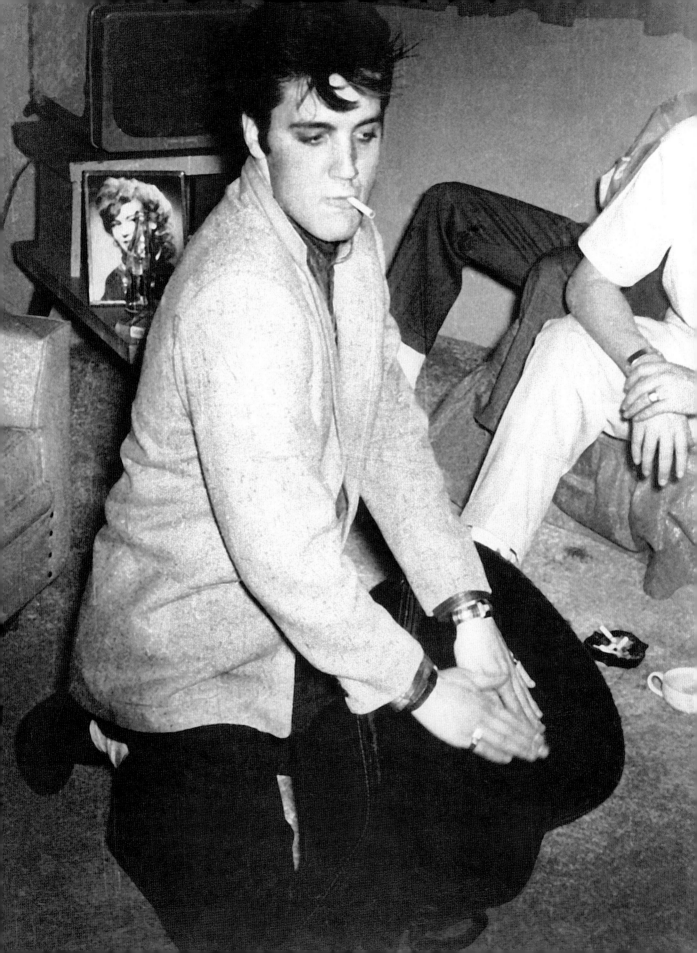

MEANWHILE, having met three years ago, the exceedingly patient Priscilla was still in Germany, still in high school, and still in the picture. After visits to L.A. and Memphis at Elvis' request, they both tired of the separation and Elvis decided she had to move to Graceland. Right now!

Priscilla. Moving to Graceland. Wow. Being driven over to Bad Nauheim to hang at 14 Goethestrasse was one thing, and it had been challenging enough persuading her father to allow her to visit from Germany, but live full-time in Memphis? Much as she adored Elvis, Priscilla did not know *how* he would pull this one off.

Well, say this for him, Elvis always loved a challenge. In March 1963, Priscilla arrived in Memphis with her father. Among other things, he promised Captain Beaulieu that Priscilla would live with Vernon and Dee at their home around the corner from Graceland and complete her senior year at the Immaculate Conception High School.

Priscilla did graduate from high school as they had agreed. But as might be expected, she stayed at Vernon and Dee's for about a week before moving into Grandma's room at Graceland and, shortly thereafter, Elvis' bedroom. Her parents were passed off as army friends of Elvis' from Germany who would be moving to Memphis shortly. To the world at large, the subterfuge worked—a seventeen-year-old girl secretly living with the most famous sex symbol in the world! As Elvis well knew and the Colonel reminded him, if the press got wind of this, it could be devastating for Elvis' career. Everyone knew how pilloried Jerry Lee Lewis was after his third marriage was discovered (to his thirteen-year-old cousin, Myrna Gale Brown), effectively ending his career.

Whatever it was, it worked. The world at large knew nothing about Priscilla, although, according to his hometown girlfriend Anita Wood, it caused a *big* scandal in Memphis.

PRISCILLA'S LIVING AT GRACELAND says a great deal about the strength of Elvis' personal vision (when he saw something and wanted it, it *happened*), his considerable charm, and the general naiveté of the era that he was able to pull it off. As Geraldine Kyle, Dee's best friend and a visitor to the Presley house, put it, "That was the way Elvis wanted it, and what Elvis wanted, Elvis got. You didn't question Elvis." In other words: Don't Ask, Don't Tell.

While Priscilla's living at Graceland may have shocked proper Memphians who were not familiar with Elvis World, it was, in fact, Elvis' way of making a commitment to his significant other. Behind it all was the very weighty—and real—assumption that, at some point, Elvis would marry Priscilla; that was what she was doing there in the first place, right? Of course, no one dared ask Elvis what his intentions were. Joan Esposito, Joe's wife at the time, thought Elvis would marry Priscilla. "I assumed he would. I don't know whether she said it or I picked it up." Her husband agreed. "We were sure that he would marry her someday," said Joe, who hastily amended his conjecture—"but nobody asked."

To heighten the *verboten* aspect of the whole thing, Priscilla was promptly enrolled in a local Catholic girls' school. Since neither Priscilla nor Elvis had any connection to the Catholic Church, someone must have thought this would give the situation a veneer of respectability. At school, Priscilla was memorable not because she studied (she didn't), but because she kept to herself, wore a great deal of makeup, and said that she was living with "a family in Whitehaven" (where Graceland was located). She identified herself as Elvis' girl in the subtlest way by wearing his *Blue Hawaii* star sapphire ring to school, wrapped with tape to fit her little finger.

In her other, far more compelling life back at Graceland, Priscilla quickly got into the swing of things, engaging in firecracker wars, staying up all night with Elvis and the boys, watching endless movies at the Memphian, going roller skating. Of course, any time spent in Memphis would not be complete without a visit to Lansky's. Bernard recalls how she and a girlfriend came in one time and got a coat on layaway for Elvis for Christmas.

"Show me something Elvis would like," she asked.

Bernard showed her a waist-length coat Elvis could lounge in. It was pretty simple, no big deal. Priscilla put two dollars down on layaway, eventually paid off the balance, and gave it to Elvis. Incidentally, Bernard still has the ticket.

FOR PRISCILLA, living with Elvis was a style education of the first order. How could it not be? Much in the way that he had a definite vision of how he wanted to present himself to the world, Presley had equally strong opinions about how his lady should look, too. A few days after coming home from making *Fun in Acapulco*, they got in his long black limousine and headed for Union Avenue, Memphis' most exclusive shopping area. With the boys hanging around and the staff trying to look nonchalant (*Elvis* is here!), Priscilla modeled one outfit after another. The dozens of dresses, suits, and coats were so seriously stylish, so grown-up, that she doubted she could wear any of them. In her mind, in spite of the circumstances in which she found herself, she was still an insecure teenager.

"Elvis," she said, wearing a gold lamé gown that emphasized every curve, "these clothes are too sophisticated for me."

"Sophisticated?" he said, regarding her admiringly, for she was Priscilla. "What's sophisticated? You could go around wearing a feather and that would be sophisticated."

"Well, bring me a feather, then."

They spent four hours in the shop, which stunned the sales help, since most men could not be bothered going shopping with their wives, let alone direct them in what to wear.

It turned out that Elvis was every bit as opinionated as Mr. Blackwell, who devised the Best (and Worst) Dressed List every year. As Priscilla tried on one outfit after another, he gave a running commentary on color, style, and fit that would do a *Vogue* editor proud. Since Priscilla was short, he liked solids, declaring that she got lost in large prints. "Too distracting," he said. Given a choice, he liked her in red, blue, turquoise, emerald green, or black and white—the same colors he himself wore. Not surprisingly, he hated her in brown and dark green, two colors he associated with drab army fatigues. He'd had enough of that in Germany.

Exhausted and a little confused with her new look, Priscilla walked out of the shop in a sleek black linen suit with four-inch high-heeled shoes to match. With Elvis sitting proudly beside her, the guys loaded the trunk of the car with armfuls of packages. As Priscilla recalls, "I felt very special."

Back at the house, he had her model her new clothes for Grandma, who patiently sat through the two-hour fashion show. You have to admit, when the man of the house decided to do something, he got into it. Years later, with the hindsight that only time and distance can provide, Priscilla recognized that in the early years of their relationship, "I was Elvis' doll, his own living doll, to fashion as he pleased." At the time, it was more than enough for her.

PRISCILLA TRIED. She tried to be and do and give Elvis everything he wanted. From the outside, her life looked so glamorous (and, at times, it often was). For all his demands—and he expected nothing less of himself—Elvis was the most charismatic human being Priscilla had ever met. When he focused his attention on her it was magic. And it was the dream, the possibility of recapturing that *feeling*, that kept her going all the long years they were separated. But for all her external disciplined perfection (which was considerable), there were times Priscilla chafed from the pressure, from trying to do all that Elvis expected of her. Can any one person fulfill all the needs of another? And even ensconced in the rarefied, upside-down world of Graceland, she knew there were a hundred women who would take her place in a second because Elvis, after all, was *Elvis*. No matter how you looked at it, hers was an impossible task.

One day, perhaps wanting to express some of her own personality, Priscilla cut her hair without asking Elvis' permission. Like most men, Elvis liked long hair. Unlike most men, he was shocked that she had done so.

"How could you cut your goddamn hair? You know I like long hair. Men love long hair." Not surprisingly, Priscilla's follicular revolt ended quickly and she grew it back.

Like his taste in clothing, Elvis had very specific ideas about Priscilla's hair. He wanted it long and jet black, dyed to match his because, as he observed, "You have blue eyes, Cilla, like mine. Black hair will make your eyes stand out more." To Priscilla, this made a lot of sense and soon her hair was dyed like his, using "Lady Clairol blue black."

Years later, Priscilla reflected on their relationship, finally recognizing that "the more we were together, the more I came to resemble him in every way. His tastes, his insecurities, his hang-ups, all became mine.

"For instance, high collars were his trademark, not because he especially liked them, but because he felt his neck was too long. He never felt comfortable unless he was in a customized high-collared shirt, though in a pinch he'd turn the collar up on a regular shirt as he had when he was in school."

Elvis once told Priscilla—who had previously had no problems with her neck—that the collar she was wearing on a particular blouse was too small for her "long, skinny neck." Say no more. She immediately began wearing high-collared shirts, too. "Why not?" she recalled. "My sole ambition was to please him, to be rewarded with his approval and affection. When he criticized me, I fell to pieces."

Elvis may have presented himself to the world as a simple man. But he had a complex personality, and a complex life, and this may have thrown Priscilla in the beginning. Jerry Schilling observes that "history has him as this good old country boy, but Elvis is about as country as Bono! He came from here, but he was not the boy next door, he was on the edge . . ." Not surprisingly, Elvis' endearing traits, what made you love him, were also the mirror images of what made him—at times—very hard to live with. His need for control, for example, positively mani- fested itself in his protective and nurturing side, as well as, creatively, his clear vision of Graceland and in the recording studio. The extraordinary self-gratification brought about by his stardom and power—the fact that, basically, *Elvis could do whatever the hell he wanted at all times*—was tempered, and probably surpassed, by his legendary generosity. His double standard about women reflected his very real tendency to place women on a pedestal. His egocentricity, when reversed, gave Elvis an almost supernatural ability to empathize with others.

No longer just the shy, raw young man who walked into Sun Studio a decade ago—although he was still that, too, sometimes, Elvis Presley was a man of many paradoxes; with his desire and his genius matched only by his need.

HAVING TAKEN the last two months off, Elvis has had his fun in Memphis— what with the all-night movie fests at the Memphian, the annual July 4 fireworks dis- play at Graceland, even Priscilla's graduation from high school. Now, on July 6, 1963, it was time to hit the road, get back to Hollywood to make another movie.

IN HIS WORLD, it was women's burden to wait. Elvis was cunning Odysseus, testing all possibility, roaming the edges of the known world battling Cyclops, caught between Scylla and Charybdis, dealing with the eternal Sirens, while Priscilla got to stay home and be Penelope without the loom or any suitors vying for her attention.

Due to start shooting his next film, *Viva Las Vegas*, with an intriguing young starlet named Ann-Margret, Elvis was anxious to leave. Impossibly handsome in his yachting cap and driving gloves (even more so because he was leaving), Elvis set- tled in the driver's seat. All anticipation, the bus had been packed and ready for hours. It was a moving party, Muddy Waters cranked out of the speakers. The man who made everything possible closed the door and adjusted the mirror, gone in his mind already. "All right—let's roll it!"

With that, the boys headed for the coast. Priscilla stood on the portico of Graceland and watched the red taillights head down the drive and Highway 51 until she could see them no more.

in the kitchen **with elvis**

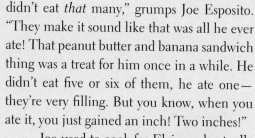

EP WAS AN early enthusiast of the Atkins diet. Of course being Elvis, he modified it and made it distinctly his own. On his plate, there was lots of protein, few vegetables, zero whole wheat. Butter was its own prized food group. He hated the smell of fish, reminding him, as it did, of childhood poverty, so it was not allowed on the premises.

At Graceland, he had three cooks at his beck and call day and night, and basically ate whatever the hell he wanted whenever he wanted it. There was the grilled PB and banana sandwich, clichéd beyond reason. "He

didn't eat *that* many," grumps Joe Esposito. "They make it sound like that was all he ever ate! That peanut butter and banana sandwich thing was a treat for him once in a while. He didn't eat five or six of them, he ate one—they're very filling. But you know, when you ate it, you just gained an inch! Two inches!"

Joe used to cook for Elvis, and actually got him to eat "pasta with vegetables—broccoli with garlic and stuff." Good Italian food, exotic for a boy from Memphis. In other chronicles of Elvisian culinary history, Joe was present when Presley had salmon for the first time and loved it. They were on a set out in California when one of the guys was having a cream cheese and lox sandwich. Elvis asked for a bite, then quickly polished it off, not realizing it was the dreaded f-i-s-h. "I knew what it was but didn't say anything," says Joe wisely.

Like Audrey or Jackie, Priscilla was vigilant about maintaining her weight, snacking on hard-boiled eggs between meals to quell her appetite. When she was pregnant with Lisa Marie, Nancy Sinatra asked her how she stayed so thin. "Whenever I get hungry, I just eat an apple," she replied sensibly.

Like his first Cadillac, Elvis' diet was basic Americana circa 1956. Basically, he was a complex guy with simple tastes. His favorite meal was a cheeseburger washed down with Pepsi (or Mountain Valley water). Onstage, he depended on Gatorade to give him the boost he needed.

We, for one, are not getting on the Sloth Elvis bandwagon. Our belief is, eat what you want, just don't bore us with the details. Any of his friends can tell you that Elvis was a man with big appetites—for food, cars, women, spending money, pleasing the crowd. For E, food was love as well as sustenance.

Besides, it made him happy. Isn't that enough?

TO GET THE full Prez dining experience, have about a dozen friends downstairs waiting for your summons. Make them wait. Make them wait some more. Throw in a few false alarms to keep them off balance. Have a tantrum if you are feeling particularly tetchy. Finally, amble downstairs at about 4:00 P.M. for breakfast and fire up the bacon. Better yet, have someone else cook it for you.

Family Buttermilk Biscuits
(from E's grandmother, Minnie May Hood Presley)

Forget giving up carbs—Elvis loved, loved, *loved* these biscuits, and brought his grandmother to Germany just so she could bake them for him. Every Southerner knows that yeast and buttermilk make all the difference.

> 5 cups self-rising flour
> 1 tsp. baking soda
> 8 tsp. sugar
> ½ tsp. salt
> 1 (¼ oz.) envelope yeast
> ½ cup lukewarm water
> 1 cup Crisco or other shortening
> 2 cups buttermilk

In a large bowl, mix together the flour, baking soda, sugar, and salt. In a teacup or small bowl, sprinkle the yeast over lukewarm water, stir to dissolve, then cover with plastic wrap and let sit for about 10 minutes. You want to keep the yeast warm. After the yeast has proofed (it will look bubbly), add the yeast mixture, shortening, and buttermilk to the flour mixture. Mix together well with a wooden spoon or use a KitchenAid with dough hook (this is far easier although historically inaccurate). Cover loosely with a tea towel and let rise in a warm place for about an hour. Knead on a floured surface just a little (do not overwork dough or it will become tough). Put back in bowl, cover with plastic wrap, and refrigerate overnight.

When ready to bake, preheat the oven to 425°F. Take out the amount needed and roll out to about ½ inch thickness on a floured surface with a floured rolling pin. Cut with biscuit cutter and place biscuits on a greased baking sheet. Bake for 12–15 minutes or until golden. Serve piping hot with lots of butter (the way Elvis liked them). Makes about two dozen.

Dough will keep about two weeks in the refrigerator, so you can have biscuits every day. Try this recipe; you'll thank us.

Grilled Peanut Butter and Banana Sandwich
(from Joe Esposito)

> 2 tablespoons smooth peanut butter
> 2 slices white bread
> 1 small ripe banana, mashed
> 2 tablespoons butter

Spread the peanut butter on one slice of bread and the mashed banana on the other. Press the slices gently together. Melt the butter over low heat in a small frying pan. Place the sandwich in the pan and fry until golden brown on both sides. Enjoy with a glass of buttermilk.

I want to go to Hollywood and
become the next James Dean.

— E P

l.a. stories

ONE MORNING, BOB WILLOUGHBY was shooting Sophia Loren on the Paramount lot. He got some amazing photos of her and Martin Ritt, the director of *Black Orchid*—she had a Frank Sinatra song playing in her dressing room, and they just went out in the hall and did the Lindy. It was an amazing moment and Bob felt really happy; everything just clicked. Later, they went to the commissary for lunch. Fortunately, Bob—who had started his career as an assistant for *Harper's Bazaar* in 1951, went on to shoot the stills for *A Star Is Born* in 1954, and along the way shot Frank Sinatra, Audrey Hepburn, Liz Taylor, Jack Lemmon, and pretty much everyone in Hollywood—had his camera with him. He was sitting with his back to the door and suddenly Sophia backed away from the table with a huge grin on her face and Bob wondered—what was going on?

Miss Loren had just seen Mr. Presley. She did not know him. She knew who he was, of course, but they had never been formally introduced. Still smiling, she got up from the table, grabbed him, and brought him back. Her trophy. She pulled him down, sat on his lap, and started kissing him right in the middle of the commissary, not caring who saw.

At first, Elvis did not know what was happening. Then he saw Bob taking pictures and got embarrassed. Sophia didn't care, she was ecstatic: "I *love* him!" she exclaimed, mussing his hair like so many other women wanted to do, except that they were not Sophia Loren on the Paramount lot that morning.

They were both so relaxed and happy with no sense of what the future might bring. It was a rare snapshot: two movie stars with nothing but youth and beauty, and this small moment for each other.

Sophia had been so impetuous, later, she and Bob laughed about it. "Anytime you would like to grab me and mess up my hair, that would be fine with me!" he joked.

No wonder Elvis loved the movies. It was that kind of a day on the Paramount lot.

ELVIS NEVER TIRED of the attention. Never. Unlike some stars today who try to pass among us incognito in sunglasses and baseball caps, Elvis welcomed the love of his fans. He *liked* being recognized. As Jerry Schilling noted, "Nothing can prepare you for that kind of fame, your whole world blows up. But you know what? I don't think Elvis wanted to be like everybody else. I think he loved being Elvis! Do you know how hard he worked—where he could have people look at him and say, 'That's Elvis'? In the beginning, it was the greatest life. He was the first, he was a pioneer. He paved the way . . . and he did love being Elvis Presley."

Patti Parry met Elvis in November 1960, on a glorious warm evening in Los Angeles. She and a girlfriend were driving down Santa Monica Boulevard when they spotted a black Bentley up ahead, and in those days, as Patti recalls, you didn't see too many of them. They pulled up and it was Elvis, on his way to record the sound track for *Flaming Star.* He was the crown prince of Hollywood. Since leaving the army twelve months earlier, he had shot *G.I. Blues, Flaming Star, Wild in the Country,* and part of *Blue Hawaii,* and was enjoying serial romances with costars Juliet Prowse, Tuesday Weld, and Hope Lange, as well as a brief affair with a script girl and his Memphis steady, Anita Wood.

Patti was in a goofy mood, pretending she didn't recognize him. "Do I know you? You look sort of familiar . . ." She was fifteen at the time. Elvis liked her sass, so he invited her to a party at the house he was renting on Perugia Way in Bel Air.

Elvis liked Patti right away. She reminded him, somehow, of the little sister he never had. As for her attraction to Elvis, "Who wouldn't be? Oh, he was so beautiful. He had the most beautiful skin and lips. He had eyes the color of the Aegean Sea. He also had the most amazing style—nobody looked like him or dressed like him. His dress was 'Memphis Style.' He wore those silky shirts with bands on the sleeves in all different colors." The night they met, Elvis wore a sailor hat. "He always wore a sailor hat in those days because he did not like to wash his hair."

In 1960, women wore girdles (even fifteen-year-old girls with no discernible figure problems to speak of). When they met again, Elvis hugged Patti and touched her butt. It had the resiliency of iron.

"What is that?" he wondered. A girdle. "Don't ever wear that again," he advised.

With that, Elvis and Patti became instant platonic friends. In time, she learned that "Elvis conveyed a different side of himself to women. With the guys, he had to be macho. With women he revealed more of himself." He gave her a nickname, Patricia (nicer than the ones most of the guys were saddled with), and folded her into his entourage as the lone, nonsexual, female.

It was a magical time, a blast. "Every night there were parties at the house, and every night the girls would drive up. It was like an open party. . . . He was dating everyone he was working with."

THE COSTUMES EDITH HEAD (or, honestly, her underlings) designed for Elvis' Paramount movies were not much to look at in terms of style. Elvis dressed far more imaginatively left to his own devices and besides, at six feet tall and a perfect size 42, he looked great in anything you put him in.

In 1960, with European polish acquired on the Continent, Elvis temporarily put aside his beloved Lansky duds for the Rat Pack gloss of legendary Hollywood tailors Sy Devore and Jack Taylor. No longer the rockabilly wild child bombing around the back roads of Georgia with Bill Black's bass strapped to the roof of the car, it was time for Elvis to look like a grown-up. Then, too, perhaps he was inspired by the fact that he was now using Clark Gable's old dressing room.

Elvis had Frank Sinatra to thank for his pivotal menswear discovery. When he landed in New Jersey after being discharged from the army, Nancy Sinatra greeted him with a gift from her father, two dress shirts from the legendary Hollywood tailor, Sy Devore. An inside secret among the best-dressed men of Hollywood, Devore started with the Rat Pack—Dean Martin (whose suit collar was slightly higher on the neck), Sammy Davis Jr. (his trousers had to be pencil thin), and, of course, that great clotheshorse, Francis Albert Sinatra (whose lapels were exactly 2 1/4 inches wide). All the greats had Devore make their suits. Nat King Cole, Bob Hope, Milton Berle, and Jimmy Durante were regulars. Jerry Lewis was the biggest Devore devotee since he was allergic to dry cleaning fluids and gave away his suits when telltale signs of soil appeared. (He also never wore a pair of socks more than once.)

Devore was a perfectionist. He had no qualms about tossing out a garment that didn't meet his standards and having his tailors start over again. He even kept Elvis' and the Rat Pack's suit patterns filed and locked in strongboxes to protect against fire.

Of course, being the best, Devore was not cheap. When he did Elvis' wardrobe for *It Happened at the World's Fair*, it cost $9,300 and included ten suits, two cashmere coats, and fifty-five ties. "In a very good year," Bob Hope used to joke, "I have my choice between a Rolls-Royce, a new house in Beverly Hills, or a suit from Sy Devore." Elvis, being Elvis, often bought fifteen suits at a clip.

Jack Taylor, who still works in L.A. and has been rediscovered by today's young Hollywood set, also suited up the King. He remembers the glory days of the 1940s and 1950s "when entertainers made a lot of money after the war and learned about clothes and how to use them in their performance." And don't forget, he adds, "In those days you would wear a suit and tie to just lounge around the house." You want stories, Jack's got stories—the Duke of Windsor, who was very particular about his tweeds. "He was a small guy, but when he walked in, you could tell from far away that he was a well-dressed man." Jackie Gleason, Taylor knew him from the old days in New York, every time they made him a suit they made three jackets in varying sizes. "He would go up and down in weight because of the booze." Cary Grant was the best-dressed man Jack had ever known, and that was saying something. Grant had been an acrobat in the circus and had a great body for clothes. "No one carried a suit like he did." Of Elvis, Jack recalls, he "always came in with an entourage and bodyguards. He wanted things for the stage that were flashy, but the fit was all mine."

NOW THAT he had his grown-up suits, it was time for E to meet a grown-up girl.

Ann-Margret—there was his equal. They met, they sang, they danced, they chased each other by motorcycle up and down Mulholland Drive in the middle of the night, they stayed up until 4:00 in the morning talking, they laughed a *lot*, they fell in love. Ann was perfect for Elvis.

And, at least in the beginning (like so many loves), he was perfect for her, too.

They met prior to rehearsals at a soundstage while a studio photographer and the boys lurked in the background. Elvis had on a conservative suit and tie, and Ann was in a white knit double-breasted jacket and an A-line skirt. They were the souped-up Jack and Jackie of the MGM lot, but still subdued, correct, the absolute opposite of their public images.

"Elvis Presley, I'd like you to meet a wonderful young lady, Ann-Margret," said George Sidney, the director, who was hoping for the best, since good chemistry between the leads would really help *Viva Las Vegas*. "Ann-Margret, this is Elvis Presley."

Ann reached out her hand and Elvis shook it gently.

"I've heard a lot about you," they said at the same time, making them laugh and breaking the ice.

Ann soon realized how alike they were. For all the hysteria surrounding Elvis, he was as shy and ill at ease at meeting new people as she was. As Ann recalled, "We were quiet, polite, and careful. But I knew what was going to happen once we got to know each other. Elvis did, too. We both felt a current, an electricity that went straight through us. It would become a force we couldn't control."

They had a blast making *Viva Las Vegas*. Elvis played Lucky, a guitar-strumming racecar driver whose life is turned upside down after a chance meeting with Rusty, a swimming instructor with show business aspirations. They get together, but then find themselves (and here is the big plot point) competing against each other in the hotel talent contest. Okay, so the story wasn't much, but they both looked totally gorgeous and you can tell they were getting a giant kick out of each other. In 99 percent of Elvis' movies, the plot, the director, the locale are almost beside the point anyway—people just wanted to *see* Elvis, like a monarchistic deity, on the big screen. They didn't care what he actually did.

Like their characters in the movie, he called her Rusty (which he amended to Rusty Ammo) and she called him Lucky. They were so alike, it was uncanny. Music moved them both viscerally, took them out of their persistent shyness. They loved to dance. Ann-Margret recalls that dancing beside Elvis "was an odd, embarrassing, funny, inspiring, and wonderful sensation. We looked at each other move and saw virtual mirror images." Each time they sang, they could not help but notice the similarities in the way they performed.

"It's uncanny," said A-M, a girl from Stockholm.

Elvis grinned.

Not long after shooting started, Elvis asked her out on a date, but not before asking around to see if she was attached to anyone. He did not want to risk hurting his ego. When word got back that she was single, he asked if she would like to go out with him and the boys to see a show.

She couldn't wait.

They slipped out, a whole group of them. It was an innocent, friendly date. How could it be anything else? They weren't alone for one second. But that was okay with Ann; she was used to having her parents accompany her.

As time went on, Elvis grew more and more trusting of her, and the boys disappeared when she came over.

"Where'd everybody go?" she asked.

"They were busy," Elvis said with a smile.

Years later, Joe confided to her that Elvis would pass the word that everybody had to clear out when she visited.

They always had the most fun together, that was the thing. One time after shooting, Elvis gave her a ride home on his Harley. They roared across the MGM lot, outside the gate, and made it as far as Venice and Overland, where the bike sputtered to a halt. Lucky had run out of gas—not cool. Fortunately, there was a gas station on the corner. When they got there, they realized that neither of them had any cash. The young attendant recognized Elvis, asked for an autograph, then filled the tank. They all thought it was pretty funny. The next day, Joe came by and settled the bill.

With E, life was many things, but it was never dull. Another time, Elvis suggested they go for a ride. Ann thought he meant another motorcycle jaunt (making sure, of course, that this time the tank was filled), but when she stepped outside, she saw he had brought along a tandem bicycle. "But that was fun, too," Ann recalled. They pedaled all over the hills of Bel Air as people waved and honked.

As Elvis opened up to Ann, she began to see what he was really like. It was interesting (but probably not surprising), this most public of men was so utterly private. He trusted very few people outside of his father and the Colonel, and a couple of the others, but no one else. As he and Ann became friends, she realized that "people think of Elvis as having everything, but that wasn't at all true. He had a great capacity to love, and he wanted to be loved in return, but he knew the world he existed in, the life he led, as well as all the people who surrounded him, who hurt him, who wanted something from him—everyone but a few—made it virtually impossible for him to ever feel that affection; and if he did, he didn't know whether or not to trust it."

His life: From the outside it looked as if he had everything, but in some ways (the ways that mattered most to him), it was a nearly impossible situation. That dreamy boy who sang for Sam Phillips on Union Avenue, could he have had any idea what was in store for him? As Plato knew, the gods do not give man the gift of prophecy—it would drive them mad.

It would be years before they realized the consequences of their actions. Right now, he and Rusty were young and in love, and the plotline of *Vegas* mirrored that nicely. At the end of the movie they were married—no, not by an Elvis impersonator since the real thing was so very present—at the Little Church of the West. After MGM released the publicity photos taken of the scene, it seemed that every Hollywood gossip columnist had them engaged.

When Ann-Margret went to London for the royal premiere of *Bye Bye Birdie*, the media had a field day. At a press conference, they had little time for the movie, but instead centered all their questions on her relationship with Elvis. They wanted to know just what, exactly, was going on.

With the aplomb of a diplomat Ann answered, "We're seeing each other. That's all."

But in the world of tabloid journalism, and particularly the British press, who know fewer bounds than the *New York Post*, this was akin to announcing your banns of marriage. In no time, the story grew that Ann had held a press conference to announce the big day. Which was totally, totally untrue.

First she was crushed, then badly hurt by the made-up story. She called Elvis as soon as she could to explain things. He was understanding; in his world these crazy stories were par for the course. He asked if she was upset by the whole thing and she said, yes, she was.

After the movie wrapped and Elvis returned to Memphis while Ann remained in Los Angeles, things just weren't the same. They tried to maintain their connection, but life, and reality, intruded. No matter how much he tried to ignore it, Elvis knew he had to give her up. There was Priscilla (clueless, faithful, accusatory as a matter of course) waiting for him back home; it was always the same old thing. Ann was perfect for him, but it would never work out. That's why it broke his heart. They both had commitments, other people waiting for them. They knew the deal going in, but it was still hard—they really were soul mates. Elvis once asked Esposito why he couldn't get Annie out of his head.

"She's the female *you*," he observed.

And she was. That was the wonderful thing, the heartbreaking thing. She really was.

He never forgot Rusty, her spirit, that buoyant laugh that lifted them both. Years later, they were both in Vegas at the same time and he had a late-night conversation with her, making it clear that the door was still open, that he had never stopped having feelings for her, but by then they were both married to other people, and Ann—*Damn, he was still gorgeous*—just couldn't bring herself to get involved again, not like that.

Ann rarely spoke of Elvis publicly; their relationship was too important to her. She realized, too, that he had been distorted into the sort of figure he feared—more myth than man. "But the Elvis Aaron Presley I knew was very much a young man at the peak of his creative powers and enjoying life to the fullest. He was happy and fun. He was loving and good. The thing that caused him the biggest problems was the enormous fame that engulfed him, because at heart Elvis was no saint or king but rather a kid."

Patti Parry thinks Ann-Margret was the great love of Elvis' life. She never tired of hearing from him and he never forgot her. Every time she opened in Vegas, there was a guitar-shaped flower arrangement from him. In ten years, he never missed one.

At the end, Lucky and Rusty—like all of us—learned that hard, great lesson: Love was not enough to get what you wanted; it never was. It broke Elvis' heart that they could not be together, but as Shakespeare could have told him, the greatest love stories are always tragedies.

IN HOLLYWOOD, as in music, Elvis was *big*. Between 1956 and 1969, he made thirty-three movies and none lost money. Some estimates put his picture profits at over $200 million. The exact figures are elusive because while Elvis could flaunt his mansions and Cadillacs, the studios (then and now) were discouraged from revealing the true worth of their product.

"Colonel Parker made some smart deals," said Art Murphy of *Variety*. "Elvis got one million per picture, and Parker made it so that Elvis co-owned the music publishing rights—not the studios."

You might never invite him to dinner (for starters, he would probably bill you), but for all of his off-putting carny persona, the Colonel's early marketing of Presley was genius. Twenty years before MTV, the movie sold the songs and the songs sold the movie. It was brilliant in its simplicity and from a strictly financial viewpoint, it worked.

Once the studios and the suits got the formula down, Elvis was busy. Many years, two or even three Presley movies were released per year, often timed to coincide with school vacations. Churning out so much product (namely himself), Elvis wasn't really making movies. They were more like episodic television shows shot in Panavision accompanied by fabulous lobby posters.

Yet almost in spite of the occasionally stultifying conditions he worked under, some great songs came out of the movie years—"Love Me Tender," "Jailhouse Rock,"

"Hard Headed Woman," "Can't Help Falling in Love," "Return to Sender," even the Euro dance remix of "A Little Less Conversation" (from 1968's *Live a Little, Love a Little*), a hit in 2002.

No matter what was put in front of him, or what drama was going on in the rest of his life, Elvis always could sing the hell out of anything.

BUT LET'S PUT ASIDE the eventual creative disappointment Elvis felt in making movies (and since when is Hollywood interested in Art—what are we, France?). Instead, here is another way of looking at the Presley *oeuvre*, whoops, cinematic output: as purely visual effects—Bachelor Elvis, Racecar Driver Elvis, Charter Helicopter Operator Elvis. Like the greatest movie stars, Clark Gable, Paul Newman, Tom Cruise, Elvis was always himself but in different guises: playboy tuna fisherman, roustabout, truculent son of a pineapple plantation owner. And no matter what he did, he looked fabulous.

But the main thing to keep in mind about Elvis and his movies (particularly those made in the mid- to late 1960s) is—*it does not matter*. It does not matter if the script was written in two weeks, if principal photography was completed in thirty-seven days, if Elvis was asked to play twins, one with risible blond hair (was hair stylist Larry Geller on staff then, or what?). All that matters is that EP is up on screen. That's it.

Elvis always wanted to be a "real" actor, like Brando or Dean, but judged under another set of criteria, could Brando sing "Can't Help Falling in Love" or "Hound Dog"? For all his twitchy mannered bisexual brilliance, could James Dean ever believably tear up the house with "One Night with You"?

We doubt it.

BACK AT GRACELAND, Priscilla was going through her own existential crisis. Like everyone else, she had been reading about Elvis' most recent romance with his beautiful leading lady. "Is it true?" she asked him directly. No. Was it? *No*.

Elvis was no fool. As with most men he gave away nothing in romantic matters and when pressed (especially by a hysterical female), he knew the best defense was a strong offense. Like a master politician, his response to poor Priscilla (and anyone else he ever dated) was absolutely Clintonian: deny, deny, deny. Just as he had downplayed his connection with Priscilla to Anita Wood, now he did the same to Priscilla about Ann-Margret.

Priscilla had always used makeup to appear older, but at the age of eighteen, with Elvis spending most of his time squiring beautiful Hollywood leading ladies, she was definitely subscribing to the "more is better" adage—way more. In the sixties, there was no subtlety for Elvis' girl. Instead, the otherwise pretty teenager (and we hate to sound like her mother, but she did not need to wear all that stuff) took on vaguely Elvira overtones. At the height of her mania, er, extreme interest in applying eye makeup, she wore two pairs of black false eyelashes in addition to jet-black eyeliner applied like Catwoman in *Batman*, with heavily penciled eyebrows to balance the look.

While some might consider this overkill, personally, we like the fact that young Priscilla had the courage to embrace her inner Elizabeth Taylor. "Give me anything," Diana Vreeland rallied, "just don't bore me!" DV would have seen a kindred spirit in Priscilla.

The same style moxie extended to her hair. In Texas, there is the saying "The higher the hair, the closer to God," and this instinct must have affected Miss (as she was still, to her endless sorrow, called) Beaulieu. Her back-combed hair, attention-getting to begin with, now grew to Brobdingnagian proportions until it resembled the powdered wigs worn by the French aristocracy during the reign of Louis XVI. The Sun King comes to Memphis—personally we say, *fabuloso*. Patti Parry, who helped style Priscilla's hair, called it "the big boomba" (while quickly adding that everyone wore their hair like this at the time).

"I used to comb her hair into this big boomba, and she would say, 'Make it bigger, bigger,' and then we would go into the den and Elvis would send her to fix it, saying 'It's too big,' and Priscilla would run back upstairs, weeping, her feelings hurt." To add to the Byzantine aura of the whole thing, Elvis would blame Priscilla, who would then blame Patti, who had no one to blame. Eventually, Patti tired of the hair imbroglio and decided to let Cilla fix her own damn hair.

On April 20, 1964, an article appeared in the *Las Vegas Desert News and Telegram*: ELVIS HELPS IN SUCCESS OF BURTON–O'TOOLE MOVIE. In the piece, producer Hal Wallis admitted that the profits from Presley's pictures enabled him to finance a prestigious vehicle like *Becket*, starring Richard Burton and Peter O'Toole. "In order to do the artistic pictures," Wallis pointed out none too obviously, "it is necessary to make the commercially successful Presley pictures." Elvis was hurt by Wallis' comments, referring to them obliquely in private over the years.

ON THE AFTERNOON of April 30, 1964, Larry Geller, a talented young hairdresser working for Jay Sebring (who ran the hippest—and only—men's salon in L.A.), got a phone call about Elvis Presley's hair. It was an introduction that would have a profound, entirely unexpected effect on each of their lives, but, as Larry would tell Elvis, "The Hindus have a saying: 'When the pupil is ready, the guru appears.'"

After coming to the house on Perugia Way to give Elvis a haircut, Larry eventually started discussing deeper matters with Elvis. "Hey, man, what are you really into?" Elvis wondered.

Larry thought, *Whoa, this is* pretty straightforward. He decided to tell him the truth, figuring that Elvis would either think he was a typical southern California nut or they'd become friends. Well, he began, "Elvis, you know I work with all these celebrities, but what is more important to me is my search for truth. My search has led me... mean, where do we come from? Do we really have souls? Where do we go when we leave this life? Is there an afterlife?"

Elvis said, "Wait a minute, man. You have no idea how I need to hear...

...for three hours. Larry explained to him about metaphysics, and... ics. Like Elvis, Larry was searching for the truth. He studied Hinduism, and Christianity. He was into health food, did yoga, and was just searching for the purpose, but I think I found my purpose...

Elvis' eyes were... did?"

"It's simple. What gives us our intelligence, and our life force and our energy, and we're supposed to dedicate our lives to discovering what our mission is and what our purpose is. So, my purpose is to discover my purpose."

Cool. Twenty years before Oprah, Larry was *very* Oprah.

Larry had no way of knowing that his concerns were the very things that Elvis was fascinated with. "What you're talking about," he said, "is what I secretly think about all the time . . . I've always known that there had to be a purpose for my life. I mean, there's got to be a reason . . . why I was chosen to be Elvis Presley."

Within days, Geller had quit his job at the salon and was installed as Elvis' hairdresser/spiritual adviser—a combination that would make any chic Californian jealous, seconded only by a hairdresser/Bikram yoga instructor or hairdresser/Manolo Blahnik salesperson.

ON AUGUST 21, 1964, it is announced that Elvis' next picture will be *Tickle Me*, to be produced for Allied Artists and directed by Norman Taurog. Because Allied is in financial trouble, Elvis will receive $750,000, more than half the total budget, and 50 percent of the profits.

JERRY SCHILLING OFFICIALLY went to work for Elvis on August 25, 1964. It was a funny thing with Elvis; you would see him a dozen nights in a row, and then, nothing for the next six months, and you would hear he was out on the coast shooting a movie with Juliet Prowse. The man liked to keep moving. But every chance Jerry got, he would hang out with him. "It was a pretty big deal then. I was Elvis' friend—he knew who I was and I could go to his house." For ten years, Jerry had been dying to go out to California with the guys, but the timing was never right and besides, in spite of his obvious intelligence and the fact that he got along so well with E (to say nothing of the way he could handle a pigskin), he was too young.

In 1964, Jerry was working a summer job at a trucking company. During the school year, he was going to Arkansas State on a football scholarship. He used to get summer jobs operating cotton gins or loading trucks because he could do that in the afternoon, and work until 10:00 or 11:00 at night. Then he would grab a change of clothes he kept in his car, go to a service station and freshen up, then meet up with Elvis and the guys who were just going out for the evening.

One night he was leaving the trucking company real late and saw all of Elvis' cars at the Memphian Theater. Something was up. Jerry went to the front door and whoever was there said, "Come on in, where've you been?" Jerry went into the theater just as Elvis was leaving. He was down by the screen walking out the side exit. Schilling saw him and thought, God, he looks tired, I'll see him tomorrow night. Elvis was on his way out anyway so Jerry didn't want to stop him, besides, he hadn't seen him in a couple of months.

Richard Davis, one of the guys working for Elvis, said, "Jerry, would you like to go with me to return this film, and then we'll go to breakfast?" Elvis had access to the entire mid-South film exchange; he could just call them up and get any film he felt like seeing.

"You know, Richard, I'll see you tomorrow—I'm kind of tired."

Richard told him they were going to California tomorrow. That changed things.

"Okay," Jerry decided. "I'll go with you."

They got to the film exchange and Elvis called Richard there and asked, "Do you know where Jerry is?" "He's here with me." "Would you ask him to come out to the house? I'd like to speak with him."

Jerry headed out to Graceland and Elvis asked him to come work for him; he only had about three people working for him at that time. Something had happened on the road with Esposito and a few others, and Jerry didn't know if they had quit or were fired (which seemed to happen with no-big-deal frequency), but at any rate, they were gone.

"When?"

"Today."

Jerry did not hesitate a second. "Do you mind if I go home and get my clothes?"

So that was that—Jerry went home, tossed a few things in a bag, and immediately returned to Graceland as directed, where, it should be admitted, he sat on the back step for about twelve hours and waited for the show to begin. Today, he laughs at the memory: Hey man, welcome to Life at Graceland. It turns out they did not leave until that night.

Jerry was thrilled to be on the team with Elvis, but others in his life were not so certain. School, for one, because Jerry was a history major and Arkansas State had great plans in store for him. He had it all worked out. He was going to be a teacher and a football coach, and he was the only one in the entire education department chosen to practice teaching his last semester. His teachers were very disappointed with his decision. Various relatives wondered—is this what you want to do? What if you're making a mistake?

To a lot of the older people who grew up with Elvis, they didn't quite *get* him. Jerry had an older brother who was Elvis' age. They hadn't lived together that much because he had grown up in an orphanage in Arkansas, but way back in 1954 he wondered, "Why are you always hanging around this guy?" And Jerry didn't know how to explain it. "Don't forget," Jerry says now, "there weren't rock idols then. It wasn't just that he was a rock idol, although that certainly had something to do with it. I loved his damn music! His interpretations just blew me away. He did some great stuff later, but boy, nothing will be as interesting as the unpredictability of his interpretation of rhythm and blues. It was just unbelievable."

Sitting on the back porch, Jerry thought about the adventure in store for him. He may have wondered briefly—what if it was too late? For what, he was not sure . . . but he put that thought out of his mind and spent the next eleven years with this man he had admired for so long.

ELVIS WAS ELOQUENT about his relationship with God, as he was about few other things, except, perhaps, his love of gospel music. "I never expected to be anybody important," he once admitted. "Maybe I'm not now, but whatever I am, whatever I will become, will be what God has chosen for me. Some people can't figure out how Elvis Presley happened. I don't blame them for wondering that. Sometimes I wonder myself . . .

"But no matter what I do, I don't forget about God. I know he's watching every move I make and in a way it's good for me. I'll never feel comfortable taking a strong drink and I'll never feel easy smoking a cigarette. I just don't think those things are right by me. I just want to let a few people know that how I live is by doing what I think God wants me to."

THE FIRST THING SCHILLING (who was quickly nicknamed "Milk" for his aggressively healthy lifestyle) had to get used to was Elvis' sense of humor. Life around Elvis was very fast and funny; the humor was sort of like Monty Python, very inside. One time, Elvis decided all the guys had to carry briefcases to impart a more professional look to the whole operation. This worked out fine until somebody discovered Gene Smith used his to carry a hairbrush and a doorknob.

Jerry was not sure he would have gotten the humor if he was not part of the gang. Elvis was never mean-spirited, but he liked to shake things up, keep himself entertained. He picked things up so quickly—people, situations, what was expected of him, that he got bored easily.

When Jerry first got out to California he was very shy, just a country boy from Memphis, and Elvis sensed this, knowing exactly how he felt. One night, they were going out to a nightclub, the Red Velvet on Sunset and, you know, Jerry wanted to make sure he fit in. He got dressed and everybody met up and Elvis said to him, in front of the whole gang, "Are you going to wear that?"

In the style of the day, Jerry was wearing a pair of tight pants and a velour shirt. And Jerry was an okay-looking guy, six foot one, in shape from playing ball; it's not like he was a schlub or anything. He thought he looked pretty good.

"No, no," he said quickly, "I was just going to change. . . ." Although this was not strictly true, Jerry was nothing if not conscientious and wanted to make sure he got with the program.

Jerry went back and changed twice until Elvis let him know that he was just putting him on. They laughed about that many times later. It was just Elvis' way of seeing if a guy could take a joke, make sure he wasn't some kind of a hardass. A guy who wasn't cool wouldn't last long with EP. "He was goofing around, he was putting me on!" Jerry laughs at his young impressionable self. "He could put you on—that's one of the reasons I knew he'd be a great actor. He knew exactly how I felt."

ON JANUARY 30, 1965, Elvis turned thirty. As was his custom, he spent the day quietly at home. Two months later, some of his reflections on growing older appeared in print in an interview with the hometown newspaper, the *Memphis Commercial Appeal*. "I can never forget the longing to be someone," he says. "I guess if you are poor you always think bigger and want more than those who have everything."

NOW THAT JERRY WAS ON THE INSIDE, he saw things a little differently than when he was just a starry-eyed kid, waiting to be called into the scrimmage. Not that it was bad, mind you, it was just a different perspective. The best thing about spending time with Elvis was the chance to have a conversation with him, to learn how his mind worked.

"I had known him for ten years, but once you got in that inner circle, it really gave you an opportunity to know him. After we played football we sat at this little table and talked about life and family and friends. Elvis—one of the unique things about him was, he didn't just talk about who won the football game, or a movie, everything that normal people talk about—he made them very personal. He made them have meaning." For Jerry, spending time with Elvis was a fascinating education.

"I learned more from this man than from all the schooling I ever did. Talking to him would make you *experience* it. It's like you have an education and then you go out and experience it. Being with him was like that, because here's a man who had seen it all at a young age."

Being with Elvis was exciting as hell—to walk into a room with Elvis *Presley*— Jerry was prouder of that than making a touchdown. But for the first time, he also saw some of the pressures Presley was subject to. Although in the beginning, during those first few years, Jerry was just thrilled to be with Elvis. He ran errands and helped with security as it came up. He had the feeling that Elvis was testing him, seeing what he was made of. Was he smart? Could he be trusted?

To the outside world, the guys hanging around Elvis might have looked just like that. Guys hanging around. But it wasn't that way at all. As Elvis said, "I run a multi-million dollar business, and I need people who can help me." In the Memphis Mafia (as they became known), everyone had his own function. Although people may have thought they were just a bunch of hangers-on, Jerry says that "Elvis didn't hire somebody because of their ability in a certain field; this person was going to have to live with him. So he hired people out of trust and friendship, and then it was up to you."

Jerry had been working for Elvis for about six months, not saying much, just keeping his head down and trying to do a good job. One time, he was in the den with Elvis, who was having a late afternoon breakfast.

Elvis looked over and said, "Jerry, you know what's going to be the hardest thing for you to learn?" And he said, "No, what are you talking about?"

"To do nothing."

It was years before Jerry realized that Elvis was talking about himself.

LARRY HAD MET ELVIS at a precipitous time in his life. Yes, he had everything, all the success and money and women you can imagine, but he was restless and searching, searching for answers. More than anything, Elvis was growing up, looking within for his purpose in life. As Jerry Schilling observes, "Jesus Christ, he's getting to be thirty, thirty-three years old—throwing firecrackers just wasn't cutting it anymore!"

The day after Elvis met Larry Geller, he delved into the metaphysical and philosophical books he gave him with an intellectual avidity he had rarely shown before. He began with *The Impersonal Life* by Joseph Benner, which posits that God is found within each person, *Autobiography of a Yogi* by Paramahansa Yogananda, and *The Initiation of the World* and *Beyond the Himalayas* by M. MacDonald-Bayne, then went on to read hundreds of books. Elvis read them again and again, underlining passages and scribbling notes in the margins. In years to come, he would acquire a library of over a thousand books, often giving away copies of spiritual texts to friends.

During the filming of *Harum Scarum* in March 1963, Larry introduced Elvis to the Self-Realization Fellowship, founded in 1920 by Paramahansa Yogananda, an

Indian holy man. The Fellowship is an ecumenical movement that teaches broad-based religious principles by which the seeker of any religious persuasion can find spiritual solace. Elvis began to spend a good deal of time at the group's Lake Shrine retreat in Pacific Palisades, where he met Sri Daya Mata, the group's spiritual leader since 1955.

Elvis loved spending time with Daya Mata. For the first time in a long while, he felt such peace with her. "I wish you could have met my mama," he said. "I wish I had, too," she replied. But the real world always beckoned.

ELVIS MET THE BEATLES (or, more properly, the Beatles met Elvis) on August 27, 1965, at the house on Perugia Way. It was a big thing for them. They had admired Elvis since forever and had been trying to get together for several years, but the timing never worked out. As Paul McCartney noticed, Colonel Parker would show up with a few souvenirs and that would have to do them for a while. "We didn't feel brushed off," he recalled, "we felt we deserved to be brushed off. After all, he was Elvis and who were we to dare to want to meet him?"

Finally, at the end of their American tour, they did.

Elvis was in the bathroom with Larry, who was doing his hair. He was wearing an electric blue, bolero-type shirt and dark pants; he looked fantastic. But he was stone quiet. He had this look in his eye that Larry had seen before. He was pensive—there was something on his mind. He sat there, drumming his fingers on the countertop, not saying anything. Larry knew to leave him alone.

Finally, he looked at Larry and said, "Man, I know what those boys are going through. They're in front of a live audience when you're making it up right on the spot!" Then he got to the real reason for his annoyance. "I'm making these teeny-bopper movies that embarrass the hell out of me and I know it! I keep telling the Colonel—'Why don't you get me in a real movie? I'm an actor—I can do it! You know I can do it! The studios know I can do it!'

"But I know their trip, I know their game, the studios just want to make their money. I'm keeping some of these studios going. But someday, man, I'm telling you, I'm going to make a movie, I'm going to win an Oscar, I'm going to do it. The Beatles, man, what they're doing—they're on that stage and they're getting energy from the audience, that's where it's at!"

So that was it: He was embarrassed. Yes, he was the King of Rock and Roll, he would always be the King, but here were the Beatles conquering America, and he was singing "Song of the Shrimp."

They walked into the den, and some of the guys were there, some of the girl-friends and one or two wives, with a few little babies, even the Colonel (who had been at the house only once or twice). A devoted gambler, he had inexplicably brought along a big roulette wheel, maybe in case the conversation flagged.

Everyone was sitting in the den, hanging out, and word had leaked out, probably by the Colonel, that the Beatles were coming and there were thousands of people outside in the street. And all of a sudden, they heard an explosion of scream-ing. The quiet Bel Air neighborhood sounded as if World War III had just broken out. The front door opened and the Beatles walked in with Brian Epstein.

John Lennon recalled, "It was very exciting, we were all nervous as hell, and we met him at his big house in L.A.—probably as big as the one we were staying in, but it still felt like 'big house, big Elvis.' He had lots of guys around him, all these guys that used to live near him. And he had pool tables! Maybe a lot of American houses are like that, but it seemed amazing to us. It was like a nightclub."

They came into the den, where Elvis was, and everyone was introduced.

Silence.

Elvis, shy to begin with, sat back down in his chair. The four Beatles sat cross-legged on the floor in front of Elvis and looked up at him with their jaws dropped, gaping at him for, like, thirty seconds. The four lads from Liverpool were just sitting there looking at Elvis and you could tell their minds were totally blown, because there was Elvis live and in person.

The Beatles made no bones about it: Presley was *the man*. As Lennon admitted, "When I first heard 'Heartbreak Hotel,' I could hardly make out what was being said. It was just the experience of hearing it and having my hair stand on end. We'd never heard American voices singing like that. They'd always sung like Sinatra or enunciated very well. Suddenly, there's this hillbilly hiccuping on tape echo and all this bluesy stuff going on. And we didn't know what Elvis was singing about. . . . It took us a long time to work what was going on. To us, it just sounded like a noise that was great."

Still, no one said anything. Elvis started to get up and said, "Well, if you guys aren't going to talk to me, I'm just going to go to bed." Everyone laughed and that broke the ice.

They started having a conversation, a little chat, "How's the tour?" and so on. And John said to him—"Oh, man, it's great, but the crowds—it gets so crazy out there, they're chasing the cars—it's just crazy out there—you get scared!"

And Elvis said, "John, let me tell you something—if *you're* scared, you all are in the wrong business." The room cracked up. Elvis had the television on with no sound and Paul looked at it and said, "Look—color telly!" Elvis had a remote control. Paul remembered that detail years later. He had never seen a remote control gadget before. It was decades before anyone he knew had one.

As the evening wore on, Brian Epstein and the Colonel went to the roulette table to talk shop (he was stunned to learn that Epstein handled anyone else but the Beatles; it took all of his time just to take care of Elvis). Ringo and the rest of the guys went to the pool table. George wandered off somewhere, which left Elvis, John, Paul, Larry, and Mal Evans, the Beatles' bodyguard, in the den.

Paul asked, "Elvis, can I pick up your guitar and strum it?" Elvis said sure, "Does anybody have a pick?"

Paul turned around and said, "Yeah, Mal's got a pick. He's always got a pick. He carries them on holiday with him."

Mal was a big man, six foot three, and he patted his pockets to get a pick. But he was so excited to meet Elvis that he had brought a suit specially to the dry cleaners so he would look sharp ("really ponce myself up," as he put it), but when the suit came back from the cleaners they had sewn the pockets shut. No bloody picks! Mal ended up in the kitchen, breaking plastic spoons, making picks for Elvis and the lads.

"It was a disappointment," Mal admitted. "I would have loved to have given Elvis a pick, had him play it, then got it back and had it framed."

Paul started to strum, just to feel it out. John picked up a guitar, Elvis picked up a guitar, and they jammed for about thirty minutes. They were playing "Johnny B Goode," real rock-and-roll stuff, and Larry was having an out-of-body experience—he's with Elvis and John and Paul, they're jamming, he's at the center of the musical universe.

It was historic, it really was. Elvis and the Beatles jamming in his den on Perugia Way. Unfortunately for us, the music ended the moment they stopped playing. No recording was ever made. For starters, there were no small cassette players, only reel-to-reel tape players, big bulky monstrosities, so recording the evening was out of the question. Besides, Colonel Parker was the ultimate control freak. He would not allow even one picture to be taken of Elvis and the Beatles.

LARRY HAD HEARD that George Harrison was into spirituality, Hinduism, meditation, things like he was, so he thought it might be cool to talk to him about it. He went to look for him but couldn't find him anywhere. He looked around the house, he wasn't there. He decided to check the backyard. It was pitch black. The minute he opened the door he smelled something, and there was George under a tree smoking a joint. George handed Larry the cigarette and he took a hit. They got into this wonderful, loopy, mildly stoned conversation, and Larry said, "I just want you to know that I'm into meditation and this, that, and the other, and so is Elvis . . ." George nodded sagely, his eyes squinty, his voice up a few notches. Cool, man.

After a while, they went back upstairs. (Larry, like, totally can't believe he just got stoned with one of the Beatles!) Elvis and everyone were together and Elvis wanted to show them his new car; he'd just gotten another Rolls-Royce. Everyone went outside to where the cars were parked and it was a mob scene—there were people up in the trees, it was wild! Then they started screaming, "Elvis, Elvis," then "The Beatles, the Beatles, we love you!" back and forth. Elvis showed them the Rolls, they waved to the fans, and it was just an amazing moment in cultural history.

After about fifteen minutes they walked back into the house because Elvis wanted to show them something else, a present he had just gotten from Parker. Everybody trooped back to the end of the hall toward Elvis' bedroom, and in the hall was a Swedish sauna—very *Rubber Soul*—the Colonel's gift.

A sauna. Cool. Everyone walked up to the sauna and Paul looked in the little window and said, "Elvis, who's that?"

They opened the door, and crouched under the bench was some fifteen-year-old girl who screamed and lunged at Elvis and everyone started laughing and somebody pulled her off Elvis, and everybody said at once: How the hell did she get in the house? It was funny, though. Typical Elvis. Just like something out of *A Hard Day's Night*.

The Beatles stayed for about two and a half hours. It was a great night for everybody, one of the best they could remember. John loved Elvis. They stayed in touch for the rest of Elvis' life.

After they left Larry walked Elvis back to his room, and Elvis said to him, "Let me ask you something. Who won?" Larry realized he was talking about the fans outside, howling their names—the fame contest.

"You won, hands down, Elvis."

"Well, let me tell you something," he said, serious now, still the ambitious boy from Memphis. "Don't forget—there's four of them and only one of me."

LIVING AT GRACELAND, more fully in his life especially now that *l'affaire* Ann-Margret was over, Priscilla was where she had dreamed all these years. Life with Elvis was exciting and all encompassing. It was thrilling to be with a man who loved her so, who cared about her. Elvis was not one of those men who would not notice if the woman in his life bought a new dress. But sometimes the attention could be exhausting. Elvis' scrutiny, while welcome, never let up.

Little fissures appeared in their relationship; Priscilla was not superhuman, after all. At Graceland, even if they dined alone (which was rare), Elvis and Priscilla dressed for dinner. After first going downstairs and making sure the cook had prepared Elvis' dinner the way he liked it (basically, char the hell out of everything), there were nights when he would send her back upstairs because her outfit was "dull," "unflattering," or "not dressy enough for him." Like a Hollywood director coaching a young starlet, everything Priscilla did came under review—he told her to walk more slowly. For a while, he even had her walking around the house with a book on her head. It was like *My Fair Lady*, except Priscilla was not Audrey Hepburn and Elvis sang ten million times better than Rex Harrison.

As Priscilla recalls, "I appreciated his interest, but I hated having him remind me of my shortcomings so many times, and each time having to promise him that he'd never have to tell me again."

For all the glamour and madcap excitement of Graceland, it had to have been an emotionally exhausting way to live. Priscilla wondered, "Would I ever be able to live up to his vision of how his ideal woman should behave and appear?" She had to be sensitive, loving, and extremely understanding, meeting unusual demands an average woman might reject.

A relationship with Elvis was pretty much—no, it was definitely—a one-way street. His way. Elvis was the most famous man in the world. He was charismatic, charming, generous, and kind, when he chose to be. But it was his show, and that is just the way it was.

For example, Elvis had a strong aversion to wearing jeans. As a poor boy, he had no choice but to wear them but he never wanted to lay eyes on another pair, and this applied not only to him, but everyone in the group. He didn't even want to see blue jeans.

Elvis' firm opinion of what his woman should and should not wear (which he pronounced with the assurance of any Seventh Avenue fashionista) did not make it easy for Priscilla to express herself sartorially. One day she came home with a dress that she had just bought, that she couldn't wait to try on and show him. It was a silk black-and-white print. She knew Elvis did not like prints, but it was so special she thought it would work.

She put the dress on. Elvis glanced at it for a nanosecond and said, "That dress doesn't suit you—it does nothing for you. It takes away from your face, your eyes. All you see is the dress." It was just like his gold suit created by Nudie, the famous Western designer, for the 1957 gig in Chicago, the one he *hated*. Priscilla wasn't wearing the dress—the dress was wearing her, couldn't she see that?

Priscilla started to cry. She really thought it would work. "Are you quite finished?" she asked stiffly, running to her bathroom and slamming the door, bolting it from the inside. It was just like a scene from one of Elvis' movies.

As she stood there crying in her poor, it's-not-working dress (almost playing a scene now), she heard a voice on the other side of the door. "You gotta keep away from those large prints. You're a small girl, Sattnin."

Sattnin, his nickname for her.

Priscilla was in no mood to be appeased. She swung the bathroom door open and snapped (again, just like in the movies!), "Okay—I'll return the *fucking* dress!"

Audrey wouldn't say it like that, but Priscilla did. Elvis fell to the floor laughing. He thought the whole thing was hilarious. Cilla (his other nickname for her) was such a spitfire. Eventually, Priscilla joined in, too.

She would relay this story in later years, to show how "once again I'd compromised my own taste." But really, Elvis meant well—everyone knows that unless you're a six-foot-tall Ford model, you've got to stay away from the large prints.

LARRY GELLER WAS LOOKING forward to visiting Graceland, his friend's home base. But when he got there, no one but his host welcomed him. Priscilla, whom he had heard so many good things about and was looking forward to meeting, was pointedly disinterested. Vernon, who didn't understand why Larry was being paid (more than anyone else in the crew, incidentally) to have incomprehensible conversations with Elvis, didn't get him either. In his opinion, Larry was just another whim of his son's, another needless expense, like the Cadillacs he insisted on giving to complete strangers to amuse himself.

No matter. Larry was there, he was going to make the best of it. And Elvis was glad to see him, that was the main thing.

Like any good houseguest, Larry got into the swing of things at G'land. Nearly every night, Elvis rented out the Memphian Theater and watched whatever movies struck his fancy. During the late afternoons, he raced go-carts, shot at targets with air rifles, and practiced karate with his bodyguards.

One day he formed his entourage into a real football team, spending thousands of dollars outfitting them with regulation helmets, kneepads, pants, and blue jerseys with "E.P. ENTP" (Elvis Presley Enterprises) sewn on the front. After rounding out two teams with a few husky professionals and deciding he would be captain and quarterback (after all, it was his football), the game began. Everything Elvis did was such a giant production now. It was a long way from that Sunday afternoon in Guthrie Park, when he couldn't get six people to play.

Elvis decided Larry would play left end. He was tall and could catch passes. But Larry had never played football before (the boys snickered, typical). That didn't matter, Elvis assured him. Football was simple, he told him. Whatever you do, just *don't drop the ball.*

Larry was a Zen Master, in touch with his inner self. He was a confident man. There were things he knew: He knew how to cut hair, he knew there was a world beyond the one we experience through our temporal senses, he knew Elvis Presley was his friend. If you wanted to talk about Rumi, Carlos Castaneda, Sun Salutations, blowing dope with George Harrison, Larry was your man. But there was one thing Larry did not know. He was in Memphis now, surrounded by Southern boys who were about to take him downtown.

You don't have to be psychic to predict what happened next. On the very first play a former Denver Bronco lineman crashed into him. Larry fell over like a redwood. If the game were televised, John Madden would hit Replay: Ouch, that's gotta hurt.

Larry's side was killing him, he had difficulty breathing. *Shit.* He limped to the sideline and a doctor was called over. His rib was broken.

Later that night he returned to Graceland, wounded but curiously proud of himself. "Well, we won," Elvis announced. In response, Larry pulled up his shirt, revealing his taped torso.

Elvis grinned. "Let's face it, Larry, you're not the athletic type."

THE COLONEL USED EVERY TRICK in his very capacious book to promote Elvis. His inventiveness knew no bounds (and more often than not, it seemed, no shame). For *Tickle Me*, he persuaded RCA to buy Elvis' gold Cadillac and ship it around the country as a vehicular stand-in for the star himself at local premieres. Customized by George Barris, the car featured two telephones (thirty-five years before cell phones were common), a complete entertainment console, a refreshment bar, and an electric shoe buffer, while the outside was stunningly finished in white-gold Murano pearl with gold plated trim.

But away from his celluloid image (which had less and less to do with him, really) Elvis searched for meaning. He knew what he wanted, he just did not know how to get there. "When you're not in love, you're not alive," he scribbled in the margin of his copy of *The Prophet.*

And yet, and yet. Amidst the seemingly boundless existence his life appeared to be was Elvis' most secret love, brought over from Germany, held close as any girl: speed and 'ludes, uppers and downers—two distaff angels balancing one another. It had started in the army to stay awake, and back in America, was enthusiastically prescribed by West Coast doctors where image was everything. It was all legal, aboveboard, Elvis made sure of that—he never got wasted in public or anything. Most important, he could handle it. Like so many things, like Lucifer's grin, it was so innocent in the beginning. This outstretched hand, this offer of help, *here, just try a few.*

He studied the *PDR* to make sure he was taking the right substance in the right amount. He didn't want to make any mistakes. There was makedexedrine, little gold triangles; and amphetamines, either pink or blue; and quaaludes, his favorite, to stop the world and help him rest. He always had trouble sleeping.

He took some now and then, as did most of Hollywood—so did Priscilla, the guys, Esposito, who ran his show, even Milk, the straightest one of all. They gave him energy, kept him trim. Kept him up so they could party all night in Vegas. His pills: his secret, his friends. No big deal, just a little something to ease the rough edges.

ON WEDNESDAY, MAY 18, 1965, Elvis and his gang rented out the Fairgrounds Amusement Park in Memphis from midnight to 7:00 A.M. While there, it was Sugar and Caffeine City as they consumed 201 Cokes, 7 Pronto Pops, 2 bags of peanuts, 16 candy bars, 58 cups of coffee, 31 ice cream sandwiches, 5 dill pickles, 16 bags of potato chips, and 12 devil's food cakes, for a total of $101.05, paid promptly by Vernon (check number 2097).

With Elvis, lately, you never knew what you might get. There were weeks, months, of real lassitude on a film set, of just not caring (or not appearing to care, which amounted to the same thing on the screen), and then, when the spirit moved him, going into a recording studio, giving everything to his performance, and reminding everyone that yes, there was a reason he was Elvis damn Presley.

On May 25, 1966, Elvis went to RCA's famed Studio B in Nashville and over the next four days (or, in Elvis' case, nights), recorded the bulk of the songs that made up his gospel album, *How Great Thou Art*. First, he met Felton Jarvis, the young producer who loved Presley; in fact, after hearing a concert of his at Norfolk, Virginia, in 1955, he had decided to get involved in the music business. Felton, thirty-one, was the producer every singer dreams of. What he may not have had in technical ability, he made up for in enthusiasm in translating what the artist wanted. He was on his feet the whole time, encouraging the artist, making sure the bass player came in on time, monitoring the board. He and Elvis hit it off right away.

What Elvis wanted, as he explained to Jarvis, was the kind of sound the Beatles and some of the English bands were getting—he wanted it hotter, he wanted people to sit up and take notice. After two and a half years of recording insipid movie sound tracks, he wanted the beat to grab them by the throat.

Felton agreed. It was a matter of feel, such a hard thing to explain, but he sensed what Elvis was getting at. "You get your excitement from the drums and the bass getting real funky, you got to have all that stuff up, and it's got to be mixed properly." Elvis nodded, fully engaged. Felton was one of his guys, for sure.

The singers gathered around the piano, interested now. There was a real sense of anticipation—with Elvis in his element and a producer who "got" him, anything was possible.

At 10:00 P.M. they started with "Run On," the traditional black spiritual that tells you, basically, God is watching you all the time. Elvis wanted a big sound, and he got it. Jake Hess, lead singer of the Imperials (and one of Elvis' gospel heroes), thought there was no way they could miss with all the enthusiasm in the room. "Elvis just really loved that sound—the adrenaline really pumped in him when he

heard it. He wanted a big sound, and we sung like Elvis wanted it sung . . . I don't think he cared so much how we blended, he just wanted that big sound."

He grabbed the song from the first note. "Well, you may run on for a long time, run on for a long time . . . what you do in the dark will be brought to the light." Elvis knew what he sang about, believed it, lived it. Backed by the Imperials, energized by precise double-beat cymbals, it wasn't the simple, old-timey piano stuff he grew up with—although, God bless her, that was Mama's favorite—this was gospel with *soul*. And Elvis delivered. "Go tell 'em God Almighty's gonna cut you down," he sang coolly, his voice deep and authoritative, living the life.

He owned the room. By the eighth take they had a master.

It was a night like that, full of mystery and surprise—a night you tossed the dice at the moon. When Elvis sang, it was really like being in love. And he loved gospel, he always had, like he loved Jesus. Ah, he had missed it—mixing it up in the studio, singing songs he believed in, everybody knowing they were creating something greater than themselves. For all the Colonel's picayune schemes and Hollywood ways, he knew *this* was what he was supposed to be doing.

Then they moved on to "How Great Thou Art," a bravura vocal performance Elvis had been practicing all spring. Elvis saw the song, as he saw every song with which he made a passionate musical connection, as an opportunity to pour out his heart and soul. And he did. To Jerry Schilling, it was almost as if Elvis was taken over by another spirit as he built to a memorable vocal crescendo that left him spent, visibly shaken.

"He didn't do a lot of takes, but something almost frightening happened on that song," Jerry recalled. "It was like he was just drained—he turned white and almost fainted when he finished. I wish I could verbalize it better, and I don't know if I'm talking about three minutes or three seconds, but it was as if something happened outside the normal experience. And I don't really think like that ordinarily—and it's not even my favorite song. But there was no question that for Elvis something really happened."

To Jake Hess, it was one more example of the conviction of Elvis' singing. "Elvis was one of those individuals, when he sang a song, he just seemed to live every word of it. There's other people that have a voice that's maybe as great or greater than Presley's . . . but he had that certain something that everyone searches for all during their lifetime."

After everyone went home around 6:00 A.M., Elvis and Felton stayed talking until the secretaries came in. They talked about the all-night gospel singings they had both grown up with. Elvis confessed his childhood ambition to sing in one of those quartets. "Everyone else had gone but him and me," Felton recalled. "I said 'Elvis, we better go, the people are starting to come to work.' He said, 'Lord, is it that late?'" and Felton walked him back to his hotel. It was a night like that, a transcendent night when everything was magic.

Over the next few sessions they did "So High," "Farther Along," "In the Garden," even Bob Dylan's "Tomorrow Is a Long Time," with all of the camaraderie of the first night. Days later, back at Graceland, Elvis must have realized what a special time it was. "Dear Felton," he wrote in a rare note to Jarvis, "Please convey how much I deeply appreciate the cooperation and consideration shown to me and my associates during my last two trips to Nashville. I would like to thank you, the engineers, musicians, singers and everyone connected with the sessions. Please see that every one of them know my feelings. And as General MacArthur once said, 'I shall return.' Gratefully, Elvis Presley."

IN THE LATE 1960S his friend Sandi Miller brought her daughter to his L.A. house for Halloween. The gates were uncharacteristically wide open and Elvis (wearing a gorilla mask) was handing out candy. "No one had any clue it was him until I drove up with my daughter who had seen him enough to recognize him with or without a mask," Sandi recalled. "Thankfully, no one really noticed when she yelled out! By the way, he was giving out Butterfinger candy bars."

ELVIS HAD ALWAYS DREAMED of being in the movies, of being the next James Dean. Real actors, he knew, didn't smile. People didn't take you seriously if you smiled too much. Now, all he did was smile all the damn time on screen, and break into song at the slightest pause. Somehow, he had gotten locked into making the same movie over and over again. It was a nightmare, like something out of *The Twilight Zone*. Elvis was professional, he expressed his concerns and always hoped for the best (figuring that these guys were pros and knew their stuff), but somehow, it never got better. Through *Girl Happy*, *Tickle Me*, *Double Trouble*, and *Clambake*, it was shit, all of it, just shit. Then there were the same old hassles when he escaped L.A. for Graceland. He was just so *tired* of it all. The only thing that interested him was his books, his spiritual study.

Joe Esposito knew how it was. "Some guys go to the factory. Elvis showed up at the studio. Making movies was his job, and as with any job, some days were better than others. I could always predict the two days that were the worst: the day he got the script and realized it was . . . a carbon copy of the last absurdity, and the day they shot the publicity stills. Elvis was always in a terrible mood on stills day. He had trouble standing in one place for very long anyway, and for stills, he had to sit on a bare stage for six or eight hours straight, changing over and over again, and smiling through it all as if he were having the time of his life."

Jerry saw the glamorous torpor of Elvis' current situation. "After you do three pictures in one year, and you've met all the people and heard all the jokes, you know the routine." The guys could leave if they felt like it, take some time off, but Elvis could not.

THERE WAS A BLOWUP. Of course there was. For starters, Larry Geller was just too out there, and under his influence, Elvis was not himself anymore. The dramatic denouement happened when Elvis fell in the bathroom of his Rocca Place home in Beverly Hills. With a great scurry of activity (Elvis was supposed to begin shooting *Clambake*), the Colonel arrived and a doctor was called. Fortunately, Elvis did not have a concussion, but he had delayed the start of production. In Hollywood, where time was money—that was not a good thing.

Was the slip in the bathroom Elvis' unconscious attempt to play hooky? It did not matter. The Colonel was furious and took charge because in the opinion of Priscilla, Vernon, and 99 percent of the guys, Elvis was becoming too passive. He was losing touch with the essential Elvis-ness that gave him his edge, made him *him*.

Was it Geller's doing? Was it Elvis' decision to try to become his most authentic self? It didn't matter. All that mattered was that this crazy meta-*whatever* stuff (which nobody except Schilling half understood or had any patience for) had to stop, and it had to stop (one imagined the Colonel banging his cane on the floor) NOW!

From here on, Larry was forbidden to give Elvis any more three-hour haircuts. Instead, he would be limited to a half-hour trim, monitored at all times by one of the guys. Curtailing Elvis' intellectual and spiritual studies, there would be no more religious discussions and no more books. "Some of you," the Colonel declared ominously, "think maybe he is Jesus Christ who should wear robes and walk down the street helping people. But that's not who he is." This contemplating the essence of life shit was over. From now on, if the Colonel had any say in the matter—and believe me, he sure as hell would—it was going to be strictly business.

THE SECOND PART of the Colonel's plan was to get the boy married. While not doubting that Elvis loved Priscilla *in his way* (and it was this last phrase that would be used to explain away many of his nonspousal erotic interludes in the future), one had to wonder why he agreed to it. Hard-nosed (but romantically inclined) historians cannot help but recall JFK's comment on the eve of his marriage to Jacqueline Bouvier: "I am both too young and too old for this," as well as Elvis' famously offhand comment to producer Hal Kanter describing his Hollywood salad days, "Why buy a cow when you can steal the milk through the fence?"

But, at the age of thirty-two, married he would be.

In great secrecy (albeit scooped by the very lucky and very prescient Rona Barrett), Elvis and Priscilla were married on May 1, 1967, at the Aladdin in Las Vegas, a place where it was simple to begin or end marital alliances. Unfortunately, neither Priscilla nor Elvis had much (if anything) to do with the actual planning of the event. The Colonel did it all, and, like so many things in Elvis' life, everything was engineered for maximum press exposure. Unbelievably (to us now), the coup de grâce was the fact that he scheduled a press conference directly after the ceremony. With stunning good patience, the newly married Mr. and Mrs. Elvis Presley went along with it.

But first, their outfits. Since he did not seem to have the standard issue Sy Devore tuxedo, his friend Marty Lacker did a rough sketch of an appropriate three-piece suit and had it made up in absolute secrecy by Lambert Marks, an MGM studio tailor.

There was no magical Vera Wang for Priscilla. Her dress came straight off a bridal salon rack. At first (disguised with a blond wig as "Mrs. Hodge"), she went with Colonel Parker's wife to look at dresses in Palm Springs, but did not find anything. She eventually found her dress in a bridal shop in Westwood, near UCLA, again, posing as Memphis Mafioso Charlie Hodge's future wife, with (and shouldn't this have tipped somebody off?) Charlie in tow. "It was just a very, very simple long dress with beaded sleeves," Priscilla recalled. "I didn't have time to stay there forever and look at dresses. I had one fitting for this dress and that was it, I was out of there."

The day of the wedding, Priscilla wore a train and full veil, held in place by a little tiara perched atop her back-combed hair. For the look she envisioned (glittery, theatrical, just like their lives together) her makeup was flawless, her pink lipstick perfectly matched her manicure.

If possible (although we should not really be surprised), Elvis outshone the bride and certainly the other groomsmen. (Is it our imagination, or does he tower a

foot over everyone else?) In addition to his black tuxedo, he wore a platinum watch subtly banded in discreet sapphires and diamonds. His cufflinks were also diamond and sapphire. It might sound a bit much, but on Elvis it all worked, big time.

The most famous sex symbol in the world had just gotten married, and all over the world, hearts would soon be breaking. "Remember," the Colonel cheerfully pointed out at the press conference, "you can't end bachelorhood without getting married." If he's going down (and, as we shall see, except for a brief respite, marriage did not perceptibly slow Elvis), he's going down looking like a champ.

IN A MOVE THAT would have horrified any devoted bibliophile, one of Priscilla's first acts as Elvis' wife was to burn all the spiritual books he had accumulated.

She and the Colonel were convinced that reading all those baffling books was sapping Elvis' energy. You can't just sit around thinking about this stuff all day—why do you think writers are all so crazy? Starting right now, changes were going to be made. The books had to go. Geller had to go. The guys had to stop treating Graceland like a combination frat house/Waldorf-Astoria, no more ordering whatever you wanted from the kitchen twenty-four hours a day. There would be discipline, order imposed on the operation. Starting today, *it was a new day.*

For all her emotional fortitude, Priscilla must have wondered, now that she was finally married to Elvis—can't we just have a quiet weekend like any other couple once in a while? Maybe rake a few leaves, go to the mall, pick up some extra lightbulbs from the hardware store on your way home, honey?

After tossing Elvis' books in an abandoned well in the backyard, she poured gasoline on them and tossed a match, convinced this would solve his ennui.

ACCORDING TO JOE ESPOSITO, the late sixties, the last of Elvis' Hollywood years, were "a matter of grab the money and run." He may have been in a creative deadlock at the moment, but with E, a good time was still had by all. They went to Hawaii as a group, "the closest thing we ever had to a normal life." Of course, being Elvis, it was never an intimate *rendezvous* with Priscilla, it was more like the usual retinue of a dozen people—the guys, their wives, and girlfriends.

Elvis loved Hawaii, he basked in the sun. He was loose, happy. He even got up early some days, wearing his "Hawaiian outfit"—an aloha shirt with white cotton pants and a yachting cap. Everyone else wore shorts, which Elvis refused to wear because he thought his legs were too skinny.

BY THE END, ELVIS MAY HAVE TIRED of his moviemaking experience, but he hid it well. His innate kindness would not allow him to behave otherwise. Norman Taurog, whose direction of Elvis' nine later pictures provided the only real continuity in his screen development, has fond memories of him. A realist, he admits, "I always felt that he never reached his peak," but says that Elvis reminded him of another screen legend—Clark Gable. As with Gable, Taurog found Elvis to be a simple man, industrious and polite, but one who rarely brought his own ideas to his pictures.

He remembers, too, his leading man's charming sense of humor. "He was a karate expert and he was breaking wood all day long. I would take home an armload every night to burn in my fireplace. His fingers were deformed from the constant karate stuff." One day, Taurog had the prop man set up a piece of balsa wood that he promptly demolished in a thousand pieces, very impressive.

Elvis put his arm around Taurog. "You know, Don, the last director, when he hit the balsa wood, he did it a little different . . ."

STARTING WITH BEALE STREET, Germany, and now Hollywood, Elvis' stylistic influences came from everything around him. Like any artist, Elvis plucked ideas from the air, from realities that did not even exist yet (his vision was so singular that he saw and heard things no one else did, and if it worked, he used it). But even more important, Elvis' style—so inherent in him—worked because it was authentic. He was inventive, not an invention.

Elvis' style came from his life, from his experience. It was everything that had happened to him thus far, and everything that might happen in the future. He carried it all with him—the death of his brother, the love of his mama, his ability to sing, every woman he had ever known. This is why, in spite of any dumbass movie he happened to find himself in the middle of, Elvis fascinated. You could not take your eyes off him, because he himself was so inherently compelling. In his personal relationships and with the audiences he seduced, he had this hold over people.

Elvis had a creative vision some people could understand, but no one could replicate. "Elvis was the most eclectic human being I've ever seen in my life," declares Jerry Schilling. "Sometimes some of the movies that we would rent, I would wonder—why are we looking at this three times? Elvis would pick up something, not from the major star necessarily, and utilize it. He would pick up little things that you would never know about," Jerry recalled. "There were no accidents in Elvis' look."

After spending so much time with him, Jerry realized that for Elvis, there was a lot of emphasis on looks, but in a subtle, not an obvious, way. More than anything, Elvis had a hell of an eye. Like Cary Grant, or Audrey Hepburn, he knew what worked for him and what didn't. "He was very particular in his casualness," said Jerry. "He could wear something very sexy casual, but you can bet that every thread was in the right place."

TO GIVE AN EXAMPLE of how Elvis picked up some of his visual influences, he used to tell Jerry stories about an L.A. character, Billy Murphy. Billy was this great-looking guy in college, he was a quarterback at UCLA, and then starred with John Wayne in *The Sands of Iwo Jima*. By the time the 1960s rolled around he had developed into a real longhair character—he wore a black hat, and always had on black boots like he was a refugee from *Gunsmoke*. But he was the real deal, too. Murphy was a friend of Bob Mitchum's, a tough guy if there ever was one.

Elvis, like a lot of the younger actors in Hollywood, got a real kick out of Billy. There were even Billy Murphy expressions they picked up. Elvis used to say *Mister!* with a menacing pause, just like he did.

In 1967, Elvis was in Arizona doing *Stay Away, Joe*, and Jerry was flown in to be his stand-in. He went to the mess hall early one morning and saw a guy dressed all in black and realized, "My God, that's got to be Billy Murphy." Just to make sure he walked up to him quietly. Even sitting alone at 5:30 in the morning, you never know what you'll get with a man like Billy Murphy. He had that smoldering quality of the very masculine.

"Excuse me, are you Mr. Murphy?"

"Sit down, son." His voice was like gravel. Even all alone in a chow tent in the middle of the Arizona desert, man, this guy was cool.

"I'm a friend of Elvis Presley's," Jerry began; he was sure he sounded like an idiot. "I'm working on Elvis' movie, and uh, Billy, what are you doing here?"

"Got in the Saint," which was the name of his car, "this morning and followed the sun. . . ." That was how he talked. Jerry just sat there, watching him. *Billy fucking Murphy!* "The Saint," that killed him. He could see why Elvis was fascinated.

It turns out that Murphy was in the neighborhood to do a part in a Robert Mitchum movie. Jerry had to tell Elvis.

"Go talk to the assistant director and get Billy a part," he said as soon as Jerry woke him. He had an idea. "And tell Billy not to go anywhere, I want to meet him."

Three days later on the set, Elvis was sitting in his director's chair close to the camera. He called Jerry over.

"You know why I wanted to get Billy a part in this movie?"

No.

"Watch this." Under the eye of the camera, Billy was crossing the street. Elvis nodded over at him. "Watch that walk." They looked: Murphy had a gait between Mitchum and John Wayne. Elvis smiled quietly, knowing exactly what he was doing. "I'm going to use that on the *Singer special*."

the memphis **mafia**

WHERE THERE IS the Alpha Male there is his crew, bound to do his bidding. The historical precedent of the Memphis Mafia (a term coined by a wiseass journalist, natch) descends from King Arthur's Knights of the Round Table, but the modern-day posse began with Humphrey Bogart.

In the 1950s Bogart and his Genevieve, Lauren Bacall, lived on Mapleton Drive in Beverly Hills. After their late-night carousing, friends knew that if their porch light was on—sort of like Gatsby's mythical green light—the party was rolling back at Bogey's. Pals like Judy Garland, David Niven, Frank Sinatra, Spencer Tracy, and agent Irving "Swifty" Lazar stayed up all night arguing politics and singing around the piano. Since they were rapidly drinking Mr. and Mrs. B out of house and home, they dubbed themselves the Free Loaders Club.

The Free Loaders became the Rat Pack in an inspired outburst after bitchy diarist Nöel Coward played a gig at the Desert Inn in Las Vegas. The wrecking crew, led by Head Pally Sinatra, boarded a bus in front of Bogey's house and were whisked to the airport, downing caviar and champers the whole way. In an inspired debauch, they dismantled Vegas with a nonstop schedule of cocktails, dinners, shopping, gambling, and show hopping. After five days of madcap partying (with Judy Garland passing out pep pills for the especially bedraggled), Bacall looked at the hungover assemblage and exclaimed, "You look like a goddamned rat pack." And so it was.

After Bogey (whom Frank idolized) died, the mantle of the Rat Pack was taken up by Sinatra, then JFK (Jackie archly called Kennedy's Irish Catholic pols "The Murphia," an *infra* dig that would score major antipapal points at Bailey's Beach in Newport), and finally, Elvis.

As Joe Esposito recalls, El's Angels was sort of like La Cosa Nostra, but without its psychotic *Sopranos* overtones. "We played a little game with the Mafia thing. Elvis was very impressed with the mob and how they operated. He didn't like what they *did*," Joe quickly points out—very PC, "but he liked the idea of loyalty to friends and family." Plus, there were the hugely cinematic possibilities of traveling around in a large group. When they went to the movies in L.A., the car would pull up and the guys would jump out and Elvis got out last. "I think he liked to make an entrance," observes Joe mildly.

Everybody played a role. If the MM were a boy band, Jerry Schilling was the Cute One with his shaggy hair and winning smile. Assuming anatomy is destiny, he, more than Billy Smith (who had a suspiciously small head), could have been Elvis' cousin. Red West looked like one tough hombre, or at least he looked like someone trying to look like one tough hombre. Like Elvis and Anna Wintour, he wore sunglasses indoors. While he always rode shotgun in the limo, it was hard to appear too menacing with red hair and a penchant for striped Dennis the Menace shirts. Charlie Hodge seemed intelligent, and Lamar Fike was definitely along for the ride.

As soon as the boys were assembled, EP decided they needed a look. They tried black cotton jumpsuits for a while, but ended up

looking like glorified gas jockeys—not the effect Elvis wanted. The 1960 Sy Devore black suits with thin ties were the most successful: Prada Secret Service agents. As the sixties turned into the seventies, the MM tried to morph into mini-Elvi with sideburns, gold sunglasses, and lots of extracurricular marital activity. Crazy times. ("We were bad boys," admits the now grandfatherly Joe Esposito.)

Like the Round Table, everyone took their cue from the top. Elvis said "Jump" and you could practically hear "How high?" Everybody chewed gum. Everyone—including Esposito, an Italian kid from the west side of Chicago—spoke in soft, slurry voices, leaving the consonants off the end of their sentences. As with any decent prep school, there were nicknames, inside jokes, water fights, internecine power struggles. Think *Lord of the Flies* with a veneer of Southern gentility. "They aren't employees," insisted Elvis. "These boys are my friends from down home. I've known them since we were kids."

They broke into close four-part harmony during any lull in conversation, laughed at every-thing Elvis said. Everything. It must have gotten so damn boring for him. With your "TCB" necklace, you were either on the team or not.

The Memphis Mafia—a never-ending Boy Scout troop. How tiresome it must have been for Priscilla. And the expense (like *any* expense) drove Vernon up the wall. But on some level, Elvis needed them, because for twenty years, whenever he hit the road, he took the show with him. While the boys provided entertainment, the comfort of home, and an unending fount of youthful hijinks, in the end, they may not have done him much good. Did the Memphis Mafia help or hinder Elvis' growth? Does it matter? In Hazelden parlance, they may have been enablers, but they were good old boys, and they served their master well—or at least, as well as they were able.

Today, Sean Combs and Leonardo Di-Caprio's meager celebrity groupings barely merit discussion. (Please, the pussy posse?) Historically, the Golden Age of Guyworld ended with Elvis—who had over a dozen friends on the payroll living with him 24/7 for over twenty years. Now that's commitment.

I'm never going to record
another song I don't believe in.

— E P

tiger **man**

"IF YOU'RE LOOKING FOR TROUBLE? You came to the right place," sang Elvis, in all his black leather splendor, during his 1968 comeback television special (underwritten by the Singer Sewing Machine Company), *Elvis*. The informal jam session, in which Elvis tore the roof off the joint with rough-hewn versions of songs from his back catalog, has lost none of its galvanic power.

After ten years of making Hollywood movies, Elvis had come back to prove that he could still rock the house. On a shaky folding chair surrounded by Scotty, D. J., and Charlie Hodge, Elvis was barely able to sit still on the stage, barely able to contain himself—"We're goin' up, goin' down, up down, down up, any way you want me"—growling. Guitars roaring.

He looked amazing, tan, and feral, more himself, no longer hiding behind goofball scripts. And all the kids who had missed him when he was first touring in 1956 got to see what all the fuss was about.

With his usual disarming honesty, Elvis said, "I'm doing a television special now because we figure the time is right and today's music is right. Also, I thought I ought to do this special before I get too old."

FROM THE LATE 1960S through 1977, Bill Belew was the King's couturier. The inspired black leather suit he wore on the 1968 special—that was Bill. The Vegas jumpsuits—Mr. Belew. The black Napoleonic suit Presley wore to meet Richard Nixon—Billy B. As Hubert de Givenchy and Coco Chanel were to Audrey and Jackie, Bill Belew was to Elvis.

Belew was in the Orient during the Korean War and ended up designing an outfit for Josephine Baker when she came through on her world tour, and when he returned to the States, he worked for Sears Roebuck doing its catalogs and fashion shows. At the time, Sears was trying to make a transition and Bill traveled to Europe to watch the collections and translate them for the aspirational yet budget conscious women back home. From there, he headed out to California, where he worked for Ray Aghayan and Bob Mackie. Although Mackie went on to design for Carol Burnett, Cher, and others, at the time Aghayan was more well known, having already done work for Judy Garland.

Bill, a personable Southerner, soon got a reputation for being able to appease the more difficult talent, not a small thing in Hollywood. He had worked with director Steve Binder on the Petula Clark special, so he was brought on board for the 1968 special. What was his take on Elvis?

"He was different from what I had seen on the screen—not that I had seen any of his movies," Bill hastens to add. "But I'd seen promos and things like that . . . he was just different from what I'd expected.

"Elvis was a very attractive man. At that period he had an absolutely wonderful body for clothes—he had a 42 chest, 32 waist, and he was almost six feet tall, he was just really built to look great in clothes. Bob Mackie had Cher, and I had Elvis!"

Everything was done from a sketch, and except for once or twice in their relationship, Elvis never questioned the wardrobe. Once he trusted Bill, that was it. He told the Colonel and everyone else to stay out of it.

The inspiration for that famous leather suit was actually a pair of women's long opera gloves. It sounds a bit kinky, but it makes sense. It turns out that Bill had a glove maker in Los Angeles and he wanted her to make a pair of long opera gloves for a client. They were discussing material, and she said, "Why don't you try cordovan leather? When a lady puts it on, once the heat starts coming out the glove adheres beautifully to the hand."

In the late 1960s, everything was denim, but Bill knew that would not work for Elvis. He remembered the glove lady and, thinking of Elvis, got an idea. At that time, Bill worked with the Ice Capades costumers, since they had the stretch gabardine he needed and built all the costumes for the '68 special. So he went to Ciro Romano, a tailor he worked with, laid his jean jacket on the workroom table, and asked, "Can you do this in black leather?"

And he did.

When he saw it, Elvis loved the black leather suit, recalls Belew. "He loved it, and it was great because it did exactly what the glove maker said it would. Once he got into it and the performance and heat and everything, it just started adhering to his body, and it just looked fabulous." In later years, Bill would read that he had gotten the idea from Jim Morrison, but scoffs, "To begin with, I didn't even know who Jim Morrison was in those days . . . that's just a silly thing some writer made up, and then it gets printed and everyone thinks it's true."

Really, it was an idea that just came to him—using his jean jacket and remembering the lady who made gloves for him in L.A. "It was just one of those things," he muses now. "Who would have ever thought that leather suit would ever have become so famous?"

During rehearsals, they were working twelve, fourteen, sixteen hours on the television show, and Elvis had a cot set up in his dressing room so he wouldn't have to go home at night. Everyone involved felt they were creating something really memorable—they were all in it together.

Elvis loved the wardrobe Bill came up with, but he did have one mildly prima donna moment. There was a segment called "Down the Road" that showed Elvis as a young boy traveling the road to success, and when he hits the big time, Bill used a design that was a takeoff on Elvis' famous gold lamé suit. The $2,500 one designed by Nudie that he first wore in 1957 at a gig in Chicago. The one he hated because it seemed like the suit was wearing *him*—a first for Elvis—and not the other way around.

One day, Bill got a phone call from Steve Binder, sounding uncharacteristically unnerved—"Bill, get down here right away!"

"Okay, Steve, what's up?"

"All I can say is, it's Elvis—get over here. . . ."

Of course, being good with the talent, Bill hustled over to wardrobe *pronto* and when he saw Presley said, "Elvis, I understand we have a problem?"

Yes, said Elvis. It was the dreaded gold suit. Of course, Bill had no way of knowing how much he hated it, but Elvis let him know now. "I am *not* wearing this suit, Billy—I hate it! I hated it the first time I wore it, and I don't ever want to have to wear this thing again!"

Bill backtracked fast. "Well, I'm sorry, I hadn't heard anything about that, I didn't know." He had a solution in mind already but first he apologized again, just to make sure Elvis understood he was on his side. "I'm sorry, I'll talk to Steve, we'll

shoot out of sequence . . . I'll give you a regular tuxedo, and do you mind if I give you a gold jacket and I will trim the lapels in black and give you black tuxedo pants, will that work for you?"

"Okay," Elvis said. He could see Bill was trying. "I can go with that," he said, even though he still wasn't happy with the gold.

When Steve heard about Bill's solution to the sartorial tsunami, he said, "No problem—whatever the King wants, we'll do." Bill was really amazed about Elvis' response to the suit, though. "I hadn't known he felt that way—he was really vehement about it."

AFTER THE TV SPECIAL, Bill and Elvis became friends. Once Bill felt they had a good rapport, he told him a story about being back home in Georgia after the war, passing a church, and there was a big crowd outside. What was going on? he wondered.

"Elvis is singing!"

The name meant nothing to him so he kept walking; he had somewhere to go. Elvis roared when he heard the story—he loved it, repeating it to everyone.

WITH THE CONFIDENCE HE GAINED from his special, Elvis was back big time. "Okay, I've done those movies, I've had a smash TV special," he declared. "I'm ready to cut some hit records." In mid-January 1969, working with producer Chips Moman at the American Studio in Memphis, Elvis would record what many consider to be his best work.

At first, the guys in the studio were not that impressed that Presley was going to come in and record. "We were thrilled about Elvis," recalls trumpet player Wayne Jackson, "but it wasn't like doing Neil Diamond." But he soon won them over with his consistent hard work.

In fact, we are going to go out on an editorial limb here and say, if you listen to no other Presley album, buy this double album (known as *Suspicious Minds: The Memphis 1969 Anthology*). If you really want to understand man's desire for women (or Elvis', at any rate), listen to the gleeful, down-home raunch of "Power of My Love." Even thirty-five years later, having been mixed on a very rudimentary mono board, his intention is clear: "There's just no stoppin' the way I feel for you. Every minute, every hour you'll be shaken by the strength and mighty power of . . . my love." While everybody's mother loves him singing gospel, this is definitely Saturday-night Elvis.

When he was singing what he wanted, and not movie songs, Elvis was comfortable, loose, in a recording studio. "I tell you what, I think I'm going to have to play the piano on this one . . ." "Elvis gon' play piana . . ." somebody in the background (probably one of the guys) translated.

For him, scraps of songs could also serve as a general conversational gambit. "Little less conversation, little more action, *please*," Elvis sang a capella to get the band behind him for "I'm Movin' On."

"Let's save that last one, Chips. . . ."

Okay.

"I'm savin' the last take for me . . ." was sung to the tune of "Save the Last Dance" as a lone electric guitar came in at the end.

Working all night, Elvis recorded "Kentucky Rain," an early writing effort by Eddie Rabbit, who had just moved to Nashville from East Orange, New Jersey. Rabbit had cut his own demo of the song and saw it as a way to launch his recording career. Then his publisher sent the demo, via Lamar Fike, to Elvis. "Elvis loved the song and said yes to it the first time he heard it," recalled Chips. This put Rabbit in a major bind. As he recalled, "I could let Elvis record it and make some money, while at the same time tossing my own recording career down the tubes, or I could record it myself and maybe starve." Rabbit chose not to starve. "Kentucky Rain" sold over a million copies.

The image of Elvis, practically the handsomest man in the entire world, walking through Kentucky in the rain, looking for some misguided woman who just left him, is too surreal to actually fathom. But his voice is so incredible, you believe it. The song is greater than some man's search for a woman (that eternal search, after all); but America's search for herself. After opening with a haunting guitar melody, "I reached out one night and you were gone . . . I want to bring you home." Home to ourselves. "Never knowing what went wrong, in the cold Kentucky rain." Elvis knows, too, that search for home.

We are Americans, all of us fated to repeat the same damn mistake over and over again. It is an amazing song that puts you on the floor every time you hear it.

On Monday, January 20, 1969, working from 9:00 in the evening until 4:00 in the morning, "In the Ghetto" took twenty-three increasingly focused takes. At first, Elvis and the Colonel were hesitant to record a "protest song" no matter how benign, but Elvis came to believe it could be a hit. "And his mama cries . . ."

There are at least another dozen amazing songs, but you will have to take our word for it. And Lisa Marie Presley's, too. In 2003, she spoke of her favorite songs of her father's. "I'm more prone to the seventies' stuff, because I was around then. They bring back more memories. The sad ones, I get into—the dark ones that weren't particularly a hit on the radio. 'Mary in the Morning,' 'In the Ghetto,' 'Just Pretend,' 'Solitaire.' Those I love."

Elvis knocked off "Suspicious Minds" in four takes. It had been a good, good session. After everyone said their good-byes at 4:00 in the morning, Elvis turned to the producer. "We have some hits, don't we, Chips?"

"Maybe some of your biggest," he said without hesitation.

Rolling Stone agreed. When it gave the album its lead review on August 23, it wrote, "The new album is great, flatly and unequivocally the equal of anything he has ever done."

ON DECEMBER 3, his television special, *Elvis*, aired at 9:00 P.M. and was seen by 42 percent of the viewing public, making it the number one show for the season and giving NBC its biggest ratings victory of the year. Elvis Presley's only child, Lisa Marie, was born on February 1, 1968.

EVERYTHING HE HAD DONE over the past few months, the television special and the album, was just a warm-up for what was to come—Las Vegas. From July 31 to August 31, 1969, in his first live appearance in eight years, Elvis headlined fifty-seven shows at the International Hotel and celebrated one of the greatest comebacks (not that he went anywhere, we hasten to add) in show business history.

But first, the Colonel arranged a press conference, which featured many Pucci-clad blond girls clutching Instamatics in the front row, trying to look reportorial. Had he gotten tired of making movies? someone wondered.

"I was getting fed up with singing to turtles."

Vegas was the big time—the damn big time—and Elvis knew it. Singing live, two shows a night, he recognized how high the stakes were. If he failed, if he succeeded, it would be in front of the whole world. But honestly, in his occasionally introspective moments, Elvis liked to be challenged and got bored if things were too easy. He was like a little boy this way: "You gotta prove yourself, prove yourself,

prove yourself," he declared once. Vegas was also, in his mind, a way to reconnect, once and for all, with the people and to show that he was *back*.

Of his return he said simply, "I'm really glad to be back in front of a live audience. I don't think I've ever been more excited than I was tonight."

In July 1970, Elvis and his band rehearsed for three days on the MGM lot in Culver City, California. Elvis was thrilled to be singing music that spoke to him again. He had on a brightly patterned silk shirt, and brown-and-white pinstriped bell-bottom trousers. He was one of the few men who looked fabulous in this Age of Aquarius attire and wore different versions of the same outfit over the next few days.

He sang full out, throaty, "Well, I'm leaving town tomorrow. I'm leaving town for sure . . ." His black Cuban boots tapped double time. James Burton, the intense lead guitarist who looked tougher than any of the Memphis Mafia, wore a white puffy shirt with long sleeves and wide open collar. On him, for some reason (perhaps because of his vast masculinity), it worked.

Elvis was—man, Elvis was happy. He sat on a black stool, rocking with three guys on guitars and the drummer really tight, sitting close together. He didn't hold anything back, using his hands and the whole deal as if he were onstage. Watching this rehearsal tape, we have not seen him freer, more buoyantly *himself*, it seems, since *Ed Sullivan*. He put so much into it that he could be singing for twenty thousand, not the four guys he was with.

His microphone flopped forward while he sang. Elvis looked down at it, visual comedy, and didn't miss a beat even though no one could hear him because of the lost sound. It was really funny. At the end of the song he dropped his guitar on the floor as a goof, just because he felt like it.

Lunch was simple; all the guys ate hamburgers and drank Cokes in tall white Styrofoam cups. They were like construction workers, taking a break at the job site, and we see how important the work was to Elvis. We see how he missed all *this*, when he was cooped up in L.A. making inane movies. How happy he was, finally— all the disappointments, the wasted time, the stupidity of the last ten years forgotten. His charisma comes off him in waves, his genius grin, and we can see how people would give anything to be in his company.

Elvis sat at a piano with a white towel draped around his neck, singing the chorus to "How the Web Was Woven," a new song he had learned for Vegas. "How I fell in love, fell in love with you . . ." he sang prettily, unself-consciously. They took up "Little Sister," with Burton's confident guitar bouncing bright and jangly beneath the words. Listening to Elvis, it was impossible to sit still.

Later, E goofed around for the camera; he almost couldn't help himself. He put his gold aviator sunglasses on upside down, looking buggy but impossibly handsome in yet another fitted silk shirt.

In Vegas at the International Hotel, the backup singers were coached by record producer Felton Jarvis. They listened to a tape of Elvis singing, so they could practice their parts separately before he arrived. In the style of the day, the Sweet Inspirations—three young women elegant as thoroughbreds, effortlessly chic—had full afros and the men, obvious sideburns. Sonny West (like Jerry Schilling, he was always on top of it stylewise) sported a goatee, giving him a slight, professorial air—now if only he would stop throwing ice cubes.

The Imperials leaned back on metal hotel chairs, mildly groovy in short black boots, striped shirts unbuttoned to their sternum, and droopy aviator glasses. Still, they were lesser Elvisians, coming across more like the Osmonds or, God forbid, Bobby Goldsboro. Although they were trying, they were softer, less predatory than the other guys in the crew and had obviously not spent as much time having sex with lots of women they had no intention of ever seeing again. The entire rhythm section of the band, for example, had seen a lot of hard nights, you just know it. They were authentic tough guys. James Burton, fiercest of the lot, looked like a Southern Keith Richards.

Since Elvis was not yet on the scene, the mood was relaxed. Myrna Smith, one of the Sweets, smoked a cigarette throughout rehearsal, as did Jarvis. The mood was congratulatory, that of the cool kids at the high school lunch table—*we're with Elvis.*

A few days later Elvis was in Vegas, rehearsing with the band, the backup singers, everyone. There, in an anonymous room decorated with red flecked Victorian wallpaper, sitting on hard-back chairs, we see the nonglamorous side of show business. The stakes were high. After ten years away, with his name on the International's marquee (the "eye test," Joey Bishop called it, so big it could be seen for miles away in the desert), the boy had to produce. Nothing was said, but we feel the ferocious pressure of that. He was on the scene fully in command now, wearing black trousers, wide metal belt, and a fitted black shirt with a white pattern on it, elastic at the cuff. The mood was no longer relaxed for Elvis or anyone surrounding him. The backup singers sat like schoolchildren, ready to give him the sound he wanted.

"Nineteen sixty-nine was Elvis' peak—he was a grown-up," says Larry Geller, and it was fascinating watching his creative process as he led the band and the singers all at once. It was like watching Matisse paint, or T. S. Eliot write. They were working on "Bridge Over Troubled Water." Elvis shook his head impatiently, hearing something we can't. He waved his hand, annoyed, the famous Presley temper coming up, as the sound came to a halt. "It sounds like we're lost—we don't have to *emphasize* it." They started up and were stopped, twice more, until the problem was worked out. Watching the tape, we are mystified, not sure what Elvis found fault with, but it was something. Clearly, he heard far more than we do.

At the end of practice, satisfied finally with the day's work, Elvis took a sip of water from a yellow teacup and entertained everyone by yodeling. The Sweets were in hysterics, watching him with disbelief. Moments later, he played air guitar (perfectly, something few white guys should attempt), singing, bluesy, the center of attention as he had always been, "It's Christmastime, pretty baby . . ."

In spite of his incessant karate practice he had beautiful hands.

At Elvis' invitation, Sam Phillips, the original Mack Daddy, rolled into town to give his opinion. In his inimitable manner he had one thing to say: Forget the backup singers, the costumes, the Polk Salad on the menu (the Colonel's idea, no damn doubt).

"I said, 'Is the goddamn rhythm section kicking you in the ass? Where is the *placement* of the rhythm section?' I said—'Just put the rhythm out there, baby, just put it out there. That is your I-den-ti-fi-cation.'

"Well," Phillips recounted modestly, "when I saw the show I want to tell you, I *never* heard a better rhythm section in my life. There was some randy ass shit. I told him that."

Before Mack Daddy split for Memphis, he had one more thing to say. "That was fabulous," he said, "but that song, 'Memories,' has got to go—goddamn, don't that motherfucker bog down the fucking show?"

Elvis had sung "Memories" on the Singer special. It was all very 1968, groovy, Summer of Love, Burt Bacharach in Malibu. He held his ground. "Mr. Phillips, I just love that song." It stayed.

ON AUGUST 7, 1970, Elvis finally rehearsed on the International's main stage, a vast behemoth seating two thousand people. It was the biggest venue on the strip. With only the stage lights up, the main showroom looked dark and endless. It was daunting to imagine it crowded with people; its three tiers hovered like bays on the *Titanic*. How would he ever fill the space with only his voice?

The Memphis Mafia, in all their wisdom, inexplicably decided this was a good time to have a water fight in the pit in front of the stage. Lamar Fike threw water on Elvis as he started a delicate romantic number, "Mary in the Morning."

Unlike the homeboys yukking it up on the sidelines, laughing like hyenas, the guys in the band were serious, serious. They never goofed around at all. Someone offstage said something and they began. Elvis turned quickly, his good nature finally trespassed. "*I say when the band starts. . . .*" His eyes flashed, he was angry—*this was his goddamn gig and don't you forget it.* He gave a short nod and they started up again.

ELVIS WANTED BILL to do his costumes for Vegas, so he was back in Los Angeles noodling around, thinking, thinking, trying to come up with something. Oh, he knew he would, of course—he always did—but what?

One day he got an idea for a high-neck collar. "I had seen some portraits and things when I was studying Napoleon and I thought about that. I saw a picture again and I thought that would be perfect for Elvis because he is the King and it would draw attention to his face . . ."

Another home run for BB. He did some sketches, explained to Elvis what he had in mind, and he got it instantly. Of course, it helped that Elvis was so physically confident. As Belew admits, "Very few men can get away with that high collar, it's very imperial. There were some men that would ask for it when I was designing, but their face never lent itself to it the way it did Elvis. It was really his thing."

Today, everybody wants a piece of Elvis' jumpsuit. Manuel of Nashville, the Dior of country music and Nudie's onetime son-in-law, has claimed authorship. So did Tony Alamo of Hollywood, before his arrest for using child labor to wardrobe the stars. Forget it, the jumpsuit (and its evolution) was pure Belew all the way.

The way it worked was, Bill made sketches and after Elvis okayed them, he took them to the tailors at IC, Nicky or Romano. Nicky was Bill's guy who did all the embroidery work and the punching of the stones—they used real Swarovski crystals imported from Czechoslovakia—because Bill wanted it to look as regal as possible,

with the jumpsuits made from Italian gabardine from Milan. Once they got the system worked out, it took about two weeks to make each costume, with the beadwork and everything.

Interestingly, once Romano got Elvis' measurements from the special, that was it. Like many of the actors Bill worked with, Elvis hated standing still long enough for a fitting. Unlike the Duchess of Windsor, who had three separate fittings just for her nightgowns, or Marlene Dietrich, who could look in the mirror and tell precisely what was wrong with the placement of the beadwork on her stage gowns, Elvis had *no* interest in being a mannequin. Bill would just take the clothes up to the house, he would go into the bathroom, try them on, come out, say "great"—and that was it.

According to Bill, Elvis loved that the clothes did what they were supposed to do, but he was more obsessed with the music. In this sense, Bill thought he was like someone else he had worked with, Lena Horne.

"Like Lena, Elvis was the same way—she'd go in, put her gown on, we'd do whatever we'd have to do, then she would stand in front of the mirror, she'd go to the left, to the right, check the back, but once she got out on the stage, she never thought about what she was wearing. Elvis was the same way. He did what he had to do, and then once he got on the stage the only thing he had to think about— which was what he wanted to think about—was his music."

TWENTY MINUTES BEFORE SHOW TIME, Elvis was up in his suite, surrounded by the posse, acquitting themselves properly now, holding a sheath of blue telegrams. "This is when it starts getting tense," he said to no one in particular, his hand beating staccato on the table. "If it don't go over we can do a medley with the costumes . . ." "Here's hoping you have a successful show and break both legs—Tom Jones," he read, as the minutes ticked by.

ELVIS WALKED BACKSTAGE with the whole crew surrounding him— the Mafia, the pretty backup singers, Jerry, Red, Joe. He was wearing a white jump-suit, his shoulders strong. Like a gladiator, like all men history shines down upon, he was utterly alone.

Elvis strode onstage, grabbed the mike, and snarled, "Well—that's all right mama, that's all right for you," the band rocking double time, and you know he's got it. In his beautiful white jumpsuit with white macramé belt, very long and flowy—he's gorgeous, better looking than any man deserved to be.

At one point he looked out at the crowd, shook his head slightly, and blew his cheeks out, like "Man, I can't believe this." His left leg ticked incessantly, nervously, while the rest of him was still. He wore a large black pearl ring. The room was in pandemonium to see him again. It had been so long.

The Sweets wore black miniskirt dresses and orange blouses with full, full sleeves underneath and black go-go boots. The guys in the band wore white Davy Crockett–type shirts with fringe across the back and matching bell-bottom trousers. Needless to say, no one looked one-*tenth* as fabulous as EP.

The women in the audience were beautifully dressed in sleeveless evening sheaths with very ornate hair; their ringlets carefully sprayed and arranged on top of their heads. It's Vegas, baby, and Elvis was the ticket in town that month.

HE ROARED INTO RAY CHARLES' BLUES NUMBER, "I got a woman, way 'cross town, and she's good to me, woah yeah. Well I gotta woman . . ." The crowd erupted. Seeing Elvis onstage high from the music and the love of the audience, so totally into it, it was unbelievable that in seven years, he would be dead from ill health, overwork, and anomie. He looked so great in Vegas tonight.

By the time he did a slow, smoky late-night version of "Heartbreak Hotel," the collar on his jumpsuit was all wilted, not stiff and straight anymore. He looked like he'd been through the wars, giving the audience everything he had.

During "Love Me Tender" it was time to kiss some beautiful babes in the front row and Elvis really got into it. Singing, he conveyed things in public that most men couldn't even say in private. Onstage, he was a better actor than he ever was in his movies, *becoming* each moment he sang about. He kissed them seriously, taking his time, taking each face gently in his hands and drawing it to him. Kiss after kiss after kiss as the room howled—there were so many women, hundreds and hundreds of them—and they were all so far away from him! "Hang loose, baby, I'll get to you . . ."

Face it: Elvis was the kind of guy who could call you *baby* and get away with it.

ON THE SPUR OF THE MOMENT he decided to go out into the audience. Sonny West and Richard Davis were right with him and Joe was there, too, in a blue shirt, looking dwarfed and terrified. Walking through the crowd like the Pope of

Love, he kissed any girl he came across, bestowing his blessing. "This is my grand-daughter, she *loves* you!" a woman cried. Elvis waded through the middle of the room where all the banquets were. The women looked like stewardesses, all frosted eye shadow and wide, expectant smiles. "Elvis, kiss me! Kiss me!" everyone cried, trying to get his attention.

Before he returned to the stage he leaned back and in one smooth motion swooped and gave one last kiss to some lucky gal before gliding onstage holding a necklace somebody gave him. "Sorry I couldn't make it up there," he motioned to the sky deck that roared its approval. Elvis had just brought Sin City to its knees. He had the whole room in the palm of his hand, showing everyone why he was Elvis damn Presley.

Elvis first came to Jerry Weintraub in a dream. He was an MCA agent who had been hustling around, producing small shows in New York, nothing major. But one night, he was lying in bed, sleeping, and he saw the Madison Square Garden sign in his mind: "Jerry Weintraub Presents Elvis." Not bad visualization, right?

So he woke his wife, singer Jane Morgan, and said, "You are not going to believe this, but I just saw a sign that says, 'Jerry Weintraub Presents Elvis' at Madison Square Garden."

"What are you talking about—you don't know Elvis Presley, go to sleep . . ."

Jerry went back to sleep, but the next day he made some calls and got Colonel Parker's phone number and (here is the agent part of the story) proceeded to call him every day for a year. Parker took Weintraub's call the first time he called him, even though he had no idea who he was.

As Weintraub recalls, "I told him I had this dream about promoting Elvis Presley, and he told me I was crazy. Little did I know he was a very spiritual guy, and he used to carry a Buddha around; he would pray to Buddha and talk to Buddha all the time. The Colonel was much deeper than people gave him credit for.

"So I kept calling him every day, and we got friendly on the phone, but he kept saying to me, 'First of all, Elvis is not going on tour. That's a given. And if he were going on tour, you wouldn't be the one to take him, because I owe tours to a lot of different people and I don't know you from a hole in the wall. You seem like a very nice guy, but I would get the best there is in the world.'"

"But I am the best in the world," Weintraub said.

"What are your credentials?" the Colonel countered politely.

"My credentials are that I want to do this. It's going to happen." He'd had this dream, after all.

One day, Jerry was in Beverly Hills and he got a call from the Colonel, "Do you still want to take my boy on tour?" He never forgot that: "my boy." Yes, of course he did. "Then show up tomorrow at 11:00 A.M. at the International Hotel in Las Vegas with a cashier's check for one million dollars, and you and I will make a deal."

Now Jerry really started working the phones, because people were always saying to him, Listen kid, I'd love to be in business with you, if you come up with anything, let me know. He started calling his contacts, but everyone said, Jesus—a million dollars? In 1969, a million dollars was, well, it was a million dollars.

Finally, he got hold of a lawyer in New York City who had an idea—"There's a man in Seattle, Washington, who owns radio stations and loves Elvis, he'll probably give you a million dollars."

Jerry called up the Seattle guy who had one question: "What do I get for my million bucks?"

He thought fast. He knew if he got this deal, his entire life would change. "We go fifty-fifty on every cent I make on my concert business." Not just Elvis, but everything from here on out.

Next thing, Jerry was in Vegas, walking into the bank with his long hair, jeans, and crocodile belt, and he said to the lady behind the counter, "I have a bank transfer coming in, and I'd like to know if it's here."

"How much is it for?" she asked.

"A million dollars." Now she looked interested. Jerry sat there for a few hours, waiting for the money. It was almost 11:00 and he didn't have the money for the Colonel yet. He called the hotel and said, "I need until one o'clock." The Colonel said, "I'll give you until three, but don't call me back."

At about noon, the president of the bank came over with the check. "Can I ask what this is for?"

"I'm going to take Elvis on the road."

"Do you need an accountant?" He was all set to leave the bank and join Team Elvis.

He and the Colonel made the deal, and Weintraub took Elvis out on tour. At the end of the gig, the Colonel took Jerry to a little electrician's room with two Samsonite suitcases full of money, like he robbed a bank. ("I hope the IRS can't bother me anymore," Weintraub says, telling the story.) The Colonel dumped the money on the table. What's this? Jerry wanted to know. Proceeds from the souvenir sales—T-shirts, key chains, scarves, and whatnot.

"We didn't agree to—" starts Jerry.

"No, no, no, when I have a partner, I have a partner." The Colonel piles all the money on the table and whacks it down the middle with his cane. "That's yours, and that's mine. Is that fair?"

The Colonel gave Jerry the check back, too. "I never really wanted it," he explained, "I just wanted to make sure you were the right guy."

ELVIS HIT THE ROAD for the documentary *Elvis on Tour*. "Fifteen towns in fifteen nights, and he's not even running for president," the warm-up comedian says as the crowd applauds, yes! "But if he did, he would win!" Elvis took his show to Detroit, Dayton, Buffalo, Hampton Roads, Richmond—places most Americans can't even find on a map. North Carolina, Arkansas, Virginia, the flyover states.

The documentary shows, for all its supposed glamour—the money, the women (well, we don't see that), the late-night parties (we don't see that, either)— the reality of life on the road. We see how small and cramped the backstage is, how gritty, how real the music world is. Like the president or the truly famous, Elvis never walks through the front door. Instead, he is always being led through underground alleys, loading docks, and kitchens, shaking hands with stunned dishwashers as he passes.

In a grim cinderblock dressing room, he demands to know why Joe Esposito got him down here so early—he hates waiting around too long before the show. Damn, *damn*—he's edgy, man, pissed. The tension Elvis feels is palpable. He shakes his hands from the wrist to rid himself of it. The other guys wait in the periphery, looking helpless. For all their TCB bravado, there is not a damn thing they can do for him. Elvis is the one, as he has always been, who has to walk out there alone and perform. Watching the scene more than thirty-five years later, our hearts clutch as we feel in some small measure the pressure he was under.

Elvis is as nervous before every show as he has ever been. Everything is for the audience. Everything. "I work absolutely to the audience, whether it's six or six

thousand, it really doesn't matter, they bring it out of me—the inspiration, the ham," he admits to filmmaker Pierre Adidge.

And what if something doesn't go over?

"I change the songs around. I'll go back and stay up all night and work—working on it, you know, worrying about it. I find out what it is that's not getting off the ground, you know, the first or five numbers. Because it's very important."

ONSTAGE NOW, SINGING "BURNING LOVE," Elvis reads the lyrics off a piece of paper. His vocal ability is so absolute that even standing still, holding a piece of paper in his left hand, he kicks it out to the back row. Roaring into the second stanza he tosses the piece of paper with a small comic flip of his wrist: He's got it now. Like a considerate host he turns his attention to the cheap seats at the back of the stage, as the backup singers soar into the chorus, "a hunka hunka burnin' love . . ." Walking past mezzo-soprano Kathy Westmoreland, still singing, he taps her on the shoulder and points skyward, as if to say: Hit the high note.

Just like in 1956, no one in the band had any idea what Elvis would sing or even do next. Trying to anticipate what song he would decide upon, they studied him with the intensity of the professionally wary. Ronnie Tutt bangs away on his drums, watching Elvis as if he were a four-year-old walking on a window ledge. Elvis is patient, encouraging with the newest member of the team, but having toured with Elvis, the veterans know one thing—follow his lead, or there would be hell to pay.

It has been said time and again, but Elvis had such a true connection with his audience, it is unthinkable that Sting, or Eminem, or Barbra Streisand would ever display themselves so completely to their public. Just like in Vegas, Elvis gave his complete attention to the fans, particularly the women, kissing them full on the lips. There was no fashionable, Euro air bussing for Elvis. "Just give me five minutes, man," he joked before leaning into an impressively peroxided blonde. After he kissed them, it was as if they had just witnessed the second coming of Christ. They were absolutely overcome. "Let 'em up," he told the policeman guarding the stage. They let a few women past.

ON THE ROAD, anything goes. And except for the occasional opening night in Vegas, Priscilla and the wives are safely stashed back home in Memphis. Whatever goes on on the road stays there, that's the rule. We see a seventies moment: Red, frilly edged panties are tossed on the stage. EP picks them up with the inevitable smoothie riposte. "Are these yours, honey?"

MORE THAN ANYTHING, Elvis' concerts were just fun. They were happenings, they were religious experiences, they were events. At one point, Elvis lies on his back with his legs crossed, singing at the ceiling. The crowd loves it—he could have read the back of a cereal box, for all they cared. Like a demon lover, he was with them right then, just that one night.

Cameras flashing, Elvis lifts his cape doing a victory walk, pacing from one end of the stage to the next, pausing at each corner to acknowledge the roar of the crowd. He wore a white suit with red lining on the inside of the cape. He was like a prizefighter, like a farmer pacing off his land.

"Wise men say, only fools rush in. But I, but I, I can't help . . ." It was the final song, always, of any Elvis concert. The audience howls in paroxysms of delight, but sorrow, too, knowing he would soon be gone. The room is in hysterics. Elvis turns and rolls his eyes, an inside joke for the boys in the band. He knew precisely what he was doing. Ever since he sang in those dark raunchy roadhouses in 1955, it was as if there were another creation that existed outside himself—the stage Elvis that made everybody go off the fucking deep end.

The crowd, howling, a raging Greek chorus wanting him to stay, to *stay*, knew he would be gone soon and they might not see him again. The true fans knew, too, that he never did an encore. If it were up to Elvis, he would probably sing for hours. He ducks down the steps at the side of the stage; the boys, Espo, Schiller, and Red, surround him. "Hey, Elvis, Hey, Elvis, Elvis," a thousand nightmare voices howl, the background to his public life. He is thrown in back of the limo and they're gone.

"How was the sound in that building?" is the first thing he wants to know. "Very good, very very good," assures Esposito, his corner man, who has assiduously shed his Chicago accent for a soft Tennessee drawl.

Elvis had a physical beauty that was almost indestructible. Like his voice, it was a force greater than himself. At the moment in the film, he looked pale, distracted, a towel draped around his neck, all his energy left onstage back in Jacksonville. On tour that time around, he seemed able to shape his external form at will. The voice was there, stronger than at nineteen, and his total engagement with the audience never wavered, but the look of him changed from day to day, hour to hour, almost—he was healthy, he was puffy, he was thin, he was jaundiced. In 1972, Elvis was a changeling.

One day he looked soft and jowly, as dissolute as Henry VIII; the next, lean and energized, the hillbilly cat. We don't understand the cause, but it is fascinating to see.

WE WATCH A PRACTICE SESSION with the background singers. Elvis wore a Belew masterwork, a lilac blue Edwardian frock coat with black edging detail. It was pure Carnaby Street in Winston-Salem. The cuffs were rolled back, revealing purple silk paisley lining. No one was dressed as extravagantly, as beautifully as EP. He moved with the ease of a visiting prince.

ANOTHER DAY, ANOTHER CITY, and everyone was dressed up. Most of the women shared the placid beauty of Tricia Nixon. We've got miniskirts in the dead of night, white go-go boots like on *Hullabaloo*, stacked Cuban heels and bells on the guys. It was an evening show. There were many, many couples out on a big date; it's like they're in a nightclub. The entire audience smoked enthusiastically throughout the show—welcome to North Carolina!

Elvis sang "Bridge Over Troubled Water," his voice much richer than when he and Scotty and Bill tested the waters for Sam Phillips. He really lived inside the music, totally lost in it. Singing, Elvis became more completely himself. He left his heart on the floor and that was what the fans paid to see.

Some people (the uninformed, mostly) might feel compelled to smirk at Elvis' jumpsuits, but if you consider it, the entire 1970s was an unfortunate era, fashion-wise. Think of leisure suits, *Starsky and Hutch*, "Broadway" Joe Namath stalking the New York Jets sideline in a full-length fur coat, Jimmy Carter, looking very nonpresidential in a button-down sweater. Out of everyone he had traveled with, Elvis always looked the best—he had the sure sartorial convictions of a Southern Beau Brummel, followed by the backup singers the Sweet Inspirations, with Jerry Schilling rounding out the general groove factor. Bandleader Joe Guercio, more typical of the time, chugged away wearing a black outfit and wide silver Navajo belt, with the requisite Vegas comb-over. And we're not even going to get into the Colonel's startling fashion choices.

Out in the heartland, Bill Belew's jumpsuits made brilliant fashion sense; playing auditoriums and indoor arenas, the flash was necessary when you saw the size of the rooms he filled. In 1970, there were no Jumbotrons projecting the headliner to the back row; they barely had decent sound systems. Belew's dazzling costumes, more than anything Elvis wore in the movies, ensured that he was seen in the mezzanine. "And pain is all around—like a bridge over troubled water, I will lay me down."

Like the best actor, the one he was never really allowed to become, Elvis fully inhabited the song. He stood very still in the middle of the stage and just belted it out. There were no histrionics, no karate moves, no flirting with the Sweets. He stood on the middle of the stage and believed: I will lay me down.

Allowed a glimpse into his private pain, the audience, for once, was stunned into submission.

If he were a mass of nerves and desire in his Lansky duds on *The Ed Sullivan Show*, now Elvis was older and knew the cost of fame and all it would ask of you. Not world weary, exactly, just wiser. He had seen it all—everything, things you cannot imagine—a thousand times over. Ronnie Tutt came in with the beat, banging his heart out. The backup joined him for the final stanza.

Perhaps conscious again of the audience before him, Elvis bounced a bit and brightened for the last line. Listening to him, you don't doubt it for one second, baby, like that bridge over troubled water, he would ease your mind.

MIRRORING THE MAN THEY ADORED, Elvis' fans were known to be the politest of people. They still are. In the documentary after Elvis asks to turn the house lights up so he can see the audience, they don't storm the stage, but just sit in their seats and look politely at him, applauding—the great mass of America: men and women on dates, single women with their hair optimistically curled as if Elvis might pick them out of Section K and ask them out after the show (well, he might). They worked hard, paid their taxes, educated their children. Elvis' people.

They were Fans with a capital *F*. God bless them. One says wispily in the background, "Elvis started the whole thing. I love him. I'll always love him." Several nod in agreement. "I wouldn't miss him for *nothin'*," says another.

It was all so touching. This was not the celebrity scrum you saw in Vegas, no high-rollers with their sense of entitlement, here to see The Man. These were the real folks. There were entire families, grandmas with canes, preschoolers in party dresses, who had come to see Elvis. They loved him openly, the way they loved God and country. There was no doubt, no irony. With the lights up they sit respectfully as Elvis meanders across the stage, singing "Ain't it funny how time slips away . . ."

Out there with the regular folk, Elvis seemed mellow and at ease. He had on an electric blue jumpsuit with studs and tiny mirrors on the bodice and down the side of the pant leg. His left hand was hooked into his jeweled belt, like he's a farmer and he's out kicking the dirt around, surveying his land. He meandered up and down the stage. All of the preshow jitters—*Joe, when the hell is the show going to start? The stage is too short and the lights are right in my goddamn eyes*—were gone. He was at home, as we have not seen him since rehearsing with the band. With the music he was, finally, at peace. *Ain't it funny how time just slips away?*

Three or four women evaded the policemen and rushed the stage. Elvis leaned over and tried to hand off his scarf, not missing a thing, still singing. "Let her have it, man."

He was just so damn cool, so absolutely removed from our late-night parodies and ridiculous impersonations of him. That night, he had broad shoulders and a solid torso. He looked amazing. His cape swung out the back and it worked for him. He looked like Superman, just singing, trying to hit the low notes like J. D. Sumner.

HOW HAPPY HE WAS. It was a small thing, but how absolutely, purely *happy* he was right then; the master of his own destiny. Who the hell would have wanted to go back to Graceland (as stultifying, at times, as any movie set), with everyone sitting like statues waiting for him to make a move? Out on the road, he was free. Out on the road feeling the love, he could look out his airplane window and go anywhere, anywhere at all.

He disembarks from the plane and walks over to the crowd straining at the chain-link fence. "We need about five minutes here," he says, leaning into an enthusiastically peroxided young lady squealing with delight. He kisses her full on the lips, as if they have just concluded a successful date.

BACKSTAGE, WEARING A RICH RED JUMPSUIT, Elvis reads the cards in the floral bouquets lined up on a homely wooden bench as his father looks on. Minutes before he is expected onstage, he takes the time to lean over and touch the flowers, checking to see who sent them.

"But this time, Lord, you gave me a mountain," and he's singing like an old blues guy on the Delta, every vein in his neck straining. He was not some lightweight pop crooner, some invented boy band. Elvis had lived it. In the 1970s, Elvis was heavier spiritually. He was darker, but he was also funnier, goofier—along with the gravitas of life, he also knew its basic insubstantiality. It was as if he had created "Elvis" and now that he knew who he was, he could play around with him. Elvis was like the Nile, like the Mississippi; both man and boy, he would outlive us all. His energy was just so much deeper than when he was this hungry kid from nowhere who wanted enough money to buy a pink Cadillac and have girls notice him.

He had no idea what was ahead of him. Like all great artists, his life, the music, asked everything of him. And he had the courage, the fearlessness, to give everything in return.

"It's not a hill, Lord—this time you gave me a mountain," he sings. The love of the audience envelops him in waves.

"Take it home," he exhorts the band, finally, as Glen D. Hardin rolls into the familiar piano opening of "Can't Help Falling in Love." The audience cries with abandon. The background singers sound like angels. He spreads his arms and gives a final pose, offering himself to them.

A woman dressed like a librarian stands and bangs the edge of the stage.

"Elvis, Elvis—over here, Elvis! Over here!" she cries above the band, throwing the tantrum of a four-year-old. Elvis in all his resplendent glory regards her for a nanosecond, watching her bang the flat of her hands against the wood, but does not slow his departure. You can almost watch the wheels turning—*I got over Natalie Wood, Ann-Margret, and soon, I'll get over Priscilla, too. I've got to move on, honey.*

He kneels on bended knee at each corner of the stage and in a flash, he is gone. Joe Esposito has a hand on his elbow, Red's on the other, the boys surround him, and he's out the door.

It looked like something out of *A Hard Day's Night*—everyone was running down the ramp, a screeching crowd in his wake. He dove, or was pushed, into the back of a long black limousine. Inside, the houselights were not even up yet, "Elvis has left the building." Thousands of fans screamed, willing him to return. Elvis was halfway to the nearest airport when most of the audience was still unconvinced the show was over. They were shouting and weeping, blinking when the houselights finally came up.

"Elvis has left the building . . ." *We want Elvis, we want Elvis, we want*—but he was long gone.

At the end, Elvis said good-bye to everyone on the tour. And we are sad that it was over, our brief glimpse into his life. But for Elvis, it was never over for very long. After a week resting up at Graceland, he would get restless and have Joe get the Colonel on the phone—Can we go out again? Set something up in Texas.

Elvis loved touring. Like a politician or the proverbial salesman, he loved being out on the road, meeting the folks. Because this was what Elvis the entertainer, the Southerner, knew in his heart—life was made up of those you loved, and spending time together. In the end, this was all that mattered. Elvis, in his unconscious genius, created experiences that people shared and never forgot. This was his gift: He brought them together, then gave them these irreducible moments in time.

Away from the screaming fans, sharing small intimacies the public will never see, Elvis seems like such a good guy. He puts out his hand to shake to Jerry Schilling, who's got kind of a doeskin leisure suit thing happening. At the last second, EP pulls back his right hand, leaving Jerry with his arm in midair. They break up laughing, as the man who made everything possible moves away to say good-bye to someone else. When days were good what fun, what fun they had together.

elvis' closet

Some people dream of having a big swimming pool—with me, it's closets.

—AUDREY HEPBURN

OF COURSE Elvis being Elvis, he had big closets *and* a swimming pool. Because he could. Born into daunting poverty, once Elvis made some money, he shopped with the enthusiastic acquisitiveness of Jackie during the Onassis Years, and never looked back.

Lansky, Lansky, Lansky—Stylewise, where it all began. Elvis frequented Lansky's when he barely had two nickels to rub together and remained a loyal client his entire life. Bernard Lansky wisely gave him a house charge early on. Next time you are at the Peabody Hotel down in Memphis, stop by and say hello to the deeply charming (especially to the ladies) proprietor. Note to overly familiar Northerners: Be like EP and call him "*Mr. Lansky*" no matter how much he protests.

The White Jumpsuit—The bane of true EP fans and Billy Belew's stroke of genius, the White Jumpsuit has become the leitmotif of Elvis impersonators worldwide, mostly because it hides a multitude of sins (generally around the midsection). Never forsake an imitation for the original. If any of these impersonators had a modicum of Presley's talent, they would go to Hollywood and become Brad Pitt.

Shoes—E had a shoe thing to rival Imelda Marcos, but there were no tassel loafers for the Memphis Flash. By the mid-1970s, he kept more than eighty pairs of size 12 shoes, with nary a lace-up in sight. Instead, his wardrobe was full of cowboy boots, Cuban heels, hand-tooled leather with "EP." Onstage, he favored shiny leather boots with customized designs. In a nod to his audience, he also wore Florsheim.

Scarves—For enticing that pretty young thing in the front row. Bill Clinton, our most Elvisian president (past, present, or future), has an autographed scarf from a 1971 concert. EP bought 'em by the dozen ($10.00 each with a courtesy discount), mainly from the IC Costume Company in Hollywood.

Ann-Margret—Camelot goes Hollywood—they were the Jack and Jackie of the MGM lot. After meeting cute on *Viva Las Vegas*, AM was more Presley than poor Pris, stuck back in Memphis (barely) attending a local Catholic girls' school. The King's most fitting consort, she and EP remained friends for the rest of his life.

"EP" Sunglasses—Truck-driver chic in 14 carat gold. Perhaps the only man (with the occasional exception of Kurt Russell) to successfully pull off this look, it helps to have Elvis' Cherokee cheekbones. Looking for an original pair today? Definitely buyer beware—there are thousands of fake-os floating around on eBay.

TCB Wear—The closest thing to a Presley coat of arms: "Taking care of business—in a flash." Women and children got the

G-rated "TLC" (Tender Loving Care). Nice. Copies abound on the Internet, and the G'land gift shop. Unless you're Linda Thompson or Joe Esposito, it is highly unlikely you possess the real thing.

Major Bling Bling—Sean Combs might give Kelly Osbourne a diamond watch for the heck of it, but nobody beat Elvis in the gift department. Like the Sun King, Elvis traveled with his own personal jeweler, Lowell Hayes. Whenever the mood hit him (which was often), EP bought ice-ice-baby for himself, his dentist, whoever he was dat-

ing at the moment, the girl he was recently obsessed with and might fly out to Vegas, a woman window shopping in the store at the same time as he. . . . There was no Cartier or Harry Winston for El Prez, but Hayes or Harry Levitch, local jewelers on Poplar Avenue in Memphis.

Creed Perfume—Revisionist Elvis is shown at the Creed store on Madison Avenue as having worn Green Irish Tweed, a very upscale Parisian scent favored by Cary Grant, Prince Charles, and Naomi Campbell. (Among fashionistas, this possibility is almost as compelling as an "I saw Elvis in a Flagstaff 7-Eleven at 3:00 A.M." sighting.) Called on this unlikely scenario, the Creed legal team backpedals (just like the Nixon White House during Watergate), saying they "cannot confirm or deny" it. Joe Esposito, keeper of the EP flame and a man who definitely knew what was in the bathroom cabinets, says, "He never wore that perfume." At the very least, we know Elvis wore Brut.

Firepower—

And to everybody who wants to change the Second Amendment—if EP had been running the NRA, we'd *all* be packing heat.

Law Enforcement Badges—

If you want to travel unencumbered through airport security, it helps to be Elvis Presley, and to have a vast assortment of law enforcement badges. Also, the reason behind his famous 1970 meeting with Richard Nixon.

Guitars—

Guitars? Yeah, Elvis had guitars, including a customized 1956 Gibson J-200 (that first appeared in *Loving You* and *King Creole*), 1960 Gibson J-200, 1976 Martin E-76 (Bicentennial Commemorative), Burns of London olive green 12-string used in *Spinout*, a classical guitar, the Gretsch Chet Atkins Country Gentleman, 1956 Gibson J-200 with customized neck and pick guard, Gibson doubleneck, Fender acoustic, Fender bass, as well as a custom guitar made for Elvis by a fan. Even though he tended to use his ax as a prop onstage, a man's gotta be able to walk the walk.

Miscellaneous Guy Stuff—

Elvis' environment was pretty much a self-contained world, and chances are, if you wanted something, anything, heck, it's kicking around here *somewhere*—Western saddles, a baseball mitt and ball signed by Hall of Famer Willie McCovey, pinball machines, jukeboxes, invitations to the presidential inaugurations of Dwight D. Eisenhower, John F. Kennedy, Lyndon B. Johnson, Richard M. Nixon, and Jimmy Carter ("thanks, but no thanks," to all of them), a pair of gold boxing gloves signed by Muhammad Ali ("You're the Greatest," wrote the champ), oxygen tanks, an oversexed chimp with a drinking problem, two-way mirrors in the women's changing area of the pool house . . . no, we're half-kidding about that last one.

Planes, Boats, and Cars—

This stuff didn't go in the closet, it went in the *garage*.

Things EP Never Wore—

Baseball caps, Dockers, boxer shorts with funny patterns, rep ties, jogging shorts, clogs, a Snugli, Earth shoes, a fanny pack, you get the idea. In Elvis World, it was never casual Friday.

ELVIS AND HIS FAMILY were pack rats, keeping everything from his sixth-grade report card (D in Arithmetic and Geography, A in Spelling and Music), a box of Crayola crayons, his favorite Yahtzee set, to a 1971 Stutz Blackhawk. While only 5 percent of Elvis' treasures can be displayed to the public at any time, the rest of his things are carefully preserved, cataloged, and kept in a secure, climate-controlled environment looked after by a full-time curatorial staff of three.

Having been granted rare access to E's stuff at the top-secret archives at Graceland (and we can't tell you where it is, because then we'd have to kill you), we can only say: Don't worry, everything—*and there is a lot of it*—is extremely well taken care of.

Celebrity is the mask that eats up your face.

—JOHN UPDIKE

midnight **rider**

ELVIS HAD BEEN WORKING practically nonstop since he was twenty, so when he had time off, he was like a four-year-old. A four-year-old with vast financial resources and the ego-enriched ability to do anything he wanted. As anyone who spent much time in the Presley inner circle could tell you, EP with too much time on his hands was not a good thing. He staged firecracker battles, had impromptu target practice in the backyard, bulldozed errant outbuildings at Graceland, then set them on fire.

After an argument with Vernon and Priscilla over his spending habits (okay, so maybe he gave his father and Charlie a Mercedes the day before, and now all the guys were standing around with their hands out—it was his goddamn money!), Elvis stormed out of the house and in true Wounded Husband fashion, decided it was time for a road trip. To Washington, D.C. To have a chat with Richard M. Nixon, president of the United States.

Priscilla and the guys were convinced he would be back. This had happened before, and after driving around for a few hours and realizing he had nowhere to go, Elvis always came home, the whole thing forgotten.

This time, things were different. After a few hours, he called Jerry Schilling, his comrade in arms, and together, they flew to D.C. He also called Sonny West and told him to meet them in Washington, but only after he had promised not to tell Team Graceland where he was. On the plane, after learning that Republican senator George Murphy was back in tourist class, Elvis dashed off a letter to Nixon, stating his wish to help the administration combat the drug culture, the hippie elements, the SDS, Black Panthers, et cetera. ("I call it America and I love it.") He did not wish to have an appointed position, he hastened to add, "but by doing it my way through my communications with people of all ages." But first and foremost, he would need federal credentials, namely a highly restricted FBI badge from the Bureau of Narcotics and Dangerous Drugs (BNDD).

After dropping his handwritten letter off with a guard at the White House at 6:30 in the morning, he headed over to FBI headquarters to try to have a meeting with J. Edgar Hoover, to see if he would give him a badge. Jerry was to wait at the hotel and if RN called, he could be reached at the Bureau.

The newly industrious Elvis was gone no more than an hour when the phone rang. Egil "Bud" Krogh, deputy counsel to the president, was on the line. He was in receipt of Mr. Presley's letter and wondered if Mr. Presley could possibly stop by his office at the Old Executive Office Building, directly next to the White House, in the next forty-five minutes?

Jerry, who up to this point had been indulging his friend's governmental whim, was flabbergasted—a call from the White House? They were going to meet the *president?* It was wild, man, wild. Yes, sir, he stammered. They would be there, scribbling down the address.

He immediately got Elvis on the phone at the Bureau of Narcotics, where he was transferred to the Deputy Director, Jerry Finlator. Elvis was elated, but not surprised, when he heard the news. He would come for Jerry in the limo in fifteen minutes, wait outside in front of the hotel. Sonny West pulled up in a cab from the airport just as Elvis arrived, and together they set out for the Old Executive Office Building.

Krogh, meanwhile, a pure pol, was having second thoughts about how the whole Elvis thing was going to play out for him. A thirty-one-year-old junior functionary who had been given some responsibility for development of a sweeping new drug policy, he had received the Presley letter from a coworker, Dwight Chapin, at about 9:00 A.M. Once he read it, he and Chapin talked about how Presley's participation could inject some much-needed sex appeal into an administration that, thus far, was sorely lacking in the je ne sais quoi of other presidential eras, namely that of those damn Kennedys. At present, Nixon had celebrities like Art Linkletter, *Dragnet* star Jack Webb, and evangelist Billy Graham in his corner. They were nice guys, sure, but they didn't exactly speak to the youth of America.

With these points in mind, Chapin wrote a memo recommending a meeting between Presley and Nixon to his boss, future Watergate fall guy H. R. Haldeman.

"It will take very little of the President's time, and it can be extremely beneficial for the President to build some rapport. In addition, if the President wants to meet with some bright young people outside the Government, Presley might be the perfect one to start with."

"You must be *kidding*," the aggressively short-haired Haldeman wrote in the margin next to the last comment. But he okayed the request. Now, it was up to Krogh to draw up a memo for the president, explaining the purpose of the meeting and providing him with talking points.

At precisely 12:30 P.M. on December 21, 1970, Krogh and Presley walked into the Oval Office, leaving Jerry and Sonny outside in an anteroom. For his meeting with the president, Elvis wore a Belew special with his own inimitable sartorial twist. There would be no anonymous K Street Brooks Brothers suit, white oxford shirt, and striped rep tie for El Prez. To begin, there was a white, high-collared shirt worn with a lion's head pendant he had just purchased from Sol Schwartz, and his Tree of Life necklace with the guys' names engraved on its roots and branches. Then, Bill fashioned a black tunic with white shirt, with an Edwardian jacket (lined with paisley silk) draped like a cape over his shoulders. To accent the entire ensemble, and to ensure he was not mistaken for a Rockefeller Republican, Elvis wore his sunglasses and the massive gold belt the International Hotel had given him in gratitude for his record-setting performance in Vegas.

Rock and roll hits the Oval! In spite of a cold that had been bothering him for several days and a neck rash from eating too much chocolate, Elvis, of course, looked fabulous. He was just so intrinsically cool, he almost couldn't help himself.

Nixon began the conversation awkwardly, as was his wont. He had none of Lyndon Johnson's folksiness. None of the hated JFK's intrinsic charm. Still, in his socially maladroit way, he tried.

In retrospect, it was amazing that Nixon and Elvis would have anything in common, other than Elvis' respect for the office of the president. Imagine: Richard Nixon—paranoid, famously disciplined, perhaps the least sybaritic man ever to occupy the White House. A political operative of such limited personal pleasures that he had cottage cheese and ketchup every day for lunch, meeting Elvis—a keen voluptuary of vast, ceaseless, and unending desires. Most of which he had fulfilled, and then some. Money, sex, a stretch Mercedes limousine, all the chocolate he wanted . . . it was all his.

Elvis was a man who welcomed new experiences, sought them out—like going to Washington and visiting the White House on the spur of the moment, right now, for example! And Nixon, a man so deeply removed from his Dionysian nature that if a woman ever threw herself at him, he would probably call Bebe Rebozo and have her hauled out, then make sure that she was audited for the next twenty years. How hilarious, how perfectly *American*, to imagine the two of them making small talk in the most powerful office in the world.

After his initial awe, Elvis quickly settled in, putting his sunglasses, autographed pictures, and various police badges on Nixon's desk (a power play akin to a dog staking out his property), while showing him his cuff links and Vegas belt.

"I know how difficult it is to play Vegas," offered the president.

Elvis said that he was just a poor boy from Tennessee who had gotten a lot from this country and wanted to repay it in some way. Then, he got to the matter of the BNDD badge that he wanted. If he had this badge, he stressed to the president, he could be a true undercover operator and could help the president without sacrificing his credibility.

The BNDD badge—Nixon did not know what he was talking about, wasn't this given to FBI employees? He turned to Krogh and said, "Can we get him a badge?"

Krogh wasn't sure how to read Nixon's request, did he want him to have it or not? "Well, sir, if you want to give him a badge, I think we can get him one."

The president nodded. "I'd like to do that. See that he gets one."

Elvis smiled his glorious smile, this being out in daylight wasn't half bad—he'd have to try it more often. "Thank you very much, sir. This means a lot to me." Elvis then moved close to the president and in a spontaneous gesture, put his left arm around him and hugged him.

Hey, *whoa*. RN was not a hugging guy. He was not, for example, Larry Geller or anything. And the Nixon presidency was not, needless to say, a hugging administration. Nixon was caught off guard. Krogh was caught off guard. The official White House photographer was caught off guard.

Nixon patted Elvis on the shoulder. "Well, I appreciate your willingness to help, Mr. Presley."

Before he left, Elvis had one more thing. Acting as if it were a spur of the moment request, he turned to the president and wondered if he wouldn't mind saying hello to his friends, Jerry Schilling and Sonny West.

When Jerry and Sonny were shown to the Oval Office, it was Elvis who now appeared in charge. "Come on, guys," he beckoned. He was so proud that he was able to set it up for them, like he had given them a gift.

"You've got a couple of big ones here," the president said, another awkward conversational gambit. "It looks like Elvis is in good hands with you guys."

"They're good friends," said Elvis, "and they're interested in helping me out, too." The president then presented them with tie clasps and cuff links with the presidential seal on them.

"They've got wives, too," Elvis helpfully reminded the president, as together, he and the president rummaged through RN's desk drawer to find suitable presents for the gals back home.

IT IS KIND OF ROMANTIC, but one of the most lasting legacies of the Presley era, stylewise, was a joint effort between Elvis and Priscilla.

Elvis knew the phrase "TCB." It had been a common expression in the black community for some time, and entered the everyday vernacular with Aretha Franklin's 1967 hit, "Respect." It meant "Taking Care of Business." Of course, Elvis being Elvis, he amended it to "Taking care of business—*in a flash*" (hence the "TCB" intersected with the lightning bolt), which is how he liked things done.

Jerry Schilling well recalls the eureka moment, which is right up there with the day Levi Strauss invented denim blue jeans, or Coco Chanel her iconographic suit. It was October 1971, and they were living in Holmby Hills in Los Angeles, when Elvis called Jerry over the intercom and asked him to come to his room. He and Priscilla were looking at a drawing of the "TCB" logo she had made. Elvis asked Jerry's opinion (he liked it!), then asked him to go to Saul Schwartz's jewelry store in Beverly Hills to have the necklaces made. There were originally seven—one for Elvis, and six for the inner sanctum working for him. At the time, it was quite a coup to have one.

"TCB" was quickly adopted as the Presley family crest. And now that he had his own logo (much hipper than Ralph Lauren's little polo playing man, that's for sure), the monogramming possibilities for "TCB" were endless. Elvis had a diamond ring of the same design (10.5 carats in the center diamond alone—it worked). "TCB" emblazoned the tail of his plane, the *Lisa Marie*. It was on the placecards at Graceland, the cocktail napkins. The ladies in the group were granted their own moniker, "TLC," for "Tender Loving Care."

And what about his famous sunglasses? One day he happened to be driving down Sunset (although as Larry would say, "There are no accidents"), when Hans Fiebig, who owned Optique Boutique, pulled up alongside and offered him his card, saying, "If you ever need glasses . . ."

Elvis came in a few days later. He had a cheap pair of aviator-style glasses with him and asked Fiebig to duplicate them. He was not interested in the quality of the frame, more in the look; although Fiebig, an exacting German, made the best for clients like Steve McQueen, Robert Evans, and Hugh Hefner—a veritable rogues' gallery of randy seventies' guys. Like those with truly developed style sensibilities, Elvis knew exactly what he wanted, and found the designers to give it to him. Hans recognized this instinct in him immediately.

"You cannot sell Elvis anything—he knows what he wants—either you have it or he won't buy . . . There's a certain character, you cannot persuade them, they know exactly where they are going. They also know what looks good, and they find the places that give service because that's what they like most."

After "TCB" came along, they changed all his glasses and later added "EP" on the side to further customize them. All the work was done in 14 karat gold and Elvis only had two colors—silver chrome and gold, but as Fiebig noted, "he liked the chrome better for the simple reason that most of his wardrobe was white and red and black, and gold wouldn't go as well as silver.

"The lenses were all kinds of colors—are you kidding? But the favorite ones were brown gradient and gray gradient. The gray gradient we used for the silver, and the brown gradient we used for the gold."

Elvis was very polite. "But the only thing is that he had no patience—when he wanted it, he wanted it yesterday!" Hans did great work and soon Priscilla and Lisa Marie and the whole gang were getting their specs from Optique, with Elvis ordering a dozen custom pairs at a time for himself.

One wonders, did anyone else get glasses like Elvis'?

Hans looks startled. "No, no, no, no, no, no—no, no," he says emphatically. "Elvis got his style, and Lisa Marie got hers, and Priscilla got hers. . . . They all got their own style. Nobody got his style. . . ." We suppose, like the right of kings, only Elvis could wear TCB glasses.

What about the guys?

"No. No, no, no—they would buy something similar, but never the same."

Today, with all the TCB sunglasses floating around on eBay (often for thousands of dollars), how can one tell if it's a real pair of sunglasses that Presley owned?

Hans says that "the ones that really belonged to him are gone . . . if someone tells you these are the original glasses that Elvis wore—you have to be very careful. After he died, I can tell you that the Colonel scooped up all his glasses and they were never seen again."

One story that Hans thinks would probably surprise a lot of people is that "Elvis was the best payer in the business. I don't think his father went to bed without paying the bills. That was incredible. Especially today, when all the stars want everything for free!"

"TCB"—by now, thanks to Elvis and Priscilla, the whole world knows what it means. Not incidentally, if you want to be a true insider, you should know that several members of the Memphis Mafia sign off their emails with "TCB." To continue EP's legacy in cyberspace, you might want to try this, too.

CHRISTMAS 1971 AT GRACELAND. When it came time to hand out gifts, Elvis jokingly gave everyone McDonald's gift certificates before giving them their real gifts. Although everything seems normal at the time, later, many of the guys will say that Priscilla and Elvis appeared distant over the holidays.

A few days later, after Priscilla and Lisa Marie flew back to Los Angeles, Elvis announced to everyone that Cilla is leaving him. She hasn't told him why, he admits, simply that she no longer loves him.

IN SPITE OF THE DISCORD in his personal life, professionally, Elvis was in good shape. Steve Binder, who directed the Singer special, spoke to a reporter from *Rolling Stone* about Elvis' response to it. "All of a sudden after the special he was on fire again. He told me he wanted to change his lifestyle. He said doing the program had given him a new feeling of confidence. 'It's the public who made me,' he said, 'but I've been away from them for too long. They've given me a lot of love and now I want to give it back to them. From now on I'm only going to do what I want.'"

After Sin City, what Elvis wanted to do was play the Big Apple. On June 9, 1972, he did.

But first, the Colonel scheduled a rare press conference, the first Elvis had held since his 1969 Vegas opening. At the Hilton, the television press corps came dressed in full battle regalia, and were soon immersed in a struggle to untangle video cables and hardware. At center stage, WABC's long-haired pride, Geraldo Rivera, led an attack to remove a NEW YORK HILTON sign from a position on the podium where it obscured their camera angles.

A Hilton functionary argued that "Colonel Parker says that there'll be no conference unless the seal stays put."

"Oh, come on—you don't really expect us to buy that bullshit. It just doesn't make any sense," Rivera countered. Hey, Geraldo—*major* attitude. And you wonder why Presley & Company was not in any rush to return to New York City?

Now there was a commotion up front. According to *Rolling Stone*, "An old-timer in a straw hat, black shirt, red cowboy boots, and cane was passing through the crowd, looking as if he'd just come from the 'guess your weight' booth at Coney Island and handing out red and blue ELVIS-NOW-72-NOW-RCA ballpoint pens."

"Come on, hurry up, this is your last chance to get an Elvis pen," Parker barked, vigorously limping down every aisle. When the pens were gone, he opened another carton and retraced his steps handing out Elvis wallet calendars.

By the time he had dispensed with the Presley *bibelots*, the Colonel had amassed a healthy press entourage. "You look terrific, Colonel," some said to him, for which they received a cordial, "Thank you, glad to see you," and another calendar.

Finally, Vernon entered stage left, followed by Elvis as the crowd (everyone in New York who had ever claimed a rock-and-roll byline) took a collective gasp of 1950s-induced nostalgia. To look at him, Presley seemed not to have aged a day, he'd just gotten bigger. Lights twinkled off his gold trim, his buttons, and his teeth before Geraldo Rivera shot the first question over the steady hum of Nikon clicks.

"Elvis, why have you waited so long to come to New York?"

"Well, sir, we had trouble finding a good building. And once we found one, we had to wait our turn."

"Mr. Presley, why have you outlasted your competition?" asked another.

"I take a lot of Vitamin B. No, actually, honey, I suppose I've just been very fortunate."

"Elvis, are you satisfied with your image?" The first question that caught him short.

He paused, thinking, then finally said the most real thing he had said publicly in years: "Well, the image is one thing and the human being another . . . it's very hard to live up to an image."

Steve Binder was pleased to hear that Elvis seemed nervous just prior to his New York City concert appearance. "That's very good—Elvis is only effective when he's somewhat unnerved. It means he's excited, there is something to give the audience. He's a very special kind of spring that has to be kept taut. He should always be kept on edge. That's how he was at his first opening in Las Vegas. He knew he was about to do something different which is what every artist has to keep doing to keep growing. Never repeat anything twice. He was fantastic then."

In New York City, motivated and energized, more than up to another challenge, Elvis rocked the joint, bringing an exceptionally jaded audience, including George Harrison, Bob Dylan, Bruce Springsteen, and John Lennon, to their feet. David Bowie, just starting his career, caught a predawn, pre-Concorde flight from London to catch the show. As he recalls, he got there about ten minutes after Elvis hit the stage. "I had the humiliating experience of walking down the center aisle to my very good RCA-provided seat while Elvis performed 'Proud Mary.' As I was in full Ziggy regalia by this time—brilliant red hair and Kabuki platform shoes—I'm sure many in the audience presumed Mary had just arrived."

Jerry Leiber, who cowrote many of Elvis' hits from so long ago, was also there at Presley's express invitation. He really did not want to go—not because of Elvis, but because he hated crowds.

As Leiber recalls, "My family was absolutely insane with excitement, so we went on a Saturday night. When we arrived, there was this enormous, elaborate box seat with boxed lunches and flowers. And he was real good. Of course, I'd seen him when he was more agile. But he was good, and the family loved it. I coaxed the family to leave early, though, before the finale, so that I could beat the crowds.

"The next morning, I get a call in my office. It's Elvis, and he asks my secretary what happened. Didn't he like the show? He actually saw me leave! Forty thousand people. He saw me leave. He had his eye on me and he saw me leave. I had no idea he was that into it."

AFTER THE TELEVISION SPECIAL and his success in Vegas, Elvis hit the road and would continue touring, extensively, for the rest of his life. Just like the barnstorming he did in the 1950s in the beginning of his career, he loved taking his show to the people. "The only time I feel alive . . . is when I'm in front of my audience, my people," he admitted. "That's the only time I really feel like a human being."

In 1970, Elvis did 137 shows. Over the next few years, the number of shows gradually increased, and his aide-de-camp, Joe Esposito, never missed a single one. In 1973, he peaked at 168 shows, the most he ever did in one year. Elvis' work ethic was extraordinary, almost superhuman. When he was on tour, he rarely took a day off; instead, they did one show a night, and on weekends, he also did matinees.

The stress on Elvis, as the man carrying the entire production, was immense. From the outside, it was a crazy life. Elvis agreed with Don Henley of the Eagles, who said, "You go out there night after night, getting all this tremendous love from twenty thousand people, and then, thirty minutes later, you're sitting in your hotel room, alone, watching the news on TV. The world tends to become either too much or not enough. Either way it can be fatal." Still, it was the life Elvis wanted.

Needless to say, this incessant touring could not have helped his relationship with Priscilla. Elvis wanted to be married, but he also wanted to be single, too; the eternal masculine struggle.

On February 23, 1972, after years of rumored marital discord, Elvis and Priscilla separated. After six years of marriage, divorce was granted on October 9, 1973, at the Los Angeles Superior Courthouse in Santa Monica. "You can love someone and be wrong for them," Elvis said at the time. Immediately after the divorce, rumors circulated about his poor health, and his long-standing weight problem became obvious.

Bernard Lansky, who knew the sartorial secrets of El Prez, and perhaps a few others, was asked if Elvis was happily married during his years with Priscilla.

"It seemed like it. Seemed like it." There are other voices in the room and laughter, inside comments we are not meant to hear. He gets back to the question at hand. "Once he got married I really, you know, I backed off. When you're with Elvis and the guys it's one kind of ball game," he said philosophically, with the tone of a man who has seen a lot of sunrises in his day.

"You got a wife, it's a different ball game. You know, you can't do like you did when you were single." You're out with Elvis in mixed company, it's complicated, you have to know what to talk about and what not to talk about. You've got to be very careful. You've got to edit yourself. Now, Lansky isn't one to judge a man, God knows; he had been married to Joyce for close to fifty-five years, but "that wasn't my ball game. So you back off—you let them do what they want to do."

In his boyishly self-dramatizing way, Elvis took Priscilla's exit and turned it into a set piece for his own personal Sturm und Drang. Almost tearfully, Elvis told Larry Geller how long he had meditated, hoping that Priscilla would stay with him. "It didn't work."

Larry may have been an extremely evolved guy, but he was still a man, and he saw what went on on the road. "But that wasn't what you truly desired. You wanted your freedom, and deep down you knew it."

Elvis acknowledged what Larry was saying with a shrug. "I'm glad you're back, Larry. You keep me from kidding myself."

Patti Parry had a similar experience. A few weeks after Priscilla had left him, she went to Elvis' hotel room and he was distraught, crying his eyes out. "Well, you cheated on her for years," she observed, not unkindly. Still, he could not believe that Cilla would leave *him*—after all he had done for her! He wept freely. He would never get over this.

Such was the King's logic.

I N J A N U A R Y 1 9 7 3 , Elvis gave a worldwide satellite concert filmed in Hawaii, and Bill Belew was called back into action.

Out of all the work Bill Belew did for Elvis, there was just one suit he was not sure of, and that was a corduroy suit. "At the time, corduroys were a big thing in fashion. And so, when he went to Hawaii I did a wide wale, light beige suit that I really wasn't sure of. Then, he gets off of the plane in Hawaii and lo and behold, what do I see? Him—getting off the plane and there he is wearing that suit, looking just gorgeous."

Once Elvis decided that Belew would take care of his wardrobe, they never really discussed clothes again. Well, there were three times when he had a specific request. The first was when he said he'd love to have a suit with a panther on it and he asked for that specifically, and Bill made that for him. The second time was when he was going to have a stained-glass window put into Graceland with the peacocks, and he said, Would you make me a peacock suit? And Bill said fine.

"The only other time we had any lengthy discussion about wardrobe was when we went to Hawaii and we sat and batted ideas around," Bill recalled. "And I remembered I had gone by the American Embassy in London and there was a huge American eagle on the top and out of somewhere in my mind that building came up and I said—I know what we need to do—we need to do the American eagle. I don't know where this just came in my mind, but I just saw this huge eagle on this building and I thought—that's it!"

Elvis saw it right away, too. "It's got to say America—that's fabulous!"

"Here's what we'll do," Bill said, he could see the whole thing so clearly in his mind, "we'll do a white jumpsuit and a cape, and the American eagle will be all in red, white and blue."

Of course, if it is an Elvis tour, there is another, funny part of the story. As Belew recalls, "I thought it would be fabulous if Elvis came out in a long cape and across the back will be this huge American eagle. And at the same time, I also made a short cape. So, Joe Esposito called me and he said, 'Billy, you're not going to believe this,' and I said 'no, Joe, what happened?'—and he said 'well, Elvis put on the cape and started out to the stage and fell over!' He said the cape was so heavy that Elvis just fell back down and couldn't get back up."

Elvis thought the whole thing was hilarious. He lay on his back, unable to move, laughing his head off.

A few days earlier, *boy, things were getting nutty in Hawaii*, Bill received another frantic phone call from the saintly Joe Esposito. Apparently, Elvis had thrown his American eagle cape into the audience one night, and gave away the jewel-encrusted belt that went with it another night. Joe is desperate—can Billy replace both items and bring them up to Hawaii?

Bill is in a bit of a bind. He also does work for comedian Flip Wilson on his popular television show and, as he explained to Joe, "Flip is doing Geraldine and I cannot leave when Flip is doing Geraldine." (This is why BB is so good with the talent.)

Bill and his team managed to reproduce both items literally overnight and Bill begged his assistant, Nicky, to please go to Hawaii with the belt and the cape for Elvis.

Of course he would.

Joe had gotten a seat for Nicky and a seat for the cape. During the entire flight, the stewardess kept coming back and looking down at the cape, wrapped so carefully in an oversized garment bag. Finally, she approached Nicky.

"Can I ask you something?"

"Yes . . ."

"Is that Elvis Presley's cape?"

"Yes," admitted Nicky, now a celebrity by association. "He threw the first one that we made away, and I am taking this to Hawaii for the concert."

"Can I touch it?" she whispered.

"Sure," he said.

She did, and then kept running up and down the aisles, "I touched Elvis' cape, I touched Elvis' cape!"

Beyond the tossed cape/stewardess debacle, the Hawaiian concert was a giant success. The concert was broadcast to most countries in the Far East, including Japan, Korea, and Hong Kong. Japan registered the highest rating ever, with a 37.8 percent share in a highly competitive market, while twenty-eight European countries linked by EuroVision would see the show on a delayed basis later in the day.

When the show was broadcast in the United States on April 4, 57 percent of the television audience watched the show. As did Elvis, from his home in Los Angeles.

ON JULY 6, 1972 (after the separation, but before the divorce was finalized), Elvis was introduced to Linda Thompson, a twenty-two-year-old Miss Tennessee, at the Memphian Theater. Captivated by her youth and beauty (and rowdy sense of humor), plus the fact that she looked fabulous in seventies' styles like hip-huggers and crocheted, midriff-baring tops, they immediately began dating. Linda was considered one of the best consorts for Elvis—a "Lifer," as opposed to the more casual conquests (dubbed "Queen for a Day" by the guys).

In the summer of 1974, Elvis started extensive refurbishment at Graceland, some of it in collaboration with Linda Thompson. At this time, the apogee of Presleyan decorating schemes was undertaken: the Jungle Room. As part of Revisionist Elvis (particularly after Caroline Kennedy brought it to the public's attention in a piece for *Rolling Stone*), it was said that Elvis bought the entire Polynesian-style décor as a joke in an afternoon from the Donald Furniture Company. Like Elvis' first appearance on *Ed Sullivan*, the Jungle Room seemed to galvanize cultural tastemakers everywhere. "It's not like he had bad taste. His girlfriends did," says music producer Jim Dickinson. Hey—spoilsport! Thanks for throwing cold water on a room that has entranced tourists since 1982.

No, no, no—we want to cry (stylishly, of course). Don't go all acceptable Colonial Williamsburg on us, instead, let's have the courage to embrace our inner Memphis Flash—we love the Jungle Room. From a technical standpoint, the JR is unerring in the overall cohesiveness of its design. The glossy carved wood, the green shag carpeting (on the floor and the ceiling), the monkey ashtrays, the unabashed Tiki-ness of the whole thing is *fabulous-o!* Frankly, the Jungle Room reminds us of the old Trader Vic's in the basement of the Plaza Hotel, where we enjoyed way too many wacky drinks with gardenias floating in them when we were heroically underage.

Trust us on this one (and if you haven't already gone out and bought *Suspicious Minds: The Memphis 1969 Anthology*, you'll thank us for that, too), it's perfect.

At the same time, the pool room was redesigned by Memphis decorator William Eubanks with 350 yards of draped and pleated bright cotton fabric. We like it, especially the Tiffany-esque light fixture over the pool table, and the framed *belle époque* prints on the wall: very Maxwell Plum's. Interestingly, famed decorator Renzo Mongiardino employed the same technique (well, he didn't have the guts to go with the pool table) when redoing the cozy drawing room of Lee Radziwill's London townhouse in the late 1960s.

We could go on. In a burst of inspired creativity, Elvis and Linda gave the television room an ultra contemporary makeover in yellow and navy blue accents. The three TV sets were an idea Elvis picked up from Lyndon B. Johnson, who used to watch all three networks simultaneously. With the seating area, mirrored ceiling (yes, we checked), mood lighting, the glossy, TCB pop art lightning flash mural on the wall, a hi-fi system, and a special storage rack for his 45s, the TV room was bachelor heaven.

Now come on, talk about style—how many guys do you know who could pull this off? Plus, Elvis was such a good sport about the whole thing, he moved into the Howard Johnson's motel down the street while the renovations were being done.

"LAST EVENING, and right in the middle of a good dream, like all at once I wake up, from something that keeps tapping on my brain. Before I go insane I pull the pillow from my head, screaming out the words I dread . . ." Okay, okay, so it's not "Heartbreak Hotel," but in 1974, Lisa Marie (like the rest of us) had a crush on David Cassidy. Only her father was Elvis, so she actually got to meet him.

There was nothing Elvis would not do for Lisa Marie. One day he called David Cassidy (the EP of the under-twelve set) on the set of *The Partridge Family* and asked if Lisa Marie could visit. At first, the current pop phenom did not believe that Presley was on the phone.

"Hey Elvis, how's Vegas?" he joked (very original) when the call came, but then it turned out it actually was the Prez. A day or so later a limo pulled up and a giant of a man got out and opened the door. He then introduced David to the two most beautiful women he had ever seen, Priscilla and Lisa Marie.

New Jersey rocker Bruce Springsteen is—like Jon Bon Jovi, who got married by an Elvis impersonator in Vegas in 1988, or New York fund-raiser Blaine Trump, who renewed her eleventh anniversary marriage vows at the Elvis Chapel in Las Vegas—a devout Elvis fan. In 1974, he was in Nashville with some time on his hands, sitting around in his hotel room with his guitar player Steve Van Zandt, tour manager Stephen Appel, and a few others when they decided to get in a taxi and go visit Elvis. They headed out to G'land, and seeing a light on in the second story, decided that Elvis must be up late reading, and that they should knock on the front door and say hello.

"Steve, man," he said to Van Zandt, "I gotta go check it out."

Now, Elvis' fans, as we know, are the politest folks in the world, and they would wait twenty years—politely, politely—at the front gate for Elvis to come down and say hello. It takes a kid from Jersey about four seconds to jump over the wall. Springsteen went running up the driveway ("with the enthusiasm of youth," he admits) and some guards came out of the woods, asking what he wants.

"Is Elvis home?" he wonders.

"No, no, Elvis isn't home now. He's in Lake Tahoe."

So Springsteen started tooting his own horn, which he would never do for anyone else, but he wanted to impress upon them that he is a real rock-and-roll guy . . . not some nutty fan (which he sort of is now, actually).

"So I started to tell 'em that I was a guitar player, and that I had my own band, and that we played in town that night, and I had made some records, and uh, I even told 'em, I told 'em I had my picture on *Time* and *Newsweek*. I had to pull out all the stops to try to make an impression, you know? So—I don't think they believed me, though, because they just kinda stood there noddin', uh huh, uh huh?"

Then one of them took him by the arm and put him back out on the street.

"When I look back on it now," he admits, "it was kind of a stupid thing to do, because I hate it when people do it at my house."

ON MARCH 1, 1973, Colonel Parker arranged for the sale of Elvis' back catalog to RCA Records. According to biographer Peter Guralnick, "the idea for the sale originally came from RCA executive Mel Ilberman, who saw it as a way for the record company to gain control over the Presley material so as to be able to have it for various uses (including the RCA Record Club and repackaging) that were consistently blocked, or thwarted, by the Colonel. RCA, of course, has exclusive rights to all of Elvis' material but has been thoroughly stymied by the Colonel's hands-on management of what can and cannot be released (and in what format) from the start. With a single, one-time payment of $5.4 million, RCA now purchases the rights to all material recorded before 1973 in perpetuity, with Elvis and the Colonel forfeiting all further royalties and control."

It was a stunningly bad business move ("right up there with the Indians selling Manhattan for twenty-four dollars," says Jack Soden, president of Elvis Presley Enterprises). And indicative of the financial pressures Elvis, with his enthusiastic spending, and Parker, with an equally enthusiastic gambling habit, found themselves under.

IN THE LAST YEARS of Elvis' life, he had his good days and bad days. But no matter what happened, he always had a great sense of humor, especially in regard to the general inanity of being him. On September 29, 1974, Louise Thompson,

Linda's sister-in-law, gave birth to a daughter at Memphis' Methodist Hospital, and Elvis insisted not only on seeing Louise and her newborn baby, but on visiting the labor room with Linda, where he was recognized, in spite of his surgical mask.

"Oh my God—you look like Elvis Presley!" says one mother-to-be, obviously thinking she was hallucinating.

"Honey, I *am* Elvis Presley," he declared.

ON APRIL 28, 1975, Barbra Streisand and her boyfriend, Jon Peters, came backstage to tell Elvis about a really great movie idea they had—a modern-day remake of *A Star Is Born*, the classic Hollywood story of success and failure. His Vegas dressing room was packed with well-wishers, and there was no place to have a private conversation, so Elvis invited Barbra, Jon, Jerry, and Joe Esposito into his walk-in closet. They ordered in food (it was actually pretty large, with a cot, and space for all his stage costumes), and Barbra made the pitch.

As Jerry recalls, "Streisand started talking about this story, and Elvis knew what a costarring role would mean. To him, this was like when Frank Sinatra got the supporting role for *From Here to Eternity*. Peters was talking too, but Barbra was really carrying the conversation. She really had the passion and Elvis got it. You were seeing two great artists loving the conversation. He was on such a high after that, it was just unbelievable. Elvis said: 'I'm doing it.' But then, of course, the negotiations started."

In Hollywood, the deal is all. And once the Colonel saw that Elvis would not get top billing, as he had in the past, there was no way the deal would go through. There was also the fact that Elvis, as the talent, was sidestepping the Colonel and initiating his own projects, which would not bode well for the course their relationship might take in the future. The Colonel was an old carny, and—unless Elvis went to the mat on this one—he would very delicately, very subtly, make sure that it never happened.

"If Elvis can make that kind of meeting and Colonel didn't stop it— Colonel's out of a job," observes Jerry. "Elvis and Colonel were very smart in their relationship. There were many bad guys, but never those two. And they would pick the bad guy for the situation. But they didn't agree on this and it almost ended the relationship. The deal wasn't good enough for the Colonel."

On April 4, Streisand's production company made a formal offer for Elvis' services, which included a $500,000 salary and 10 percent of the profits and no participation in other music or recording rights. However, Elvis and the Colonel are offered the opportunity to produce the two live concerts at the heart of the picture and to profit from them.

On April 14, the Colonel responds. If Elvis is to make this picture, he must be paid $1 million in salary, plus $100,000 in expenses and 50 percent of the profits from the first dollar . . . well, you know where this is going. As the Colonel so artfully put it in his letter, "Mr. Presley has indicated that he would like to make this movie, [but] I advised him not to allow this to become part of making a cheap deal."

We look at this now and think: This could have helped Elvis to *finally* make a decent movie, another comeback. But by overlooking the creative aspects of the movie, and asking for the moon, the Colonel made sure it never happened.

What might have been.

Asked his opinion of the professional relationship between Elvis and the Colonel, Jerry Schilling admits that he had a "love/hate relationship" with Parker (he grew very

close to the Colonel in the last twenty years of his life, even speaking at his funeral). "The Colonel was not a bad person," admits Jerry, "but I don't know if the Colonel ever understood rock-and-roll." Parker came from the age of Bing Crosby, and with all the great things that he did for Elvis, there was also the fear that you had to keep the talent within your managerial parameters. So, it would not do for Elvis (and Joe, and Jerry) to be taking meetings with Barbra Streisand and her hairdresser/boyfriend/future movie producer Jon Peters, in a walk-in closet at the Las Vegas Hilton.

In Jerry's opinion, "I think the Colonel did some brilliant stuff, certainly at the beginning. At the end, Elvis outgrew the Colonel, but I think society outgrew the Colonel, too."

IN 1974 ALONE, Elvis' concert tours netted him approximately $4 million, to be divided two-thirds, one-third with the Colonel. Income from Las Vegas and Tahoe appearances came to $700,000, again split two-thirds, one-third, with an additional $750,000 income from RCA split fifty-fifty. Elvis' personal expenses were so excessive that on September 25, 1975, in need of cash as a result of his recent purchases of airplanes, cars, racquetball courts, and jewelry, as well as a sizable payroll that included almost every one of his relatives, increased medical bills, expensive upkeep on various houses, and unchecked gifts to friends, family, and casual acquaintances, Elvis borrowed $350,000 from the National Bank of Commerce in Memphis, putting Graceland up as collateral. The loan was to be repaid in two equal installments in November of 1976 and 1977.

ONE DAY WHEN SHE WAS SEVEN or eight, Lisa Marie told her father, "I don't want you to die."

"Don't worry about me," she remembers he told her. "I'm not going anywhere."

"I just had a feeling," she says now. "He wasn't doing well." A feeling. "All I knew was that I had it, and it happened."

ON JANUARY 20, 1976, Jerry Schilling quit for good, telling Elvis that "friendship is more important than the job."

On August 13, 1976, Vernon fired Red West and his cousin, Sonny West, from Elvis' employ with one week's pay. They are understandably upset since they have worked for Elvis for sixteen years and Red has known Elvis since Humes High and his early days on the road. Shortly thereafter, Red, Sonny, and karate expert Dave Hebler collaborated with reporter Steve Dunleavy on an insiders' biography of Presley.

BY 1976, MOST OF the original crew had left. Joe Esposito and Larry Geller were living in California with their families. Lamar Fike lived and worked in Nashville. Jerry Schilling, Red, and Sonny West were gone. Now, alone in Graceland, Elvis was surrounded by a bunch of new guys. They were serviceable, they did what was asked of them, but that was all.

On August 4, 1977, *Elvis: What Happened?*, an eviscerating account of Presley's life, was published. After Elvis' death, Sonny would express outrage at the tone its author, Steve Dunleavy, took, calling him a "sensationalist." But since Dunleavy was a reporter for *The Star* and the *New York Post*, one wonders, of course, what tone they were expecting.

As an adult, Lisa Marie was furious with some of her father's "friends." After all, Elvis had fed, housed, and clothed most of them for close to twenty years and in the end, they took his generosity, his talent, and his hard work and twisted it into something mirroring themselves: small-minded and unrecognizable. "His dignity was one of the most important things to him, and you are trying to take it away from him," she said of them.

Jerry Schilling calls it the "and then I told Elvis" syndrome. "We've all become far more important in Elvis' life! [Presley biographer] Peter Guralnick and I have this joke—'and then I told Elvis!' Nobody told Elvis, *nobody* told Elvis what to do!" In the end, Iagos all, they were small men whose only fortune was that they once drew close to greatness.

IN AUGUST OF 1977, with the book's publication, Elvis anguishes over what his daughter and fans will think of him.

WELL, I'M TIRED AND SO WEARY, *but I must go alone . . .* "We pay the price for fame with our nerves, don't we?" Elvis said to John Lennon in a rare moment of introspection. In the last year of his life, Elvis was not himself. Joe Esposito says, "He was just a wonderful person, but the last couple of years were tough. It was tough for all of us because we know that was not the Elvis we knew! It was almost like he was sick and this other person took over—that was not him."

In 1976, concert tours were occasionally interrupted because of his exhaustion. On May 29, 1977, Elvis left the stage for the first time during a concert in Baltimore, returning after thirty minutes. On June 26, 1977, he gave his last performance at the Market Square Arena in Indianapolis.

Bernard Lansky is asked, what does he think happened to Elvis in his final years?

"Only the Lord knows. I really don't. But I know one thing—if his mama was living he'd be living." As he got older, Lansky thought it was a "different ball game," for Elvis—"he was nervous, you know, uptight all the time, on everybody's neck. Can't ask him a question, he'd get real hot at you, uptight, really excited, jump off the handle real quick. There were two different Elvises."

In Lansky's opinion, two events affected Elvis greatly—"after his mother died. Then after he got divorced from Priscilla . . . You know, different things build up on you, you get to thinking about it, and nothing's going right, and everything just falls apart. This is not the regular Elvis, this is a different Elvis."

Wasn't it strange that someone could be unhappy with all the talent, and the fans, and the material success that he had?

"Hey," said the seer of Beale Street, "money ain't everything. If you ain't got that with the home, you don't have that love and things like that—that's the main thing. You can get out there, man, and do everything in the world—if it's not there, it's not there."

TODAY, PEOPLE TAKE such good care of themselves physically that it is said, "Forty is the new thirty," but for Elvis, it wasn't. For him, turning forty might as well have been a hundred. Joe Esposito says that "when Elvis turned forty, it made a big difference in his life. Turning forty was a very hard time for him. He wouldn't admit it, but I think he was just worried about the future—were they still going to like me? Were they still going to love me? Where am I going to be when I am fifty or sixty? There was the *National Enquirer* headline—'Elvis at 40—Paunchy, Depressed and Living in Fear.' That really upset him."

For someone so extraordinarily physically blessed, his weight gain depressed Elvis along with the thought of getting old. His mother had died at forty-six, and this may have preyed on him. Offstage, now, in the mid to late seventies, his wardrobe tended to stretchy warm-up suits, sunglasses, and tennis hats. When he wanted, he could still sing—and the fans loved him as much as ever—but it broke your heart to see him. On his last concert tour in the spring of 1977, Elvis looked,

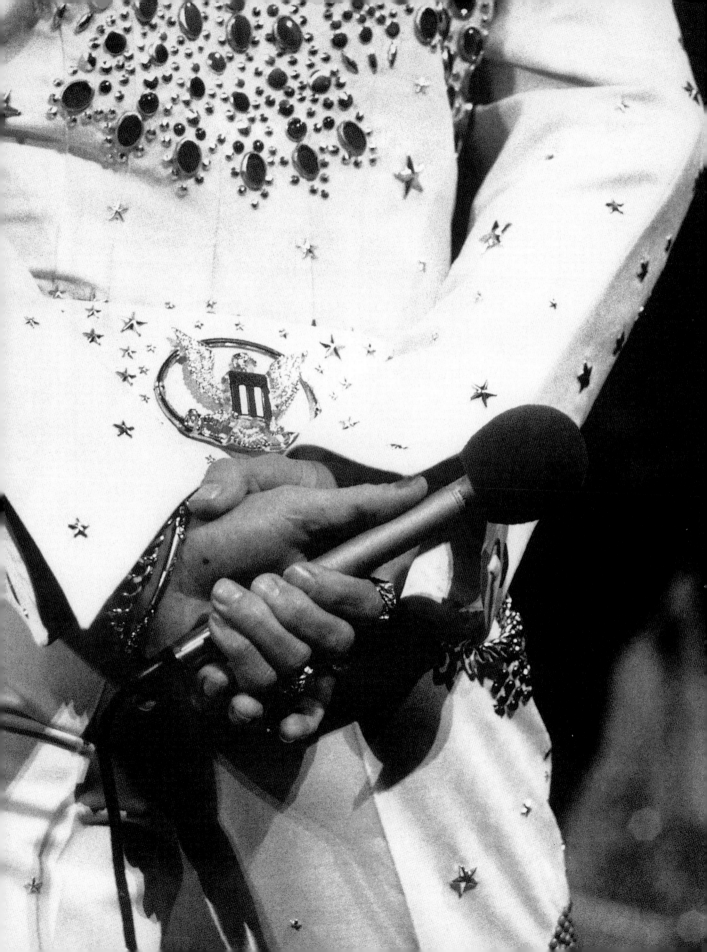

unbelievably, like a more bloated version of his nemesis Robert Goulet. Even up on stage, his home, his eyes looked terrified, as if to say: What am I doing here?

It is heartbreaking to watch. The Elvis we knew is gone.

WHAT HAPPENED TO THE DREAM? It seemed so clear when he walked into Sam Phillips' little place on Union, Jesus—what was it, twenty years ago? Now everything was cloudy, overwhelming. There were so many people in his life making decisions, too much fear and regret fogging his mind. He needed to make a change. Regain control of the situation. Tomorrow, for sure.

Why couldn't it just be him and Scotty and Bill, and Mr. Phillips, woodshedding in that little white room in Memphis, with nothing, *nothing* but the joy of the next note in front of them. Like the old days, man. And what was the name of the girl lying next to him?

Like an old general, his glorious days were behind him and would not come again. Still he had known greatness, was still great. No one could take all that he had accomplished from him. *Don't touch the radio, Mama*, as he drifted off to sleep, his mind a blessed blank.

ON AUGUST 16, 1977, at 2:30 in the afternoon, Elvis Presley was found unconscious in his bathroom at Graceland. He was pronounced dead an hour later at Baptist Memorial Hospital after doctors failed to revive him. Dr. Jerry Francisco, the Shelby County coroner who performed the autopsy, said, "He had coronary disease and mild hypertension. Butter probably produced more damage on his heart than drugs."

Years of overwork, bad habits, and an excessive lifestyle had finally caught up with Presley. Interviewed by Chet Flippo of *Rolling Stone*, a Baptist hospital employee said, "Elvis had the arteries of an eighty-year-old man. His body was just worn out. His arteries and veins were terribly corroded.

"He had been hospitalized here on five occasions," the employee said. "Usually he would go home to Graceland first. But in April, they flew him directly here from Louisiana. Every time, security got tighter. This time, when he was dead, it was tight.

"He was hospitalized here from April first to sixth of this year, after cutting short a tour. And Elvis was here for two weeks in January and February of '75, for two weeks in August and September of '75, for two weeks in October of '73," the hospital employee continued. "They were treating him for everything—hypertension, enlarged colon, gastroenteritis, stomach inflammation. He was getting cortisone treatments, and I heard that was for arthritis. . . . He also had a severe liver condition. Cortisone might have explained his weight—he was a big man; he was weighing at least two hundred thirty pounds."

HOW HE DIED, why he died—the drugs in his system, his faltering will, his failed heart—in the end, did it matter? At forty-two, Elvis Presley was gone.

DEATH CAPTURES CROWN OF ROCK AND ROLL read the headline of the *Memphis Commercial Appeal*, the hometown newspaper.

AS NEWS OF ELVIS PRESLEY'S DEATH was made public at 4:00 in the afternoon, a sad, quiet crowd of about 150 people gathered outside the emergency room entrance of Baptist Memorial Hospital. Although most of the people in the crowd had never met Elvis, most called him by his first name.

Their faith in Elvis and his supremacy was touching; completely removed from the reality of the situation. They watched the emergency room doors as if they expected some newer announcement that earlier reports had been wrong. "Are you sure?" asked Winston Meek, sixty-three, of Memphis. "Have you confirmed it for sure? There's no mistake?"

Twice a police helicopter buzzed overhead, and later, fire trucks answered a false alarm at the hospital lobby. But nothing deterred their attention from the emergency room door.

"I think everybody's just stunned," said a young woman in a white lab coat.

A group of Memphis police officers hustled other emergency cases into the hospital and kept the drive clear for ambulances. Hospital security guards and maintenance workers kept spectators and the press out of the emergency room and the main hospital. A group of spectators watched from inside the main lobby, where large tinted-glass windows looked down on the emergency room area.

"I feel very depressed right now," said Therisia Mosley, who was in a hospital waiting room when she heard that Presley was dead.

"I just can't believe it. This is terrible," said Anthony Stella of Corinth, Mississippi. "There goes a great one, I swear." Stella said he had been at the hospital since noon and had seen "all the commotion and people running around, but I didn't know what had happened."

Meek said he, like almost everyone outside the emergency room, was an Elvis fan. "Yeah, sure I was a fan. I think everybody in town was. Shoot, I never saw the man, but you can bet I'm a fan. He conquered the world with just a guitar and his voice."

THAT AFTERNOON, driving from Knoxville to Nashville on Interstate 40, Tennessee's main thoroughfare, everything becomes still, like the moments before a tornado. It is as if there is no more air to breathe. Even the horizon seems tilted. Something is very wrong, and you don't know what it is. There is a sense, suddenly, that everything has stopped, as if your little car is the only one in the whole world. Up ahead and all around, vehicles pull off the highway, jerking to a stop as the inhabitants spill out, clutching their faces, keening. What is going on? Whatever it is, it had to be something cataclysmic. Your earliest memory is the day JFK was shot, and this feels the same. Were we at war?

You punch a button, ejecting your boxy eight-track cassette, and turn on the radio. "Elvis Presley died at his home at Graceland this afternoon at the age of forty-two," the announcer says. Your heart stops. It is like your cousin, or a favorite uncle, has just gone. Jesus, you turn to your friend—*Elvis*? You shake your head, hands fearful, saying nothing as you point the car in the direction of home, his perfect voice filling the air.

PRISCILLA WAS ON THE *LISA MARIE*, heading to Memphis from her home in Los Angeles, thinking of a man she would not see again. She could not imagine her world without him. It was unthinkable—like the sun not rising tomorrow.

"He taught me everything: how to dress, how to walk, how to apply makeup and wear my hair, how to behave, how to return love—his way. Over the years he became my father, husband, and very nearly God. Now he was gone and I felt more alone and afraid than ever in my life," she recalled. Knowing Elvis changed Priscilla; certainly he changed her life. Like all loves, he pushed the boundaries of her heart, asking more of her than she ever imagined.

Now, at thirty-two, having loved him since she was fourteen, in the moment of his death, Elvis' little girl grew up.

WITH FIFTY THOUSAND FANS crowding the gates of Graceland, Elvis was buried wearing a white suit, light blue shirt, and a white tie that his father had bought him. "I knew Elvis would like what I picked for him," says Bernard Lansky, "that was his last suit."

AS WITH ALL COMPLEX MEN, there were many sides to Elvis. Which is to say, there was always one essential Elvis with varying facets. Even his closest friends acknowledge both his essential goodness, and his multiplicity. Larry Geller was struck by Elvis' vulnerability, Jerry Schilling his personal power, while Joe Esposito viewed Elvis simply as "a great guy." Then there were Priscilla, Lisa Marie, and the other women he loved, and allowed himself to be far more emotionally accessible with.

And of course, all of these myriad perceptions stand alongside Elvis' vast public persona that is far greater (and certainly more lasting) than the fleeting opinion of anyone who knew him personally. Years after Elvis' death, Bruce Springsteen reflected on what Presley meant to him. "Later on I used to wonder what I would've said if, you know, if I'd knocked on the door and Elvis had come to the door—because it wasn't Elvis I was going to see . . . It was like he came along and whispered some dream in everybody's ear, and somehow we all dreamed it."

Elvis, the first modern superstar when he was alive, is even more popular today, twenty-seven years after his death. Does Joe Esposito think Elvis would be surprised at how big he is now?

He laughs. "Oh, I'm sure he is! If he's up in heaven, he's saying, boy—look at all those crazy people out there still listening to me! Still writing books about me!"

As we see with the impersonators (creepy) or those who want so greatly to believe that he still walks among us (sad, in spite of their faith), people want to remain connected with Elvis.

Years after Elvis' death, Larry Geller tells of getting on an airplane to return to Los Angeles after meetings in New York City. As he got into his seat, he noticed a man coming toward him wearing a TCB necklace with his hair dyed and shaped sort of like Elvis'. Larry looked at him and said, "Wow—where'd you get that?"

"Elvis gave it to me," the man said confidently.

"You knew Elvis?"

"Sure did—I was his drummer and bodyguard for seven years. . . ."

"Oh my God—really? Then you probably know all the people who work for Elvis—Joe Esposito and Charlie Hodge, and you probably know Larry Geller, too."

"Sure do," he said, and winked at Larry and sat down.

"I couldn't pop his bubble, you know?" Larry says, laughing. "What can you say to a guy like that? He was Elvis' bodyguard *and* his drummer—if he says that to me, can you imagine what he says to other people?"

IN LIFE, ELVIS WAS A LEGEND. In death, he became that thing he feared most, a myth. What can he mean to us? How do we see him? His talent sets him apart, as it always will. But with his foibles and his grace, his generosity and his temper, and most of all, his striving to be good, he is very human. And it is his humanity—not his perfection—that draws us to him, even today.

But perhaps, in the final telling, how we view Elvis (fun-loving, decadent, lonely, willful, loving, or tragic) says far more about ourselves than it ever will about him. After all, he was merely living his life. And what can anyone's experience possibly mean to those who love him from afar?

Joe Esposito remembers Elvis singing, always singing. "He would sit alone in Graceland and sing for hours. That's what made him happy." Remarkably for us, Esposito doesn't think Elvis had a sense of his own charisma. "He just knew that people loved him when he sang. And that's why today, when young kids hear his music, they don't know who he is, they just like it. When Elvis sings, you just feel better."

Like so many friends (and a few strangers), Bill Belew thinks of Elvis' vaunted generosity. He gave him his car, a 450 SL Mercedes convertible with the license plate 2BBFREP. He is always getting stopped. One time in L.A., he heard this beeping and Ernest Borgnine pulled up alongside him. "What does your license mean, it's been driving my wife and me crazy!"

"To Bill Belew from Elvis Presley."

"If I have one wish," admits Jerry Schilling, "it's to stay up all night and talk to Elvis, and not have any agenda, which was the way it was with him. You never know—we might laugh all night or we might cry all night."

Lisa Marie, perhaps most like him, was nine and at Graceland when he died. Her father—with his darkness, his talent, his humility, and his greatness right up alongside each other—affected her always, perhaps in ways she can barely comprehend. For years, she kept her watch set two hours ahead to Memphis time.

Elvis. He was generous, he was kind, he was rambunctious, and, at times, lonely, but who among us is not? By any measure, he lived a full life. And even today, he does not fail to live.

acknowledgments

SOME PEOPLE warrant special recognition. I begin with Darac—who saw this possibility before I did. His bonhomie and humor show true Elvis Style. I treasure his friendship.

Priscilla Presley, who is the guiding spirit behind Elvis Presley Enterprises, was immeasurably helpful. Her memories, insight, and observations about Elvis aided this book greatly.

At Graceland and EPE, I would like to acknowledge Jack Soden and the ever-patient Pete Davidson, who hosted many memorable meals in Memphis and shepherded this project through to its completion. Carol Butler, LaVonne Gaw, Sheila James, Angie Marchese, and Todd Morgan gave a very close reading of the text, as well as a rare backstage tour. Kelly Hill and, in particular, Susan Sherwood of the photo department were incredibly helpful in culling forty thousand EP photos; truly, the man did not take a bad picture.

With this, my third book, I am enormously grateful to my agents Joanna Pulcini and Linda Chester—nothing happens without them. Their faith and encouragement of my ability (as well as picking up the tab at Michael's) is a great treasure. As always, Gary Jaffe gets major kudos for keeping the wheels greased. I would also like to thank Greer Hendricks, my editor at Atria Books; her associate editor, Suzanne O'Neill; our saintly production editor, Linda Roberts; and Carla Little. Greer's insight improved this book enormously. I look forward to working with her in the future.

As I met the people who knew Elvis, I was touched by their generosity and help. I had so much fun with them, there were times I just wanted to head down to Memphis to give tours at Graceland, or stock the shelves at Lansky's. All of Elvis' friends were so giving of their time and memories, it was as if the host of a great party had just stepped outside for a moment. Their camaraderie was—and still is— amazing, and enabled me to get a sense of EP's spirit.

Tony Aiello, Carl Sferrazza Anthony, Stephen Appel, Madalyn Aslan, Peter Bacanovic, Letitia Baldrige, Billy "Lord" Bedford, Bill Belew, Bettye Berger, Manolo Blahnik, Jon Bon Jovi, Alan Braverman, Jamie Curtis, Dennis D'Antonio, Wayne

Dowdy, Tiffany Dubin, Lisa Eisner, Joe Esposito, Juliana Etheridge, Daniel Ferguson, Hans Fiebig, John M. Florescu, Larry Geller, David Ashley Gibbin, James de Givenchy, John Gordon, Thomas "FX" Gorman, Campbell Lane Hart, Laura Helper-Ferris, William A. Henry III, Bill Hogeland, James Katz, Ward Landrigan, Bernard Lansky, Hal Lansky, Brian Lewis, Maggie McMahon, Beth Mendelson, Carol Rawlings Miller, Sandi Miller, Steve Millington, Joseph Montebello, Joseph Natoli, Pamela Needham, Richard Nelson, Patti Parry, Mary Parson, Frank Pompea, Stephen Quinn, Sugar Rautbord, Dennis Roberts, Cynthia Rowley, Linda Semans, Jerry Schilling, Caroline Sharp, Jill Siegel, Hope Smith, W. Roger Stiltz, Jack Taylor, Dr. William Taylor, Blaine Trump, June Weir.

I am also indebted to Pete Daniel and Charlie McGovern, for sharing the interviews of D. J. Fontana, Sam Phillips, and Scotty Moore that they conducted on behalf of the Smithsonian Institution.

In researching this work, I read a great many books, magazines, and contemporary newspaper articles. Peter Guralnick's two volumes, of course, trump all the rest, but (in alphabetical order) I would also like to gratefully acknowledge the work of journalists and authors David Bowie, Peter La Chapelle, Amy Fine Collins, Pete Daniel, Adam Gopnick, June Juanico, Terry Keeter and Otis L. Sanford, Larry King, Jennifer Larson, Karal Ann Marling, Dave Marsh, Charlie Rose, Ann-Margret Smith, Steven Soderbergh, Bruce Springsteen, Alfred Wertheimer, Bill Wyman, and Bill Zehme.

Additionally, I would like to thank Liz McNeil of *People* magazine, a friend with a Rolodex on a par with mine. Patrick Raynor and Mark Piel at the New York Society Library—a beautiful place to work. Mitch Blank, who has one of the most comprehensive Elvis video and audio collections I have ever seen. His West Village apartment rivals the Museum of Television & Radio. Jann Wenner and Robert Love for their generous use of *Rolling Stone*'s library. The Huntington Public Library, where much of this book was written. And, once again, Cynthia Cathcart at the Condé Nast Library.

I am thrilled to again be working with designer par excellence Susi Oberhelman. Susi developed the beautiful (and much imitated) look of my first book, *Audrey Style*. Like Elvis, she has an unerring eye, and her mother, I hear, is a giant EP fan.

I would particularly like to thank Bob Willoughby for generously sharing his rare, beautiful images of EP and Sophia Loren, as well as the story behind them. He is an immensely talented and great friend.

Finally, there is one thing that I actually have in common with Elvis (other than the delightful Creed rumor)—I would be remiss if I did not mention my twin sister, Patricia, who would have gotten a kick out of this entire project. *Fait de mieux*, this book belongs to her.

illustration **credits**

ii: *Love Me Tender* studio still, 1956.

vi: BMOC—EP in front of G'land. Memphis, 1965.

viii: EP rocking out on *The Ed Sullivan Show*, 1956.

4: While cycling around the Paramount studio lot (the bike was presented to him during *Loving You*), EP ran into a young group of fans. Gladys and Vernon Presley visited the set, appearing as extras in one scene. Paramount Studios, 1957.

7: EP and the boys (and his guitar fret) rehearsing at the MGM Studios for Vegas. Los Angeles, 1970.

8: EP in downtown Memphis, 1956. You *know* he's not getting a ticket.

13: Lansky Bros. on Beale Street, ca. 1949.

16: EP shopping at Lansky's, 1956.

27: The boys in the band at an early recording session at Sun Studio, 1955. From left to right: EP, Bill Black, Scotty Moore, Sam Phillips.

32: EP onstage, 1956.

36: Original watercolor by Bill Bailey, 706 *Union Avenue*.

37: Photo of 706 Union Avenue.

38: EP at the age of two, and his parents, East Tupelo, 1937.

45: Elvis and his parents outside their clapboard house on Maple Street, East Tupelo, around the time EP started grade school in the fall of 1941.

48: EP in his Sunday best, 1946.

51: EP and his cousin, Gene Smith, in western gear at the Mid South Fair in Memphis, September 1953.

52: EP sits on a Memphis sidewalk with one of his first girlfriends Betty Anne McMahon, who lived in the same housing project, Lauderdale Courts, circa 1950.

55: Perhaps the only man in the entire world who looks good in a photo booth picture. EP, 1953.

57: EP leaving the Richmond train station, June 30, 1956, en route to a concert. In his right hand, he carries an RCA Victor "Transistor Seven" radio that looked, according to photographer Alfred Wertheimer, "like a briefcase with knobs on it." When he got to the upper level, he changed stations and country music poured out. No one noticed him.

58: EP singing "Anyway You Want Me" during a recording session in RCA Victor Studio One. New York City, July 2, 1956. Image also appeared on the cover of *TV Guide*, September 1956.

61: EP and Bernard Lansky, Lansky Bros., Memphis, 1956.

64: EP and Scotty Moore, performing "Blue Suede Shoes" live for the Dorsey show (Bill Black on bass and D. J. Fontana, drums, were also onstage), New York City, 1956.

67: Tampa, Florida, 1955. EP and Bill Black rockin' the joint at the Fort Homer Hesterly Armory. The photo became even more famous when it was used on the cover of his debut RCA album, *Elvis Presley*.

72: Dress rehearsal for *The Steve Allen Show*. EP tries on the dreaded white tie. Tom Diskin, the Colonel's right-hand man, is seated at left. June 30, 1956, New York City.

75: "If you can't come around, at least, please, telephone." Who is he calling? Who cares? EP in New York City, June 1956.

76: EP shaving in Room 527 of the Warwick Hotel before he leaves for the Dorsey Brothers' *Stage Show*, produced at CBS Studio 50. March 17, 1956, New York City.

79: EP belts out "You Ain't Nothin' but a Hound Dog." July 2, 1956, New York City.

80: Elvis, his musicians, and the Jordanaires listen to another take of "You Ain't Nothin' but a Hound Dog." It took nearly thirty takes before EP was satisfied. July 2, 1956, New York City.

83: The hometown hero returns: This concert, at the Mississippi-Alabama Fair and Dairy Show (where he first performed at the age of ten) in Tupelo, Mississippi, is considered by fans as one of the most sensational he had ever given. Natalie Wood's dressmaker made the blue velvet shirt he is wearing. September 26, 1956, Tupelo.

84: Exhausted after a matinee performance given at the Auditorium in St. Paul, Minnesota. EP went on to give an evening performance in Minneapolis. May 13, 1956, St. Paul, Minnesota.

91: EP performing on *The Ed Sullivan Show*. New York City, 1956.

92: EP relaxing in his bedroom on Audubon Drive, 1956.

93: EP backstage before his Richmond concert. Everyone (still) wonders who the lucky girl is. June 30, 1956, Richmond, Virginia.

94: EP's enthusiastic fans see him off as he leaves the country after having been drafted into the army. September 1958.

96: EP and his parents, Vernon and Gladys, at Graceland, taken when EP visits on leave from the army in June 1958, a few months before Gladys' untimely death.

99: The buzz heard 'round the world: EP receives his army haircut, 1958.

100: EP and Vernon on the front steps of Graceland, sharing their grief over Gladys' death, August 13, 1958.

103: EP reading mail in the army. Bad Nauheim, Germany, 1959.

104: EP and his father (with Grandmother Minnie Presley) eating breakfast at 14 Goethestrasse. Bad Nauheim, Germany, 1959.

107: Engineered like no other car in the world—EP and his MB on Goethestrasse, Bad Nauheim, Germany, 1959.

108: EP and two showgirls at the Moulin Rouge in Munich, Germany, March 1959.